NCERT SOLUTIONS

with Chapterwise **Study Notes**

MATHEMATICS 9th

NCERT SOLUTIONS

with Chapterwise **Study Notes**

MATHEMATICS 9th

Author

Rakesh Pandey
Sunil Kumar Rathor

Including Selected Questions of **DIKSHA**

arihant
SUCCESS AND NOTHING LESS

ARIHANT PRAKASHAN (Series), MEERUT

卐 **Administrative & Production Offices**

Regd. Office

'Ramchhaya' 4577/15, Agarwal Road, Darya Ganj, New Delhi -110002
Tele: 011- 47630600, 43518550

卐 **Head Office**

Kalindi, TP Nagar, Meerut (UP) - 250002
Tel: 0121-7156203, 7156204

卐 **Sales & Support Offices**

Agra, Ahmedabad, Bengaluru, Bareilly, Chennai, Delhi, Guwahati, Hyderabad, Jaipur, Jhansi, Kolkata, Lucknow, Nagpur & Pune.

卐 **PRICE** ₹255.00

卐 **PO No :** TXT-59-T062580-01-25

Published by Arihant Publications (India) Ltd.

For further information about the books published by Arihant, log on to www.arihantbooks.com or e-mail at info@arihantbooks.com

Follow us on

Preface

Feeling the immense importance and value of NCERT books, we are presenting this book, having the **NCERT Exercises Solutions**. For the overall benefit of the students we have made this book unique in such a way that it presents not only solutions but also detailed explanations. Through these detailed and through explanations, students can learn the concepts which will enhance their thinking and learning abilities.

We have introduced some Additional Features with the solutions which are given below:

- **Explanatory Solutions** Along with the solutions to questions we have given all the points that tell how to approach to solve a problem. Here we have tried to cover all those loopholes which may lead to confusion. All formulae and hints are discussed in full detail.
- Also included **Thinking Process** and **Mistake Alert** to understanding 'How to solve question' and points of mistakes.
- **Note** We have provided notes also to solutions in which special points are mentioned which are of great value for the students.

Apart from all those who helped in the compilation of this book a special note of thanks to all. With the hope that this book will be of great help to the students, we wish great success to ou readers.

Rakesh Pandey
Sunil Kumar Rathor

Contents

1.	Number Systems	1-28
2.	Polynomials	29-58
3.	Coordinate Geometry	59-69
4.	Linear Equations in Two Variables	70-78
5.	Introduction to Euclid's Geometry	79-89
6.	Lines and Angles	90-106
7.	Triangles	107-135
8.	Quadrilaterals	136-162
9.	Circles	163-190
10.	Heron's Formula	191-205
11.	Surface Areas and Volumes	206-232
12.	Statistics	233-249

Number Systems

CHAPTER 01

Important Points

01 Natural Numbers Counting of numbers starting from one (1) and increasing by 1 forever is known as natural numbers. The collection of all natural numbers is denoted by N.

$$N = \{1, 2, 3, 4, ...\}$$

02 Whole Numbers Counting of numbers starting from zero (0) and increasing by 1 forever is known as whole numbers. The collection of all whole numbers is denoted by W.

or

If '0' is included in the collection of natural numbers, then the collection is known as whole numbers.

$$W = \{0, 1, 2, 3, ...\}$$

03 Integers The collection of all whole numbers (natural numbers + zero) and negative of natural numbers is called integers. It is denoted by Z.

$$Z = \{..., -3, -2, -1, 0, 1, 2, 3, ...\}$$

04 Rational Numbers A number r is called a rational number, if it can be written in the form $\frac{p}{q}$, where p and q are integers and $q \neq 0$.

The collection of rational numbers is denoted by Q. *e.g.*, $\frac{1}{2}, \frac{3}{5}, ...$

05 Equivalent Rational Numbers The rational number whose numerator and denominator both are equal or they are reducible to equal.

e.g., $\frac{1}{2} = \frac{2}{4} = \frac{10}{20} = \frac{25}{50} = \frac{47}{94}$

06 Irrational Numbers A number s is called an irrational number, if it cannot be written in the form $\frac{p}{q}$, where p and q are integers and $q \neq 0$, and its decimal representation is non-terminating and non-repeating.

e.g., $\sqrt{2}, \sqrt{5}, \pi, \ldots$

Note Symbol $\sqrt{\ }$ indicate the square root of the number *e.g.*, $\sqrt{4} = 2$, though both 2 and -2 are square roots of 4.

07 Real Numbers The collection of all rational numbers and irrational numbers is called real numbers, which is denoted by R. Therefore, a real number is either rational or irrational.

Note Every real number is represented by a unique point on the number line. Also, every point on the number line represents a unique real number.

08 Real Numbers and their Decimal Expansions For all rationals of the form $\frac{p}{q}$ $(q \neq 0)$. On division of p by q, two main things happen, either the remainder becomes zero or never becomes zero and we get a repeating string of remainders.

***Case* I. The remainder becomes zero**

In this case, the decimal expansion terminates or ends after a finite number of steps. We call the decimal expansion of such numbers terminating.

e.g., $\frac{7}{8}, \frac{1}{2}, \frac{3}{4}$, etc.

***Case* II. The remainder never becomes zero**

In this case, we have a repeating block of digits in the quotient, this expansion is called non-terminating recurring.

e.g., $\frac{2}{3} = 0.666\ldots$

$$\frac{22}{7} = 3.142857142857\ldots$$

The repeated digits are written as $\frac{2}{3} = 0.\overline{6}$

$$\frac{22}{7} = 3.\overline{142857}$$

Note • The decimal expansion of rational number is either terminating or non-terminating recurring. Moreover, a number whose decimal expansion is terminating or non-terminating recurring is rational.

• The decimal expansion of an irrational number is non-terminating non-recurring. Moreover, a number whose decimal expansion is non-terminating non-recurring is irrational.
$s = 0.10110111011110...$ (non-terminating and non-recurring).

09 Operations on Real Numbers Rational numbers satisfy the commutative, associative and distributive laws for addition and multiplication. Moreover, if we add, subtract, multiply or divide (except by zero) two rational numbers, then we still get a rational number (*i.e.*, rational numbers are 'closed' with respect to addition, subtraction, multiplication and division).

Irrational numbers also satisfy the commutative, associative and distributive laws for addition and multiplication. However, the sum, difference, quotients and products of irrational numbers are not always irrational.

e.g., $\sqrt{5} + (-\sqrt{5}) = 0$ and $\dfrac{\sqrt{15}}{\sqrt{15}} = 1$ are rational.

$\because \sqrt{3}$ is irrational.

Hence, $(5 + \sqrt{3})$ is also irrational.
($\because \sqrt{3}$ has a non-terminating, non-recurring decimal expansion).

Note • The sum or difference of a rational number and an irrational number is irrational.

• The product or quotient of a non-zero rational number with an irrational number is irrational.

• If we add, subtract, multiply or divide two irrationals, the result may be rational or irrational.

10 Radicand If $\sqrt[n]{a}$ is a surd, then n is known as order of surd, a is known as radicand and symbol '$\sqrt{\ }$' is known as radical sign.

11 Laws of Radicals Let a and b be positive real numbers. Then,

(i) $\sqrt{ab} = \sqrt{a}\sqrt{b}$

(ii) $\sqrt{\dfrac{a}{b}} = \dfrac{\sqrt{a}}{\sqrt{b}}$

(iii) $(\sqrt{a} + \sqrt{b})(\sqrt{a} - \sqrt{b}) = (a - b)$ $\quad [\because (a+b)(a-b) = a^2 - b^2]$

(iv) $(a + \sqrt{b})(a - \sqrt{b}) = a^2 - b$

(v) $(\sqrt{a} + \sqrt{b})(\sqrt{c} + \sqrt{d}) = \sqrt{ac} + \sqrt{ad} + \sqrt{bc} + \sqrt{bd}$

(vi) $(\sqrt{a} + \sqrt{b})^2 = a + 2\sqrt{ab} + b$ $\quad [\because (a+b)^2 = a^2 + b^2 + 2ab]$

12 Rationalising the Denominator When the denominator of an expression contains a term with a square root (or a number under a radical sign), the process of converting it to an equivalent expression whose denominator is a rational number is called rationalising the denominator.

To rationalise the denominator of $\frac{1}{\sqrt{a}+b}$, it is multiplied by $\frac{\sqrt{a}-b}{\sqrt{a}-b}$, where a and b are integers.

13 Laws of Exponents

(i) $a^m \cdot a^n = a^{m+n}$

(ii) $(a^m)^n = a^{mn}$

(iii) $\frac{a^m}{a^n} = a^{m-n}, m > n$

(iv) $a^m b^m = (ab)^m$

(v) $a^{-m} = \frac{1}{a^m}$

(vi) $\left(\frac{a}{b}\right)^{-m} = \left(\frac{b}{a}\right)^m$

(vii) $\left(\frac{a}{b}\right)^m = \frac{a^m}{b^m}$

(viii) $a^0 = 1$

Here a, b, n and m are natural numbers. Here, a is called base and m and n are the exponents.

e.g.,

(i) $(17)^2 \cdot (17)^{-5} = (17)^{2-5} = (17)^{-3} = \frac{1}{(17)^3}$

(ii) $(5^2)^{-7} = 5^{2\times(-7)} = 5^{-14}$

(iii) $2^{\frac{2}{3}} \cdot 2^{\frac{1}{3}} = 2^{\frac{2}{3}+\frac{1}{3}} = 2^{\frac{3}{3}} = 2$

Exercise 1.1

Question 1 Is zero a rational number? Can you write it in the form $\frac{p}{q}$, where p and q are integers and $q \neq 0$?

Sol. Yes, zero is a rational number. It can be written in the form $\frac{p}{q}$. $0 = \frac{0}{1}$ (where 0 and 1 are integers and $q = 1$ which is not equal to zero).

Question 2 Find six rational numbers between 3 and 4.

Sol. A rational number between 3 and 4 $= \frac{3+4}{2} = \frac{7}{2}$

$$\therefore \quad 3 < \frac{7}{2} < 4$$

A rational number between 3 and $\frac{7}{2}$

$$= \frac{3 + \frac{7}{2}}{2} = \frac{13}{4}$$

$$\therefore \quad 3 < \frac{13}{4} < \frac{7}{2} < 4$$

A rational number between $\frac{7}{2}$ and 4

$$= \frac{\frac{7}{2} + 4}{2} = \frac{15}{4}$$

$$\therefore \quad 3 < \frac{13}{4} < \frac{7}{2} < \frac{15}{4} < 4$$

A rational number between $\frac{13}{4}$ and $\frac{7}{2}$

$$= \frac{\frac{13}{4} + \frac{7}{2}}{2} = \frac{\frac{13+14}{4}}{2} = \frac{27}{8}$$

$$\therefore \quad 3 < \frac{13}{4} < \frac{27}{8} < \frac{7}{2} < \frac{15}{4} < 4$$

A rational number between $\frac{7}{2}$ and $\frac{15}{4}$

$$= \frac{\frac{7}{2} + \frac{15}{4}}{2} = \frac{\frac{14+15}{4}}{2} = \frac{29}{8}$$

$$\therefore \quad 3 < \frac{13}{4} < \frac{27}{8} < \frac{7}{2} < \frac{29}{8} < \frac{15}{4} < 4$$

A rational number between $\frac{13}{4}$ and $\frac{27}{8}$

$$= \frac{\frac{13}{4} + \frac{27}{8}}{2} = \frac{\frac{26 + 27}{8}}{2} = \frac{53}{16}$$

$\therefore \quad 3 < \frac{13}{4} < \frac{53}{16} < \frac{27}{8} < \frac{7}{2} < \frac{29}{8} < \frac{15}{4} < 4$

So, the six rational numbers between 3 and 4 are $\frac{13}{4}, \frac{53}{16}, \frac{27}{8}, \frac{7}{2}, \frac{29}{8}$ and $\frac{15}{4}$.

Quick Solution

We have to find 6 rational numbers between 3 and 4, we multiply and divide both the numbers by 6 + 1 = 7

$\therefore \quad 3 = 3 \times \frac{7}{7} = \frac{21}{7}$

and $\quad 4 = 4 \times \frac{7}{7} = \frac{28}{7}$

As $\quad 21 < 22 < 23 < 24 < 25 < 26 < 27 < 28$

$\Rightarrow \quad \frac{21}{7} < \frac{22}{7} < \frac{23}{7} < \frac{24}{7} < \frac{25}{7} < \frac{26}{7} < \frac{27}{7} < \frac{28}{7}$

So, the six rational number between $\frac{21}{7} = 3$ and $\frac{28}{7} = 4$ are $\frac{22}{7}, \frac{23}{7}, \frac{24}{7}, \frac{25}{7}, \frac{26}{7}$ and $\frac{27}{7}$.

Question 3 Find five rational numbers between $\frac{3}{5}$ and $\frac{4}{5}$.

Sol. We have to find 5 rational numbers between $\frac{3}{5}$ and $\frac{4}{5}$, we multiply and divide both the numbers by 5 + 1 = 6.

$\therefore \quad \frac{3}{5} = \frac{3}{5} \times \frac{6}{6} = \frac{18}{30}$

and $\quad \frac{4}{5} = \frac{4}{5} \times \frac{6}{6} = \frac{24}{30}$

As $\quad 18 < 19 < 20 < 21 < 22 < 23 < 24$

$\Rightarrow \quad \frac{18}{30} < \frac{19}{30} < \frac{20}{30} < \frac{21}{30} < \frac{22}{30} < \frac{23}{30} < \frac{24}{30}$

So, the five rational numbers between $\frac{18}{30} = \frac{3}{5}$ and $\frac{24}{30} = \frac{4}{5}$ are $\frac{19}{30}, \frac{20}{30}, \frac{21}{30}, \frac{22}{30}$ and $\frac{23}{30}$.

Question 4 State whether the following statements a :e true or false. Give reasons for your answers.

(i) Every natural number is a whole number.

(ii) Every integer is a whole number.

(iii) Every rational number is a whole number.

Sol. (i) True, because natural numbers are 1, 2, 3, 4,...., ∞ and whole numbers are 0, 1, 2, 3, 4, 5,....,∞.

or

The collection of whole numbers contain all the natural numbers.

(ii) False, negative integers are not included in the list of whole numbers.

(iii) False, a rational number is a number that can be written in the form $\frac{p}{q}$, where $q \neq 0$ and q does not divide p completely that are not whole numbers.

Exercise 1.2

Question 1 State whether the following statements are true or false. Justify your answers.

(i) Every irrational number is a real number.

(ii) Every point on the number line is of the form $\sqrt{m}$, where m is a natural number.

(iii) Every real number is an irrational number.

Sol. (i) True

$\because$ Real numbers = Rational numbers + Irrational numbers.

(ii) False

$\because$ Negative number cannot be the square root of any natural number.

(iii) False

$\because$ Rational numbers are also present in the set of real numbers.

Question 2 Are the square roots of all positive integers irrational? If not, give an example of the square root of a number that is a rational number.

Sol. No, the square roots of all positive integers are not irrational.

e.g., $\sqrt{16} = 4$

Here, '4' is a rational number.

Question 3 Show how $\sqrt{5}$ can be represented on the number line.

Sol. We know that, $\sqrt{5} = \sqrt{4+1} = \sqrt{2^2 + 1^2}$

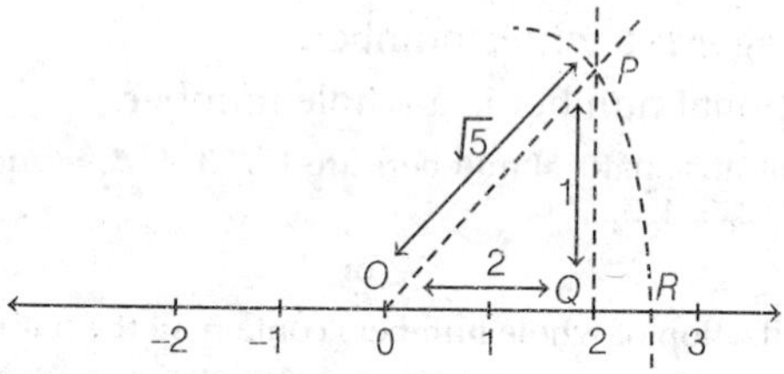

Draw a right angled triangle OQP, such that

$$OQ = 2 \text{ units}$$
$$PQ = 1 \text{unit and } \angle OQP = 90^\circ$$

Now, by using Pythagoras theorem, we have

$$OP^2 = OQ^2 + PQ^2 = 2^2 + 1^2$$

$$\Rightarrow \quad OP = \sqrt{4+1} = \sqrt{5}$$

Now, take O as centre $OP = \sqrt{5}$ as radius, draw an arc, which intersects the line at point R.

Hence, the point R represents $\sqrt{5}$ on the number line.

Question 4 Classroom activity (constructing the 'square root spiral'). Take a large sheet of paper and construct the 'square root spiral' in the following fashion. Start with a point O and draw a line segment OP_1 of unit length. Draw a line segment P_1P_2 perpendicular to OP_1 of unit length (see figure).

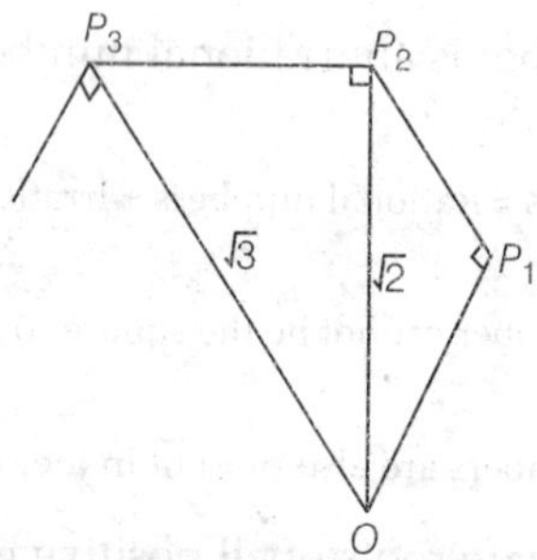

▲ Constructing square root spiral

Now, draw a line segment P_2P_3 perpendicular to OP_2. Then draw a line segment P_3P_4 perpendicular to OP_3. Continuing in this manner, you can get the line segment $P_{n-1}P_n$ by drawing a line segment of unit length perpendicular to OP_{n-1}. In this manner, you will have created the points $P_2, P_3, \ldots, P_n, \ldots$, and joined them to create a beautiful spiral depicting $\sqrt{2}, \sqrt{3}, \sqrt{4}, \ldots$

Sol. Do it yourself.

Exercise 1.3

Question 1 Write the following in decimal form and say what kind of decimal expansion each has

(i) $\frac{36}{100}$ (ii) $\frac{1}{11}$

(iii) $4\frac{1}{8}$ (iv) $\frac{3}{13}$

(v) $\frac{2}{11}$ (vi) $\frac{329}{400}$

Sol. (i) Clearly, $\frac{36}{100}$ can be written as 0.36

$\therefore$ The decimal expansion $\frac{36}{100}$ is terminating.

(ii) Dividing 1 by 11, we get

$$\begin{array}{r} 0.0909... \\ 11\overline{)1.00} \\ -99 \\ \hline 100 \\ -99 \\ \hline 1 \end{array}$$

$\therefore \frac{1}{11} = 0.090909.... = 0.\overline{09}$

So, the decimal expansion of $\frac{1}{11}$ is non-terminating repeating.

(iii) We have, $4\frac{1}{8} = \frac{4 \times 8 + 1}{8} = \frac{33}{8}$

Dividing 33 by 8, we get

$$\begin{array}{r} 4.125 \\ 8\overline{)\ 33} \\ -32 \\ \hline 10 \\ -8 \\ \hline 20 \\ -16 \\ \hline 40 \\ -40 \\ \hline 0 \end{array}$$

$\therefore \frac{33}{8} = 4.125$

So, the decimal expansion of $4\frac{1}{8}$ is terminating.

(iv) We have, $\frac{3}{13}$.

Dividing 3 by 13, we get

$$\begin{array}{r|l} & 0.2307692... \\ 13 & 30 \\ & -26 \\ \hline & 40 \\ & -39 \\ \hline & 100 \\ & -91 \\ \hline & 90 \\ & -78 \\ \hline & 120 \\ & 117 \\ \hline & 30 \\ & -26 \\ \hline & 4 \end{array}$$

$\therefore \frac{3}{13} = 0.2307692... = 0.\overline{230769}$

So, the decimal expansion of $\frac{3}{13}$ is non-terminating repeating.

(v) We have, $\frac{2}{11}$

Dividing 2 by 11, we get

$$\begin{array}{r|l} & 0.1818... \\ 11 & 2.0 \\ & -11 \\ \hline & 90 \\ & -88 \\ \hline & 20 \\ & -11 \\ \hline & 90 \\ & -88 \\ \hline & 2 \end{array}$$

$\therefore \quad \frac{2}{11} = 0.181818... = 0.\overline{18}$

So, the decimal expansion of $\frac{2}{11}$ is non-terminating repeating.

(vi) We have, $\frac{329}{400}$

Dividing 329 by 400, we get

$$\begin{array}{r} 0.8225 \\ 400\overline{)\ 329.0} \\ \underline{-3200} \\ 900 \\ \underline{-800} \\ 1000 \\ \underline{-800} \\ 2000 \\ \underline{-2000} \\ 0 \end{array}$$

$\therefore \quad \frac{329}{400} = 0.8225$

So, the decimal expansion of $\frac{329}{400}$ is terminating.

Question 2 You know that $\frac{1}{7} = 0.\overline{142857}$. Can you predict what the decimal expansions of $\frac{2}{7}, \frac{3}{7}, \frac{4}{7}, \frac{5}{7}, \frac{6}{7}$ are, without actually doing the long division? If so, how?

[**Hint** Study the remainders while finding the value of $\frac{1}{7}$ carefully.]

Sol. We have, $\frac{1}{7} = 0.\overline{142857}$

$\therefore$

$$\frac{2}{7} = 2 \times \frac{1}{7} = 2 \times 0.\overline{142857} \Rightarrow \frac{2}{7} = 0.\overline{285714}$$

$$\frac{3}{7} = 3 \times \frac{1}{7} = 3 \times 0.\overline{142857} \Rightarrow \frac{3}{7} = 0.\overline{428571}$$

$$\frac{4}{7} = 4 \times \frac{1}{7} = 4 \times 0.\overline{142857} \Rightarrow \frac{4}{7} = 0.\overline{571428}$$

$$\frac{5}{7} = 5 \times \frac{1}{7} = 5 \times 0.\overline{142857} \Rightarrow \frac{5}{7} = 0.\overline{714285}$$

$$\frac{6}{7} = 6 \times \frac{1}{7} = 6 \times 0.\overline{142857} \Rightarrow \frac{6}{7} = 0.\overline{857142}$$

Question 3 Express the following in the form $\frac{p}{q}$, where p and q are integers and $q \neq 0$.

(i) $0.\overline{6}$ (ii) $0.4\overline{7}$ (iii) $0.\overline{001}$

Sol. (i) Let $x = 0.\overline{6} = 0.666...$ ...(i)

On multiplying Eq. (i) by 10, we get

$$10x = 6.666... \quad ...(ii)$$

On subtracting Eq. (i) from Eq. (ii), we get

$$10x - x = 6.666... - 0.666...$$

$$\Rightarrow \quad 9x = 6$$

$$\Rightarrow \quad x = 6/9 \Rightarrow x = 2/3$$

$$\therefore \quad 0.\overline{6} = \frac{2}{3}$$

(ii) Let $x = 0.4\overline{7} = 0.4777...$ ...(iii)

On multiplying Eq. (iii) by 10, we get

$$10x = 4.777... \quad ...(iv)$$

On subtracting Eq. (iii) from Eq. (iv), we get

$$10x - x = 4.777... - 0.4777...$$

$$\Rightarrow \quad 9x = 4.3 \Rightarrow x = \frac{4.3}{9} \Rightarrow x = \frac{43}{90}$$

$$\therefore \quad 0.4\overline{7} = \frac{43}{90}$$

(iii) Let $x = 0.\overline{001} = 0.001001001...$ ...(v)

On multiplying Eq. (v) by 1000, we get

$$1000x = 1.001001001... \quad ...(vi)$$

On subtracting Eq. (v) from Eq. (vi), we get

$$1000x - x = 1.001001001.... - 0.001001001....$$

$$999x = 1 \Rightarrow x = \frac{1}{999}$$

$$\therefore \quad 0.\overline{001} = \frac{1}{999}$$

Question 4 Express 0.99999... in the form $\frac{p}{q}$. Are you surprised by your answer? With your teacher and classmates discuss why the answer makes sense.

Sol. Let $x = 0.99999...$ ...(i)

Multiplying Eq. (i) by 10, we get

$$10x = 9.99999... \quad ...(ii)$$

On subtracting Eq. (i) from Eq. (ii), we get

$$10\,x - x = 9.99999... - 0.99999...$$

$$\Rightarrow \quad 9x = 9 \Rightarrow x = \frac{9}{9} \Rightarrow x = 1$$

The difference between 1 and 0.99999 is 0.00001 which is negligible.

$\therefore$ The answer $x = 1$ is very close to $0.\overline{99999}$.

Question 5 What can the maximum number of digits be in the repeating block of digits in the decimal expansion of 1/17? Perform the division to check your answer.

Sol. The maximum number of digits in the repeating block of digits in the decimal expansion of $\frac{1}{17}$ is $17 - 1 = 16$.

We have,

$$
\begin{array}{r}
0.0588235294117647 \\
17\,\overline{)\;1.00} \\
-85 \\ \hline
150 \\
-136 \\ \hline
140 \\
-136 \\ \hline
40 \\
-34 \\ \hline
60 \\
-51 \\ \hline
90 \\
-85 \\ \hline
50 \\
-34 \\ \hline
160 \\
-153 \\ \hline
70 \\
-68 \\ \hline
20 \\
-17 \\ \hline
30 \\
-17 \\ \hline
130 \\
-119 \\ \hline
110 \\
-102 \\ \hline
80 \\
-68 \\ \hline
120 \\
-119 \\ \hline
1
\end{array}
$$

Thus, $\frac{1}{17} = 0.\overline{0588235294117647}$ a block of 16 digits is repeated.

So, there are 16 digits in the repeating block in the decimal expansion of $\frac{1}{17}$.

Hence Proved.

Question 6 Look at several examples of rational numbers in the form $\frac{p}{q}$ $(q \neq 0)$. Where, p and q are integers with no common factors other than 1 and having terminating decimal representations (expansions). Can you guess what property q must satisfy?

Sol. Consider many rational numbers in the form $\frac{p}{q}$ $(q \neq 0)$, where p and q are integers with no common factors other than 1 and having terminating decimal expansion.

Let the various such rational numbers be $\frac{1}{2}, \frac{1}{4}, \frac{5}{8}, \frac{36}{25}, \frac{7}{125}, \frac{19}{20}, \frac{29}{16}$ etc.

In all cases, we think of the natural number which when multiplied by their respective denominators gives 10 or a power of 10.

$$\frac{1}{2} = \frac{1 \times 5}{2 \times 5} = \frac{5}{10} = 0.5$$

$$\frac{1}{4} = \frac{1 \times 25}{4 \times 25} = \frac{25}{100} = 0.25$$

$$\frac{5}{8} = \frac{5 \times 125}{8 \times 125} = \frac{625}{1000} = 0.625$$

$$\frac{36}{25} = \frac{36 \times 4}{25 \times 4} = \frac{144}{100} = 1.44$$

$$\frac{7}{125} = \frac{7 \times 8}{125 \times 8} = \frac{56}{1000} = 0.056$$

$$\frac{19}{20} = \frac{19 \times 5}{20 \times 5} = \frac{95}{100} = 0.95$$

$$\frac{29}{16} = \frac{29 \times 625}{16 \times 625} = \frac{18125}{10000} = 1.8125$$

From the above, we find that the decimal expansion of above numbers are terminating. Along with we see that the denominator of above numbers are in the form $2^m \times 5^n$, where m and n are natural numbers.

Question 7 Write three numbers whose decimal expansions are non-terminating non-recurring.

Sol. Irrational numbers are the numbers whose decimal expansion is non-terminating and non-recurring. Hence, the three numbers whose decimal expansion is non-terminating and non-recurring are as follows.

0.74074007400074000074...

0.66506650066500066500000...

0.70700700070000...

Question 8 Find three different irrational numbers between the rational numbers $\frac{5}{7}$ and $\frac{9}{11}$.

◎ *Thinking Process* First find the decimal expansion of $\frac{5}{7}$ and $\frac{9}{11}$, then find the three different irrational numbers between them.

Sol. To find irrational numbers, firstly we shall divide 5 by 7 and 9 by 11,. So,

```
     0.714285...
13 ) 50
    -49
     10
     -7
      30
     -28
      20
     -14
      60
     -56
      40
     -35
       5
```

Thus, $\frac{5}{7} = 0.714285... = 0.\overline{714285}$

```
     0.8181...
11 ) 90
    -88
     20
    -11
      90
     -88
      20
     -11
       9
```

Thus, $\frac{9}{11} = 0.8181... = 0.\overline{81}$

We can find infinite number of irrational numbers between these two numbers.

∴ The required numbers are

0.73073007300073000073...

0.76507650076500076500000...

0.808008000800000...

Question 9 Classify the following numbers as rational or irrational

(i) $\sqrt{23}$ (ii) $\sqrt{225}$ (iii) 0.3796 (iv) 7.478478...

(v) 1.101001000100001...

Sol. (i) $\because \sqrt{23}$ is not a perfect square.

So, $\sqrt{23}$ is rational number.

(ii) $\sqrt{225} = 15$, which is rational.

(iii) 0.3796 is terminating.

So, 0.3796 is a rational number.

(iv) $7.478478... = 7.\overline{478}$, which is non-terminating repeating.

So, 7.478478... is a rational number.

(v) 1.101001000100001... is non-terminating non-repeating.

So, 1.101001000100001..... is an irratinal number.

Mistake Alert Students may assume all non-terminating decimals are irrational, forgetting that non-terminating repeating decimals are rational.

Exercise 1.4

Question 1 Classify the following numbers as rational or irrational.

(i) $2-\sqrt{5}$ (ii) $(3+\sqrt{23})-\sqrt{23}$ (iii) $\frac{2\sqrt{7}}{7\sqrt{7}}$

(iv) $\frac{1}{\sqrt{2}}$ (v) 2π

Sol. (i) $\because$ 2 is a rational number and $\sqrt{5}$ is an irrational number.

$\therefore 2-\sqrt{5}$ is an irrational number.

[$\because$ The difference of a rational number and an irrational number is irrational.]

(ii) $3+\sqrt{23}-\sqrt{23} = 3$ (rational)

(iii) $\frac{2\sqrt{7}}{7\sqrt{7}} = \frac{2}{7}$ (rational)

(iv) $\because$ $1 \neq 0$ is a rational number and $\sqrt{2}$ is an irrational number.

$\therefore \frac{1}{\sqrt{2}}$ is an irrational number.

[$\because$ The quotient of a non-zero rational number with an irrational number is irrational.]

(v) $\because$ 2 is a rational number and π is an irrational number.

$\therefore 2\pi$ is an irrational number. [$\because$ The product of a non-zero rational number with an irrational number is an irrational]

Question 2 Simplify each of the following expressions

(i) $(3+\sqrt{3})(2+\sqrt{2})$ (ii) $(3+\sqrt{3})(3-\sqrt{3})$

(iii) $(\sqrt{5}+\sqrt{2})^2$ (iv) $(\sqrt{5}-\sqrt{2})(\sqrt{5}+\sqrt{2})$

Thinking Process Use the formula $(a+b)(a-b)=a^2-b^2$ and $(a+b)^2=a^2+2ab+b^2$.

Sol. (i) $(3+\sqrt{3})(2+\sqrt{2}) = 3(2+\sqrt{2})+\sqrt{3}(2+\sqrt{2})$
$= 6+3\sqrt{2}+2\sqrt{3}+\sqrt{6}$

(ii) $(3+\sqrt{3})(3-\sqrt{3}) = 3^2-(\sqrt{3})^2$ [$\because (a+b)(a-b)=a^2-b^2$]
$= 9-3 = 6$

(iii) $(\sqrt{5}+\sqrt{2})^2 = (\sqrt{5})^2+2\sqrt{5}\times\sqrt{2}+(\sqrt{2})^2$ [$\because (a+b)^2=a^2+2ab+b^2$]
$= 5+2\sqrt{10}+2$
$= 7+2\sqrt{10}$

(iv) $(\sqrt{5}-\sqrt{2})(\sqrt{5}+\sqrt{2}) = (\sqrt{5})^2-(\sqrt{2})^2 = 5-2 = 3$
[$\because (a-b)(a+b)=a^2-b^2$]

Question 3 Recall, π is defined as the ratio of the circumference (say c) of a circle to its diameter (say d). That is $\pi = \frac{c}{d}$. This seems to contradict the fact that π is irrational. How will you resolve this contradiction?

Sol. Actually $\frac{c}{d} = \frac{22}{7}$ which is an approximate value of π. With a scale we get only approximate rational number as a result of measurement.

Question 4 Represent $\sqrt{9.3}$ on the number line.

Sol. Firstly we draw $AB = 9.3$ units. Now, from B, mark a distance of 1 unit. Let this point be C. Let O be the mid-point of AC. Now, draw a semi-circle with centre O and radius OA. Let us draw a line perpendicular to AC passing through point B and intersecting the semi-circle at point D.

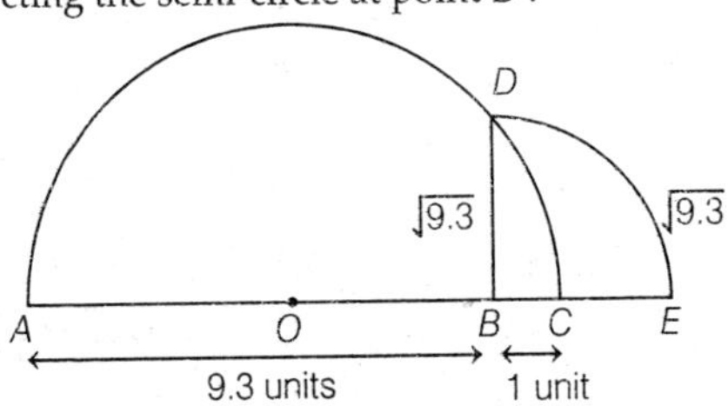

$\therefore$ The distance $BD = \sqrt{9.3}$.

Draw an arc with centre B and radius BD, which intersects the number line at point E, then the point E represents $\sqrt{9.3}$.

Question 5 Rationalise the denominator of the following

(i) $\frac{1}{\sqrt{7}}$ (ii) $\frac{1}{\sqrt{7}-\sqrt{6}}$

(iii) $\frac{1}{\sqrt{5}+\sqrt{2}}$ (iv) $\frac{1}{\sqrt{7}-2}$

Sol. (i) $\frac{1}{\sqrt{7}} = \frac{1}{\sqrt{7}} \times \frac{\sqrt{7}}{\sqrt{7}} = \frac{\sqrt{7}}{7}$ (Multiplying and dividing by $\sqrt{7}$) $[\because \sqrt{a}\cdot\sqrt{a} = a]$

(ii) $\frac{1}{\sqrt{7}-\sqrt{6}} = \frac{1}{\sqrt{7}-\sqrt{6}} \times \frac{\sqrt{7}+\sqrt{6}}{\sqrt{7}+\sqrt{6}}$

(Multiplying and dividing by $\sqrt{7}+\sqrt{6}$)

$$= \frac{\sqrt{7}+\sqrt{6}}{(\sqrt{7})^2-(\sqrt{6})^2} = \frac{\sqrt{7}+\sqrt{6}}{7-6} = \sqrt{7}+\sqrt{6} \quad [\because (a+b)(a-b) = a^2-b^2]$$

(iii) $\frac{1}{\sqrt{5}+\sqrt{2}} = \frac{1}{\sqrt{5}+\sqrt{2}} \times \frac{\sqrt{5}-\sqrt{2}}{\sqrt{5}-\sqrt{2}}$

(Multiplying and dividing by $\sqrt{5}-\sqrt{2}$)

$$= \frac{\sqrt{5}-\sqrt{2}}{(\sqrt{5})^2-(\sqrt{2})^2} = \frac{\sqrt{5}-\sqrt{2}}{5-2} = \frac{\sqrt{5}-\sqrt{2}}{3}$$

$[\because (a+b)(a-b) = a^2-b^2]$

(iv) $\frac{1}{\sqrt{7}-2} = \frac{1}{\sqrt{7}-2} \times \frac{\sqrt{7}+2}{\sqrt{7}+2}$

(Multiplying and dividing by $\sqrt{7}+2$)

$$= \frac{\sqrt{7}+2}{(\sqrt{7})^2-2^2} = \frac{\sqrt{7}+2}{7-4} = \frac{\sqrt{7}+2}{3} \quad [\because (a+b)(a-b) = a^2-b^2]$$

Mistake Alert Do not forget to multiply both numerator and denominator by $\sqrt{7}+2$.

Exercise 1.5

Question 1 Find

(i) $64^{\frac{1}{2}}$ (ii) $32^{\frac{1}{5}}$ (iii) $125^{\frac{1}{3}}$

Sol. (i) $64^{\frac{1}{2}} = (8 \times 8)^{\frac{1}{2}} = (8^2)^{\frac{1}{2}} = 8^{2 \times \frac{1}{2}} = 8$ $[\because (a^m)^n = a^{mn}]$

(ii) $32^{\frac{1}{5}} = (2 \times 2 \times 2 \times 2 \times 2)^{\frac{1}{5}} = (2^5)^{\frac{1}{5}} = 2^{5 \times \frac{1}{5}} = 2$ $[\because (a^m)^n = a^{mn}]$

(iii) $125^{\frac{1}{3}} = (5 \times 5 \times 5)^{\frac{1}{3}} = (5^3)^{1/3} = 5^{3 \times \frac{1}{3}} = 5$ $[\because (a^m)^n = a^{mn}]$

Question 2 Find

(i) $9^{\frac{3}{2}}$ (ii) $32^{\frac{2}{5}}$ (iii) $16^{\frac{3}{4}}$ (iv) $125^{-\frac{1}{3}}$

Sol. (i) $9^{\frac{3}{2}} = (3^2)^{\frac{3}{2}} = 3^{2 \times \frac{3}{2}} = 3^3 = 27$ $[\because (a^m)^n = a^{mn}]$

(ii) $32^{\frac{2}{5}} = (2^5)^{\frac{2}{5}} = 2^{5 \times \frac{2}{5}} = 2^2 = 4$ $[\because (a^m)^n = a^{mn}]$

(iii) $16^{\frac{3}{4}} = (2^4)^{\frac{3}{4}} = 2^{4 \times \frac{3}{4}} = 2^3 = 8$ $[\because (a^m)^n = a^{mn}]$

(iv) $125^{-\frac{1}{3}} = (5^3)^{-\frac{1}{3}} = 5^{3 \times \left(\frac{-1}{3}\right)} = 5^{-1} = \frac{1}{5}$ $\left[\because (a^m)^n = a^{mn} \text{ and } a^{-m} = \frac{1}{a^m}\right]$

Question 3 Simplify

(i) $2^{\frac{2}{3}} \cdot 2^{\frac{1}{5}}$ (ii) $\left(\frac{1}{3^3}\right)^7$ (iii) $\frac{11^{\frac{1}{2}}}{11^{\frac{1}{4}}}$ (iv) $7^{\frac{1}{2}} \cdot 8^{\frac{1}{2}}$

◎ ***Thinking Process*** Use the laws of radicals as $x^a \cdot x^b = x^{a+b}$, $(x^a)^b = x^{ab}$, $\frac{x^a}{x^b} = x^{a-b}$ and $x^a \cdot y^a = (xy)^a$

Sol. (i) $2^{\frac{2}{3}} \cdot 2^{\frac{1}{5}} = 2^{\frac{2}{3} + \frac{1}{5}} = 2^{\frac{10+3}{15}} = 2^{\frac{13}{15}}$ $(\because x^a \cdot x^b = x^{a+b})$

(ii) $\left(\frac{1}{3^3}\right)^7 = \frac{1}{3^{3 \times 7}} = \frac{1}{3^{21}} = 3^{-21}$ $[\because (x^a)^b = x^{ab}]$

(iii) $\frac{11^{\frac{1}{2}}}{11^{\frac{1}{4}}} = 11^{\frac{1}{2} - \frac{1}{4}} = 11^{\frac{2-1}{4}}$ $\left(\because \frac{x^a}{x^b} = x^{a-b}\right)$

$= 11^{\frac{1}{4}}$

(iv) $7^{\frac{1}{2}} \cdot 8^{\frac{1}{2}} = (7 \cdot 8)^{\frac{1}{2}} = (56)^{\frac{1}{2}}$ $[\because x^a \cdot y^a = (xy)^a]$

DIKSHA APP Questions

☐ Multiple Choice Questions

Q.1 Write the natural number is 'a' for $5^{a-3} \times 3^{2a-8} = 225$

(a) 10 (b) 5 (c) –5 (d) 2

◎ *Thinking Process* If $a^m = b^n$, then $m = n$.

Sol. (b) We have,

$$5^{a-3} \times 3^{2a-8} = 225$$

$$\Rightarrow \frac{5^a}{5^3} \times \frac{3^{2a}}{3^8} = (15)^2 = (3 \times 5)^2$$

$$\Rightarrow 5^a \times 3^{2a} = 5^3 \times 3^8 \times 3^2 \times 5^2$$

$$\Rightarrow 5^a \times 3^{2a} = 5^{3+2} \times 3^{8+2}$$

$$\Rightarrow 5^a \times 3^{2a} = 5^5 \times 3^{10}$$

On comparing both sides, we get

$$a = 5$$

Q.2 Which of the following is irrational?

(a) $\sqrt{\frac{4}{9}}$ (b) $\sqrt{5c}$

(c) $\frac{\sqrt{12}}{\sqrt{3}}$ (d) $\sqrt{16}$

Sol. (b) We have, (a) $\sqrt{\frac{4}{9}} = \frac{2}{3}$ (rational)

(b) $\sqrt{5c}$ = (irrational)

(c) $\frac{\sqrt{12}}{\sqrt{3}} = \sqrt{\frac{12}{3}} = \sqrt{4} = 2$ [rational]

(d) $\sqrt{16} = 4$ [rational]

Q.3 $\sqrt{10} \times \sqrt{15}$ is equal to

(a) $6\sqrt{5}$ (b) $5\sqrt{6}$

(c) $10\sqrt{5}$ (d) $\sqrt{25}$

Sol. (b) We have, $\sqrt{10} \times \sqrt{15} = \sqrt{150}$

$$= \sqrt{25 \times 6} = 5\sqrt{6}$$

Q.4 Decimal representation of a rational number cannot be

(a) terminating
(b) non terming
(c) non-terminating repeating
(d) non terminating non-repeating

Sol. (d) Decimal representation of a rational number cannot be non-terminating non-repeating.

Q.5 The number 1.01001001 ... is

(a) a natural number
(b) a whole number
(c) a rational number
(d) an irrational number

Sol. (d) As the given number is non-terminating non-repeating decimal, so it is an irrational number.

Q.6 On simplifying $(5+\sqrt{2})(3+\sqrt{5})$, we get

(a) $15+9\sqrt{10}$ (b) 105
(c) $15+5\sqrt{5}+3\sqrt{2}+\sqrt{10}$ (d) 123

Sol. (c) We have, $(5+\sqrt{2})(3+\sqrt{5}) = 5(3+\sqrt{5})+\sqrt{2}(3+\sqrt{5})$

$$= 15+5\sqrt{5}+3\sqrt{2}+\sqrt{10}$$

Q.7 Irrational number between 1.011243...and 1.012243 ... is

(a) 1.011143... (b) 1.012343...
(c) 1.01152243 ... (d) 1.013243 ...

Sol. (c) As 1.011243... < 1.01152243... < 1.012243...

So, the irrational number between 1.011243... and 1.012243... is 1.01152243...

Q.8 $2\sqrt{3}+\sqrt{3}$ is equal to

(a) $2\sqrt{6}$ (b) 6 (c) $3\sqrt{3}$ (d) $4\sqrt{6}$

Sol. (c) We have, $2\sqrt{3}+\sqrt{3} = 3\sqrt{3}$

Q.9 Which of the following numbers are rational?

(a) $\frac{0}{1}$ (b) $\frac{1}{0}$ (c) $\frac{2}{0}$ (d) $\frac{4}{0}$

Sol. (a) A rational number is in the form $\frac{p}{q}$ and $q \neq 0$.

So, $\frac{0}{1}$ is a rational number.

☐ Subjective Type Questions

Q.1 Simplify $\sqrt[3]{16}+\sqrt[3]{54}+\sqrt[3]{192}-\sqrt[3]{375}$.

Sol. We have

$$\sqrt[3]{16}+\sqrt[3]{54}+\sqrt[3]{192}-\sqrt[3]{375}=\sqrt[3]{8\times2}+\sqrt[3]{27\times2}+\sqrt[3]{64\times3}-\sqrt[3]{125\times3}$$
$$=\sqrt[3]{8}\cdot\sqrt[3]{2}+\sqrt[3]{27}\cdot\sqrt[3]{2}+\sqrt[3]{64}\cdot\sqrt[3]{3}-\sqrt[3]{125}\cdot\sqrt[3]{3}$$
$$=2\times\sqrt[3]{2}+3\times\sqrt[3]{2}+4\times\sqrt[3]{3}-5\times\sqrt[3]{3}$$
$$=5\cdot\sqrt[3]{2}-\sqrt[3]{3}$$

Q.2 Every whole number is a .... number but not *vice-versa.*

Sol. Every whole number is a rational number but the *vice-versa* is not always true is a whole number and also a rational number. But $\frac{4}{5}$ is neither whole number.

So, every whole number is rational number but not *vice-versa.*

Q.3 Evaluate $2\sqrt[3]{4}+7\sqrt[3]{32}-\sqrt[3]{500}$.

Sol. We have, $2\sqrt[3]{4}+7\cdot\sqrt[3]{2\times2\times2\times4}-\sqrt[3]{5\times5\times5\times4}$

$$=2\sqrt[3]{4}+7\times2\sqrt[3]{4}-5\sqrt[3]{4}$$
$$=\sqrt[3]{4}\,(2+14-5)$$
$$=\sqrt[3]{4}\times11$$
$$=11\sqrt[3]{4}$$

Q.4 If $x=9+4\sqrt{5}$, find the value of $\sqrt{x}-\frac{1}{\sqrt{x}}$.

◎ *Thinking Process* First find the value of $\frac{1}{x}$, then use the formula $(a-b)^2=a^2-2ab+b^2$ to get the required result.

Sol. We have, $x=9+4\sqrt{5}$

$$\Rightarrow \quad \frac{1}{x}=\frac{1}{9+4\sqrt{5}}$$
$$=\frac{1}{9+4\sqrt{5}}\times\frac{9-4\sqrt{5}}{9-4\sqrt{5}}=\frac{9-4\sqrt{5}}{(9)^2-(4\sqrt{5})^2} \qquad [\because (a+b)(a-b)=a^2-b^2]$$
$$=\frac{9-4\sqrt{5}}{81-80}=9-4\sqrt{5}$$

Now, $\left(\sqrt{x}-\frac{1}{\sqrt{x}}\right)^2=(\sqrt{x})^2+\left(\frac{1}{\sqrt{x}}\right)^2-2\times\sqrt{x}\times\frac{1}{\sqrt{x}}$

$$\Rightarrow \quad \left(\sqrt{x}-\frac{1}{\sqrt{x}}\right)^2=x+\frac{1}{x}-2$$

$$\Rightarrow \quad \left(\sqrt{x} - \frac{1}{\sqrt{x}}\right)^2 = 9 + 4\sqrt{5} + 9 - 4\sqrt{5} - 2$$

$$\Rightarrow \quad \left(\sqrt{x} - \frac{1}{\sqrt{x}}\right)^2 = 16$$

$$\Rightarrow \quad \sqrt{x} - \frac{1}{\sqrt{x}} = \pm 4$$

Q.5 Determine a and b if

$$\frac{7+\sqrt{5}}{7-\sqrt{5}} - \frac{7-\sqrt{5}}{7+\sqrt{5}} = a + \frac{7\sqrt{5}b}{11}$$

Sol. We have, $\dfrac{7+\sqrt{5}}{7-\sqrt{5}} - \dfrac{7-\sqrt{5}}{7+\sqrt{5}} = a + \dfrac{7\sqrt{5}b}{11}$

$$\Rightarrow \quad \frac{(7+\sqrt{5})^2 - (7-\sqrt{5})^2}{(7-\sqrt{5})(7+\sqrt{5})} = a + \frac{7\sqrt{5}b}{11}$$

$$\Rightarrow \quad \frac{(49+5+14\sqrt{5}) - (49+5-14\sqrt{5})}{(7)^2 - (\sqrt{5})^2} = a + \frac{7\sqrt{5}b}{11}$$

$$\Rightarrow \quad \frac{54+14\sqrt{5} - 54 + 14\sqrt{5}}{49-5} = a + \frac{7\sqrt{5}b}{11}$$

$$\Rightarrow \quad \frac{28\sqrt{5}}{44} = a + \frac{7\sqrt{5}b}{11}$$

$$\Rightarrow \quad \frac{7\sqrt{5}}{11} = a + \frac{7\sqrt{5}b}{11}$$

On comparing the equation, we get

$$a = 0 \text{ and } b = 1$$

Q.6 Find two irrational numbers between 1.12 and 1.13.

Sol. The number of irrational numbers between two rational numbers is infinite.

So, two irrational numbers between 1.12 and 1.13 are 1.121221222.... and 1.12212221..... .

Q.7 Divide $\sqrt[3]{128}$ by $\sqrt[5]{64}$.

Sol. We have, $\dfrac{\sqrt[3]{128}}{\sqrt[5]{64}} = \dfrac{\sqrt[3]{64 \times 2}}{\sqrt[5]{32 \times 2}} = \dfrac{\sqrt[3]{64} \times \sqrt[3]{2}}{\sqrt[5]{32} \times \sqrt[5]{2}}$

$$= \frac{4\sqrt[3]{2}}{2\sqrt[5]{2}} = \frac{2\sqrt[3]{2}}{\sqrt[5]{2}}$$

Q.8 Evaluate $\dfrac{(36)^{\frac{7}{2}}-(36)^{\frac{9}{2}}}{(36)^{\frac{5}{2}}}$.

◎ *Thinking Process* Use $\dfrac{a^m}{a^n}=(a)^{m-n}$ and $(a^m)^n=a^{mn}$ to get the required value.

Sol. We have, $\dfrac{(36)^{\frac{7}{2}}-(36)^{\frac{9}{2}}}{(36)^{\frac{5}{2}}}=\dfrac{(6^2)^{\frac{7}{2}}-(6^2)^{\frac{9}{2}}}{(6^2)^{\frac{5}{2}}}$

$$=\frac{(6)^{2\times\frac{7}{2}}-(6)^{2\times\frac{9}{2}}}{(6)^{2\times\frac{5}{2}}}=\frac{6^7-6^9}{6^5}=\frac{6^7(1-6^2)}{6^5}$$

$$=6^2\,(1-36)=36\times(-35)=-1260$$

Q.9 Simplify $\dfrac{6-4\sqrt{2}}{6+4\sqrt{2}}$.

Sol. We have, $\dfrac{6-4\sqrt{2}}{6+4\sqrt{2}}=\dfrac{6-4\sqrt{2}}{6+4\sqrt{2}}\times\dfrac{6-4\sqrt{2}}{6-4\sqrt{2}}=\dfrac{(6-4\sqrt{2})^2}{(6)^2-(4\sqrt{2})^2}$

$[\because (a+b)(a-b)=a^2-b^2]$

$$=\frac{(6)^2+(4\sqrt{2})^2-2\times6\times4\sqrt{2}}{36-32}$$ $[\because (a-b)^2=a^2+b^2-2ab]$

$$=\frac{36+32-48\sqrt{2}}{4}=\frac{68-48\sqrt{2}}{4}=\frac{4(17-12\sqrt{2})}{4}=17-12\sqrt{2}.$$

Q.10 Express the $0.\overline{418}$ as a rational number in $\dfrac{p}{q}$ form.

Sol. Let $x=0.418418.....$ ...(i)

Since, periodicity is 3 that is three digits (418) is repeating.

So, on is multiplying Eq. (i) by 1000, we get

$$1000x=1000\times0.418418....$$

$\Rightarrow$ $1000x=418.418418...$ ...(ii)

On subtracting Eq. (i) form Eq. (ii), we get

$$1000x-x=418.418418....-0.418418....$$

$\Rightarrow$ $999x=418$

$\Rightarrow$ $x=\dfrac{418}{999}$

$\therefore$ $0.\overline{418}=\dfrac{418}{999}$

Q.11 Express 5.222 ... in the form $\frac{p}{q}$.

Sol. Let $x = 5.222...$ ... (i)

Since, periodicity is 1 that is one digit (2) is repeating.

So, on is multiplying Eq. (i) by 10, we get

$$10x = 10 \times 5.222\ldots$$

$$\Rightarrow \quad 10x = 52.222\ldots \quad \ldots \text{(ii)}$$

On subtracting Eq. (i) from Eq. (ii), we get

$$10x - x = 52.222\ldots - 5.222\ldots$$

$$\Rightarrow \quad 9x = 47$$

$$\Rightarrow \quad x = \frac{47}{9}$$

$$\therefore \quad 5.222\ldots = \frac{47}{9}$$

Q.12 Simplify $4\sqrt{3} - 3\sqrt{12} + 2\sqrt{75}$

Sol. We have, $4\sqrt{3} - 3\sqrt{12} + 2\sqrt{75} = 4\sqrt{3} - 3\sqrt{2 \times 2 \times 3} + 2\sqrt{5 \times 5 \times 3}$

$$= 4\sqrt{3} - 2 \times 3\sqrt{3} + 2 \times 5\sqrt{3}$$

$$= 4\sqrt{3} - 6\sqrt{3} + 10\sqrt{3} = 8\sqrt{3}$$

Q.13 Simplify $\frac{4 + \sqrt{5}}{4 - \sqrt{5}}$

Sol. We have, $\frac{4+\sqrt{5}}{4-\sqrt{5}} = \frac{4+\sqrt{5}}{4-\sqrt{5}} \times \frac{4+\sqrt{5}}{4+\sqrt{5}} = \frac{(4+\sqrt{5})^2}{(4)^2 - (\sqrt{5})^2}$

$[\because (a+b)(a-b) = a^2 - b^2]$

$$= \frac{(4)^2 + (\sqrt{5})^2 + 2 \times 4 \times \sqrt{5}}{16 - 5} \quad [\because (a+b)^2 = a^2 + b^2 + 2ab]$$

$$= \frac{16 + 5 + 8\sqrt{5}}{11} = \frac{21 + 8\sqrt{5}}{11}$$

Q.13 Represent $\sqrt{2}$ on the number line.

Sol. We know that $\sqrt{2} = \sqrt{1+1}$

Draw a right angled triangle OQP such that

$$OQ = 1\,\text{unit},\ PQ = 1\,\text{unit and } \angle OQP = 90°$$

Now, using Pythagoras theorem, we have

$$OP^2 = OQ^2 + PQ^2 = (1)^2 + (1)^2 = 2 \Rightarrow OP = \sqrt{2}$$

Now, take O as centre and $OP = \sqrt{2}$ as radius, draw an arc which intersect the line at point R.

Hence, the point R represents $\sqrt{2}$.

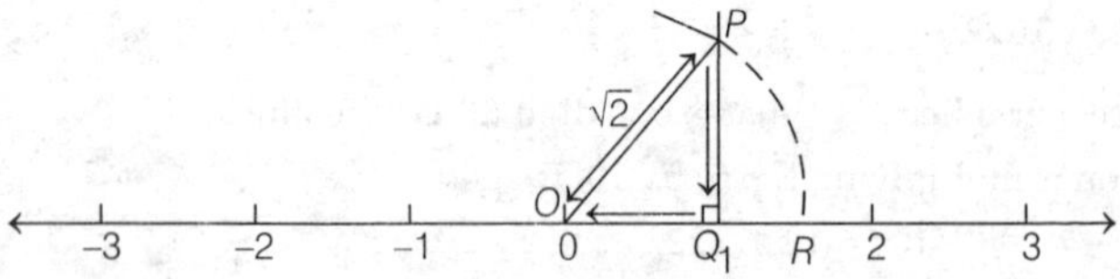

Q.15 Evaluate $\dfrac{\left(\dfrac{81}{16}\right)^{-3/4} \times \left(\dfrac{25}{9}\right)^{-3/2} \times \left(\dfrac{2}{5}\right)^{-3}}{(125)^{2/3} \times (8)^{4/3}}$

Sol. We have, $\dfrac{\left(\dfrac{81}{16}\right)^{-3/4} \times \left(\dfrac{25}{9}\right)^{-3/2} \times \left(\dfrac{2}{5}\right)^{-3}}{(125)^{2/3} \times (8)^{4/3}} = \dfrac{\left[\left(\dfrac{3}{2}\right)^4\right]^{\frac{-3}{4}} \times \left[\left(\dfrac{5}{3}\right)^2\right]^{\frac{-3}{2}} \times \left(\dfrac{2}{5}\right)^{-3}}{(5^3)^{\frac{2}{3}} \times (2^3)^{\frac{4}{3}}}$

$$= \frac{\left(\dfrac{3}{2}\right)^{-3} \times \left(\dfrac{5}{2}\right)^{-3} \times \left(\dfrac{2}{5}\right)^{-3}}{5^2 \times 2^4}$$

$$= \frac{\left(\dfrac{3}{2} \times \dfrac{5}{2} \times \dfrac{2}{5}\right)^{-3}}{25 \times 16} = \frac{\left(\dfrac{3}{2}\right)^{-3}}{400} = \frac{\left(\dfrac{2}{3}\right)^{3}}{400} = \frac{8}{27 \times 400} = \frac{1}{1350}$$

Q.16 Rationalise the denominator $\dfrac{1}{(\sqrt{7} + \sqrt{6}) - \sqrt{13}}$.

◎ **Thinking Process** Use the formula $(a+b)(a-b) = a^2 - b^2$ and $(a+b)^2 = a^2 + b^2 + 2ab$ to get the required value.

Sol. We have, $\dfrac{1}{(\sqrt{7} + \sqrt{6}) - \sqrt{13}} = \dfrac{1}{(\sqrt{7} + \sqrt{6}) - \sqrt{13}} \times \dfrac{(\sqrt{7} + \sqrt{6}) + \sqrt{13}}{(\sqrt{7} + \sqrt{6}) + \sqrt{13}}$

$$= \frac{(\sqrt{7} + \sqrt{6}) + \sqrt{13}}{(\sqrt{7} + \sqrt{6})^2 - (\sqrt{13})^2} \qquad [\because (a + b)(a - b) = a^2 - b^2]$$

$$= \frac{\sqrt{7} + \sqrt{6} + \sqrt{13}}{((\sqrt{7})^2 + (\sqrt{6})^2 + 2 \times \sqrt{7} \times \sqrt{6}) - 13} \qquad [\because (a + b)^2 = a^2 + b^2 + 2ab]$$

$$= \frac{\sqrt{7} + \sqrt{6} + \sqrt{13}}{7 + 6 + 2\sqrt{42} - 13} = \frac{\sqrt{7} + \sqrt{6} + \sqrt{13}}{2\sqrt{42}}$$

Again rationalise the denominator by multiplying and dividing by $\sqrt{42}$

$$= \frac{\sqrt{7}+\sqrt{6}+\sqrt{13}}{2\sqrt{42}} \times \frac{\sqrt{42}}{\sqrt{42}} = \frac{(\sqrt{7}+\sqrt{6}+\sqrt{13})(\sqrt{42})}{2\times 42}$$

$$= \frac{\sqrt{294}+\sqrt{252}+\sqrt{546}}{84} = \frac{7\sqrt{6}+6\sqrt{7}+\sqrt{546}}{84}$$

Q.17 Simplify $\frac{7\sqrt{3}}{\sqrt{10}+\sqrt{3}} - \frac{2\sqrt{5}}{\sqrt{6}+\sqrt{5}} - \frac{3\sqrt{2}}{\sqrt{15}+3\sqrt{2}}$.

Sol. For further simplification rationalise the denominator of all terms, we get

$$\left[\frac{7\sqrt{3}}{\sqrt{10}+\sqrt{3}} \times \frac{\sqrt{10}-\sqrt{3}}{\sqrt{10}-\sqrt{3}}\right] - \left[\frac{2\sqrt{5}}{\sqrt{6}+\sqrt{5}} \times \frac{\sqrt{6}-\sqrt{5}}{\sqrt{6}-\sqrt{5}}\right] - \left[\frac{3\sqrt{2}}{\sqrt{15}+3\sqrt{2}} \times \frac{\sqrt{15}-3\sqrt{2}}{\sqrt{15}-3\sqrt{2}}\right]$$

$$= \left[\frac{7\sqrt{3}(\sqrt{10}-\sqrt{3})}{(\sqrt{10})^2-(\sqrt{3})^2}\right] - \left[\frac{2\sqrt{5}(\sqrt{6}-\sqrt{5})}{(\sqrt{6})^2-(\sqrt{5})^2}\right] - \left[\frac{3\sqrt{2}(\sqrt{15}-3\sqrt{2})}{(\sqrt{15})^2-(3\sqrt{2})^2}\right]$$

$[\because (a+b)(a-b) = a^2 - b^2]$

$$= \left[\frac{7\sqrt{30}-21}{10-3}\right] - \left[\frac{2\sqrt{30}-10}{6-5}\right] - \left[\frac{3\sqrt{30}-18}{15-18}\right]$$

$$= \left[\frac{7(\sqrt{30}-3)}{7}\right] - (2\sqrt{30}-10) - \left[\frac{3(\sqrt{30}-6)}{-3}\right]$$

$$= \sqrt{30} - 3 - 2\sqrt{30} + 10 - (6 - \sqrt{30})$$

$$= \sqrt{30} - 3 - 2\sqrt{30} + 10 - 6 + \sqrt{30} = 10 - 9 = 1$$

Q.18 Simplify $\sqrt[4]{81} - 8\sqrt[3]{216} + 15\sqrt[5]{32} + \sqrt{225}$.

Sol. We have, $\sqrt[4]{81} - 8\sqrt[3]{216} + 15\sqrt[5]{32} + \sqrt{225}$

$$= \sqrt[4]{3\times3\times3\times3} - 8\sqrt[3]{6\times6\times6} + 15\sqrt[5]{2\times2\times2\times2\times2} + \sqrt{15\times15}$$

$$= 3 - 8\times6 + 15\times2 + 15$$

$$= 3 - 48 + 30 + 15 = 48 - 48 = 0$$

Q.19 Find three rational numbers between 3 and 4.

Sol. A rational number between 3 and 4 $= \frac{3+4}{2} = \frac{7}{2}$

$\therefore \quad 3 < \frac{7}{2} < 4$

A rational number between 3 and $\frac{7}{2} = \frac{3+\frac{7}{2}}{2} = \frac{13}{4}$

$\therefore \quad 3 < \frac{13}{4} < \frac{7}{2} < 4$

A rational number between 4 and $\frac{7}{2} = \frac{4+\frac{7}{2}}{2} = \frac{15}{4}$

$$\therefore \qquad 3 < \frac{13}{4} < \frac{7}{2} < \frac{15}{4} < 4$$

So, the three rational number between 3 and 4 are $\frac{13}{4}, \frac{7}{2}$ and $\frac{15}{4}$

Quick Solution

We have to find 3 rational numbers between 3 and 4. Now, multiply and divide both numbers by $3 + 1 = 4$.

$$\therefore \qquad 3 = 3 \times \frac{4}{4} = \frac{12}{4} \text{ and } 4 = 4 \times \frac{4}{4} = \frac{16}{4}$$

As $\qquad 12 < 13 < 14 < 15 < 16$

$$\Rightarrow \qquad \frac{12}{4} < \frac{13}{4} < \frac{14}{4} < \frac{15}{4} < \frac{16}{4}$$

So, the three rational numbers between $\frac{12}{4} = 3$ and $\frac{16}{4} = 4$ are $\frac{13}{4}, \frac{14}{4}$ and $\frac{15}{4}$.

Polynomials

CHAPTER 02

Important Points

01 Polynomial A polynomial $p(x)$ in one variable x is an algebraic expression in x of the form

$$p(x) = a_n x^n + a_{n-1} x^{n-1} + a_{n-2} x^{n-2} + \ldots + a_2 x^2 + a_1 x + a_0$$

where $a_0, a_1, a_2, \ldots, a_n$ are constants and $a_n \neq 0$.

$a_0, a_1, a_2, \ldots, a_n$ are respectively the coefficient of $x^0, x, x^2, \ldots, x^n$ and each of $a_n x^n, a_{n-1} x^{n-1}, \ldots, a_0$ with $a_n \neq 0$ is called term of the polynomial $p(x)$.

e.g.,

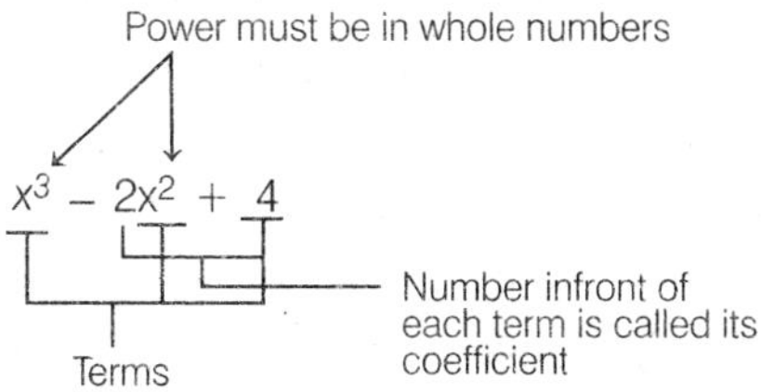

02 Terms The several parts of a polynomial separated by '+' or '–' operations are called the terms of the expression.

03 Types of Polynomial

(i) **Constant polynomial** A polynomial containing one term only, consisting of a constant is called a constant polynomial. In other words, it is a polynomial that does not have any variables term.

e.g., $-6, 4, \frac{2}{3}, -\frac{3}{4}$ etc., are all constant polynomials.

Note Generally, each real number is a constant polynomial.

(ii) **Zero polynomial** A polynomial consisting of one term, namely zero only, is called a zero polynomial or a zero polynomial whose value is zero.

(iii) **Monomial** Polynomials having only one term are called monomials ('mono' means 'one').

e.g., $x^3, \frac{7}{3}xz$ and -2 are all monomials.

(iv) **Binomial** Polynomials having only two terms are called binomials ('bi' means 'two').

e.g., $(x^2+x), (y^{30}+\sqrt{2})$ and $(5x^2y+6xz)$ are all binomials.

(v) **Trinomial** Polynomials having only three terms are called trinomials ('tri' means 'three').

e.g., $(x^4+x^3+\sqrt{2}), (\mu^{43}+\mu^7+\mu)$ and $(8y-5xy+9xy^2)$ are all trinomials.

04 Degree of a Polynomial Highest power of the variable in a polynomial is called the degree of a polynomial.

(i) **In one variable** In the polynomial of one variable, the highest power of the variable is called the degree of the polynomial.

e.g.,

- $\sqrt{2}-y^3+y^5+2y^6$ is a polynomial in y of degree 6.
- $6x+\sqrt{3}$ is a polynomial in x of degree 1.

(ii) **In two or more variables** In the polynomials of more than one variable, the sum of the powers of the variables in each term is taken up and the highest sum so obtained is called the degree of the polynomial.

e.g.,

- $3x^3-7x^2y^2+8$ is a polynomial in x and y of degree 4.
- $8a^8b-4ab+\sqrt{2}$ is a polynomial in a and b of degree 9.

Note • The degree of a non-zero constant polynomial is 'zero'.
• The degree of a zero polynomial is not defined.

05 Linear Polynomial A polynomial of degree one is called a linear polynomial and it is expressed in the form of $ax+b$, where a and b are real constants and $a \neq 0$.

e.g.,

- $x+\sqrt{7}$ is a linear polynomial in x.
- $\sqrt{2}y+3$ is a linear polynomial in y.

06 Quadratic Polynomial A polynomial of degree two is called a quadratic polynomial and it is expressed in the form of $ax^2 + bx + c$ where a, b and c are real constants and $a \neq 0$

e.g.,

- $y^2 + 6y + 3$ is a quadratic polynomial in x.
- $x^2 + 9x - \frac{3}{2}$ is a quadratic polynomial in x.

07 Cubic Polynomial A polynomial of degree three is called a cubic polynomial and it is expressed in the form of $ax^3 + bx^2 + cx + d$ where a, b, c and d are real constant and $a \neq 0$

e.g.,

- $2y^3 + 3$ is a cubic polynomial in y.
- $9x^3 + x^2 - 4$ is a cubic polynomial in x.

08 Value of a Polynomial Value of a polynomial $p(x)$ at $x = a$ is $p(a)$.

e.g., If $p(x) = x^2 + 2x + 6$, then at $x = 2$, $p(2) = 2^2 + 2 \times 2 + 6 = 14$

09 Zeroes of a Polynomial Zero of a polynomial $p(x)$ is a number a such that $p(a) = 0$.

(i) Zero may be a zero of a polynomial.

(ii) Every linear polynomial has one and only one zero.

(iii) Zero of a polynomial is also called the root of polynomial.

(iv) A non-zero constant polynomial has no zero.

(v) Every real number is a zero of the zero polynomial.

(vi) A polynomial can have more than one zero.

Note Maximum number of zeroes of a polynomial is equal to its degree.

10 Factor Theorem Let $q(x)$ be a polynomial of degree $n \geq 1$ and a be any real number, then

(i) $(x - a)$ is a factor of polynomial $q(x)$, if $q(a) = 0$ and $(x + a)$ is a factor of polynomial $q(x)$ if $q(-a) = 0$.

(ii) $q(a) = 0$, if $x - a$ is a factor of $q(x)$.

11 Factorisation of Quadratic Polynomials

(i) **By splitting the middle term** Suppose a quadratic polynomial is $x^2 + lx + m$, where l and m are constants.

Now, we split the middle term lx as $ax + bx$, so that $ab = m$.
Then,

$$x^2 + lx + m = x^2 + ax + bx + ab = x(x + a) + b(x + a)$$
$$= (x + a)(x + b)$$

(ii) **By using factor theorem** Suppose, $ax^2 + bx + c$ be a quadratic polynomial where a, b and c are constants. Let two factors be $(x - \alpha)$ and $(x - \beta)$

$\therefore \quad a(x - \alpha)(x - \beta) = ax^2 + bx + c$

$\Rightarrow ax^2 - a(\alpha + \beta)x + a\alpha\beta = ax^2 + bx + c$

On equating the coefficient of x and constant term, we get

$$\alpha + \beta = -\frac{b}{a} \text{ and } \alpha\beta = \frac{c}{a}$$

On simplifying, we get the values of α and β.

(iii) **Factorisation of cubic polynomials** The splitting middle term method is not applicable for cubic polynomials. Its need to find atleast one factor first, and then adjust the given polynomial such that it becomes the product of term in which one of them is that factor and the other is a quadratic polynomial. Now, solve this quadratic polynomial by previous method.

12 Algebraic Identities An algebraic identity is an algebraic equation that is true for all values of the variable occurring in it.

Some Algebraic Identities are Given Below

(i) $(x + y)^2 = x^2 + 2xy + y^2$

(ii) $(x - y)^2 = x^2 - 2xy + y^2$

(iii) $x^2 - y^2 = (x + y)(x - y)$

(iv) $(x + a)(x + b) = x^2 + (a + b)x + ab$

(v) $(x + y + z)^2 = x^2 + y^2 + z^2 + 2xy + 2yz + 2zx$

(vi) $(x + y)^3 = x^3 + y^3 + 3xy(x + y)$

(vii) $(x - y)^3 = x^3 - y^3 - 3xy(x - y)$

(viii) $x^3 + y^3 + z^3 - 3xyz = (x + y + z)(x^2 + y^2 + z^2 - xy - yz - zx)$

If $x + y + z = 0$, then $x^3 + y^3 + z^3 = 3xyz$

(ix) $x^3 + y^3 = (x + y)(x^2 - xy + y^2)$

(x) $x^3 - y^3 = (x - y)(x^2 + xy + y^2)$

Exercise 2.1

Question 1 Which of the following expressions are polynomials in one variable and which are not? State reasons for your answer.

(i) $4x^2 - 3x + 7$ (ii) $y^2 + \sqrt{2}$

(iii) $3\sqrt{t} + t\sqrt{2}$ (iv) $y + \frac{2}{y}$

(v) $x^{10} + y^3 + t^{50}$

Sol. (i) $4x^2 - 3x + 7$ is an expression having only non-negative integral powers of x. So, it is a polynomial in one variable.

(ii) $y^2 + \sqrt{2}$ is an expression having only non-negative integral power of y. So, it is a polynomial in one variable.

(iii) $3\sqrt{t} + t\sqrt{2}$ is an expression in which one term namely $3\sqrt{t}$ has rational power of t. So, it is not a polynomial.

(iv) $y + \frac{2}{y}$ is an expression in which one term namely $\frac{2}{y}$ *i.e.*, $2y^{-1}$ has negative power of y. So, it is not a polynomial.

(v) $x^{10} + y^3 + t^{50}$ is an expression which has 3 variables. So, it is not polynomial in one variable.

Question 2 Write the coefficients of x^2 in each of the following.

(i) $2 + x^2 + x$ (ii) $2 - x^2 + x^3$

(iii) $\frac{\pi}{2}x^2 + x$ (iv) $\sqrt{2}\,x - 1$

Sol. (i) The coefficient of x^2 in $2 + x^2 + x$ is 1.

(ii) The coefficient of x^2 in $2 - x^2 + x^3$ is -1.

(iii) The coefficient of x^2 in $\frac{\pi}{2}x^2 + x$ is $\frac{\pi}{2}$.

(iv) The coefficient of x^2 in $\sqrt{2}x - 1$ is 0.

Question 3 Give one example each of a binomial of degree 35, and of a monomial of degree 100.

Sol. (i) $y^{35} + 2$ is a binomial of degree 35.

(ii) y^{100} is a monomial of degree 100.

Question 4 Write the degree of each of the following polynomials.

(i) $5x^3 + 4x^2 + 7x$ (ii) $4 - y^2$

(iii) $5t - \sqrt{7}$ (iv) 3

Sol. (i) In a polynomial $5x^3 + 4x^2 + 7x$, the highest power of variable x is 3, hence the degree of the polynomial is 3.

(ii) In a polynomial $4 - y^2$, the highest power of variable y is 2, hence the degree of the polynomial is 2.

(iii) In a polynomial $5t - \sqrt{7}$, the highest power of variable t is 1, hence the degree of the polynomial is 1.

(iv) In a polynomial 3, the highest power of variable $y = 0$, hence the degree of the polynomial is 0.

Question 5 Classify the following as linear, quadratic and cubic polynomials.

(i) $x^2 + x$ (ii) $x - x^3$ (iii) $y + y^2 + 4$ (iv) $1 + x$
(v) $3t$ (vi) r^2 (vii) $7x^3$

Sol. (i) The degree of polynomial $x^2 + 2$ is 2, hence it is a quadratic polynomial.

(ii) The degree of polynomial $x - x^3$ is 3, hence it is a cubic polynomial.

(iii) The degree of polynomial $y + y^2 + 4$ is 2, hence it is a quadratic polynomial.

(iv) The degree of polynomial $1 + x$ is 1, hence it is a linear polynomial.

(v) The degree of polynomial $3t$ is 1, hence it a linear polynomial.

(vi) The degree of polynomial r^2 is 2, hence it is a quadratic polynomial.

(vii) The degree of polynomial $7x^3$ is 3, hence it is a cubic polynomial.

Mistake Alert Do not forget that the degree of the polynomial is based on the highest power of the variable not the sum of powers.

Exercise 2.2

Question 1 Find the value of the polynomial $5x - 4x^2 + 3$ at

(i) $x = 0$ (ii) $x = -1$ (iii) $x = 2$

Sol. Let $p(x) = 5x - 4x^2 + 3$

(i) $p(0) = 5 \times 0 - 4 \times 0^2 + 3$

$\Rightarrow$ $p(0) = 3$

(ii) $p(-1) = 5(-1) - 4(-1)^2 + 3 = -5 - 4 + 3$

$\Rightarrow$ $p(-1) = -6$

(iii) $p(2) = 5(2) - 4(2)^2 + 3 = 10 - 16 + 3$

$\Rightarrow$ $p(2) = -3$

Question 2 Find $p(0)$, $p(1)$ and $p(2)$ for each of the following polynomials.

(i) $p(y)=y^2-y+1$

(ii) $p(t)=2+t+2t^2-t^3$

(iii) $p(x)=x^3$

(iv) $p(x)=(x-1)(x+1)$

Sol. (i) We have, $p(y)=y^2-y+1$

$\therefore \quad p(0)=0^2-0+1$

$\Rightarrow \quad p(0)=1$

$p(1)=1^2-1+1$

$\Rightarrow \quad p(1)=1$

and $\quad p(2)=2^2-2+1=4-2+1$

$\Rightarrow \quad p(2)=3$

(ii) We have, $p(t)=2+t+2t^2-t^3$

$\therefore \quad p(0)=2+0+2\times 0^2-0^3$

$\Rightarrow \quad p(0)=2$

$p(1)=2+1+2\times 1^2-1^3$

$\Rightarrow \quad p(1)=3+2-1$

$\Rightarrow \quad p(1)=4$

and $\quad p(2)=2+2+2\times 2^2-2^3$

$=4+8-8$

$\Rightarrow \quad p(2)=4$

(iii) We have, $p(x)=x^3$

$\Rightarrow \quad p(0)=0^3 \Rightarrow p(0)=0$

$\Rightarrow \quad p(1)=1^3 \Rightarrow p(1)=1$

and $\quad p(2)=2^3 \Rightarrow p(2)=8$

(iv) We have, $p(x)=(x-1)(x+1)$

$p(0)=(0-1)(0+1)$

$\Rightarrow \quad p(0)=-1$

$p(1)=(1-1)(1+1)$

$\Rightarrow \quad p(1)=0$

and $\quad p(2)=(2-1)(2+1)$

$\Rightarrow \quad p(2)=3$

Question 3 Verify whether the following are zeroes of the polynomial, indicated against them.

(i) $p(x)=3x+1, x=-\frac{1}{3}$ (ii) $p(x)=5x-\pi,\ x=\frac{4}{5}$

(iii) $p(x)=x^2-1, x=1,-1$ (iv) $p(x)=(x+1)(x-2), x=-1,2$

(v) $p(x)=x^2, x=0$ (vi) $p(x)=lx+m, x=-\frac{m}{l}$

(vii) $p(x)=3x^2-1, x=-\frac{1}{\sqrt{3}}, \frac{2}{\sqrt{3}}$

(viii) $p(x)=2x+1, x=\frac{1}{2}$

◎ ***Thinking Process*** If $x=a$ is a zero of pollynomial $p(x)$, then $p(a)=0$.

Sol. (i) We have, $p(x) = 3x + 1$

If $x=-\frac{1}{3}$ is a zero of $p(x)$, then $p\left(-\frac{1}{3}\right)=0$

So, $$p\left(-\frac{1}{3}\right)=3\times\left(-\frac{1}{3}\right)+1=-1+1$$

$\Rightarrow$ $$p\left(-\frac{1}{3}\right)=0$$

Hence, $x=-\frac{1}{3}$ is a zero of $p(x)$.

(ii) We have, $p(x) = 5x-\pi$

If $x=\frac{4}{5}$ is a zero of $p(x)$, then $p\left(\frac{4}{5}\right)=0$

So, $p\left(\frac{4}{5}\right)=5\times\frac{4}{5}-\pi \Rightarrow p\left(\frac{4}{5}\right)=4-\pi$

Hence, $x=\frac{4}{5}$ is not a zero of $p(x)$.

(iii) We have, $p(x)=x^2-1$

If $x=-1$ and $x=1$ are zeroes of $p(x)$, then $p(-1)=0$ and $p(1)=0$

So, $$p(-1)=(-1)^2-1=1-1$$

$\Rightarrow$ $$p(-1)=0$$

and $$p(1)=(1)^2-1=1-1\Rightarrow p(1)=0$$

Hence, $x=-1$ and 1 are the zeroes of $p(x)$.

(iv) We have, $p(x)=(x+1)(x-2)$

If $x=-1$ and $x=2$ are zeroes of $p(x)$, then $p(-1)=0$ and $p(2)=0$

So, $$p(-1)=(-1+1)(-1-2)=0(-3)$$

$\Rightarrow \quad p(-1) = 0$

and $\quad p(2) = (2+1)(2-2) = 3(0)$

$\Rightarrow \quad p(2) = 0$

Hence, $x = -1$ and $x = 2$ are the zeroes of $p(x)$.

(v) We have, $p(x) = x^2$

If $x = 0$ is a zero of $p(x)$, then $p(0) = 0$

So, $p(0) = 0^2 \Rightarrow p(0) = 0$

Hence, $x = 0$ is a zero of $p(x)$.

(vi) We have, $p(x) = lx + m$

If $x = -\frac{m}{l}$ is a zero of $p(x)$, then $p\left(-\frac{m}{l}\right) = 0$

So, $\quad p\left(-\frac{m}{l}\right) = l \times \left(\frac{-m}{l}\right) + m$

$\Rightarrow \quad p\left(-\frac{m}{l}\right) = -m + m$

$\Rightarrow \quad p\left(-\frac{m}{l}\right) = 0$

Hence, $x = -\frac{m}{l}$ is a zero of $p(x)$.

(vii) We have, $p(x) = 3x^2 - 1$

If $x = -\frac{1}{\sqrt{3}}$ and $x = \frac{2}{\sqrt{3}}$ are zeroes of $p(x)$, then

$$p\left(-\frac{1}{\sqrt{3}}\right) = 0 \text{ and } p\left(\frac{2}{\sqrt{3}}\right) = 0$$

So, $\quad p\left(-\frac{1}{\sqrt{3}}\right) = 3\left(-\frac{1}{\sqrt{3}}\right)^2 - 1 = 3 \times \frac{1}{3} - 1$

$\Rightarrow \quad p\left(-\frac{1}{\sqrt{3}}\right) = 1 - 1 = 0$

and $\quad p\left(\frac{2}{\sqrt{3}}\right) = 3\left(\frac{2}{\sqrt{3}}\right)^2 - 1 = 3 \times \frac{4}{3} - 1$

$\Rightarrow \quad p\left(\frac{2}{\sqrt{3}}\right) = 4 - 1 = 3$

Hence, $x = -\frac{1}{\sqrt{3}}$ is a zero of $p(x)$ but $x = \frac{2}{\sqrt{3}}$ is not a zero of $p(x)$.

(viii) We have, $p(x) = 2x + 1$

If $x = \frac{1}{2}$ is zero of $p(x)$, then $p\left(\frac{1}{2}\right) = 0$

So, $\quad p\left(\frac{1}{2}\right) = 2 \times \frac{1}{2} + 1 \Rightarrow p\left(\frac{1}{2}\right) = 1 + 1 = 2$

Hence, $x = \frac{1}{2}$ is not a zero of $p(x)$.

Question 4 Find the zero of the polynomial in each of the following cases.

(i) $p(x)=x+5$ (ii) $p(x)=x-5$

(iii) $p(x)=2x+5$ (iv) $p(x)=3x-2$

(v) $p(x)=3x$ (vi) $p(x)=ax, a\neq 0$

(vii) $p(x)=cx+d, c\neq 0$ where c and d are real numbers.

Sol. (i) We have, $p(x)=x+5$

Now, $p(x)=0$

$\Rightarrow$ $x+5=0$

$\Rightarrow$ $x=-5$

$\therefore$ -5 is a zero of the polynomial $p(x)$.

(ii) We have, $p(x)=x-5$

Now, $p(x)=0$

$\Rightarrow$ $x-5=0$

$\Rightarrow$ $x=5$

$\therefore$ 5 is a zero of the polynomial $p(x)$.

(iii) We have, $p(x)=2x+5$

Now, $p(x)=0$

$\Rightarrow$ $2x+5=0$

$\Rightarrow$ $x=-\frac{5}{2}$

$\therefore$ $-\frac{5}{2}$ is a zero of the polynomial $p(x)$.

(iv) We have, $p(x)=3x-2$

Now, $p(x)=0$

$\Rightarrow$ $3x-2=0$

$\Rightarrow$ $x=\frac{2}{3}$

$\therefore$ $\frac{2}{3}$ is a zero of the polynomial $p(x)$.

(v) We have, $p(x)=3x$

Now, $p(x)=0$

$\Rightarrow$ $3x=0$

$\Rightarrow$ $x=0$

$\therefore$ 0 is a zero of the polynomial $p(x)$.

(vi) We have, $p(x)=ax,\ a\neq 0$

Now, $p(x)=0 \Rightarrow ax=0$

$\Rightarrow$ $x=0$ $(\because\ a\neq 0)$

$\therefore$ 0 is a zero of the polynomial $p(x)$.

(vii) We have, $p(x) = cx + d, c \neq 0$

Now, $p(x) = 0$

$\Rightarrow$ $cx + d = 0$

$$x = -\frac{d}{c}$$

$\therefore -\frac{d}{c}$ is a zero of the polynomial $p(x)$.

Mistake Alert Students may incorrectly interpret a zero of a polynomial as a factor rather than the value of x that makes the polynomial zero.

Exercise 2.3

Question 1 Determine which of the following polynomials has $(x+1)$ a factor.

(i) $x^3 + x^2 + x + 1$ (ii) $x^4 + x^3 + x^2 + x + 1$

(iii) $x^4 + 3x^3 + 3x^2 + x + 1$ (iv) $x^3 - x^2 - (2 + \sqrt{2})x + \sqrt{2}$

Thinking Process

- First find zero of $(x + a)$, then put the value of x in the given polynomial $p(x)$.
- If $p(a) = 0$, then $(x + a)$ is a factor of $p(x)$.

Sol. The zero of $x + 1$ is $x = -1$.

(i) Let $p(x) = x^3 + x^2 + x + 1$

Then, $p(-1) = (-1)^3 + (-1)^2 + (-1) + 1$

$= -1 + 1 - 1 + 1$

$\Rightarrow$ $p(-1) = 0$

So, by the factor theorem $(x + 1)$ is a factor of $x^3 + x^2 + x + 1$.

(ii) Let $p(x) = x^4 + x^3 + x^2 + x + 1$

Then, $p(-1) = (-1)^4 + (-1)^3 + (-1)^2 + (-1) + 1$

$= 1 - 1 + 1 - 1 + 1$

$\Rightarrow$ $p(-1) = 1$

So, by the factor theorem $(x + 1)$ is not a factor of $x^4 + x^3 + x^2 + x + 1$.

(iii) Let $p(x) = x^4 + 3x^3 + 3x^2 + x + 1$

Then, $p(-1) = (-1)^4 + 3(-1)^3 + 3(-1)^2 + (-1) + 1$

$= 1 - 3 + 3 - 1 + 1$

$\Rightarrow$ $p(-1) = 1$

So, by the factor theorem $(x + 1)$ is not a factor of $x^4 + 3x^3 + 3x^2 + x + 1$.

(iv) Let $p(x) = x^3 - x^2 - (2 + \sqrt{2})x + \sqrt{2}$

Then, $p(-1) = (-1)^3 - (-1)^2 - (2 + \sqrt{2})(-1) + \sqrt{2}$

$= -1 - 1 + 2 + \sqrt{2} + \sqrt{2}$

$= 2\sqrt{2}$

So, by the Factor theorem $(x + 1)$ is not a factor of

$x^3 - x^2 - (2 + \sqrt{2})x + \sqrt{2}$.

Question 2 Use the Factor Theorem to determine whether $g(x)$ is a factor of $p(x)$ in each of the following cases.

(i) $p(x) = 2x^3 + x^2 - 2x - 1, g(x) = x + 1$

(ii) $p(x) = x^3 + 3x^2 + 3x + 1, g(x) = x + 2$

(iii) $p(x) = x^3 - 4x^2 + x + 6, g(x) = x - 3$

Sol. (i) The zero of $g(x) = x + 1$ is -1.

Then, $p(-1) = 2(-1)^3 + (-1)^2 - 2(-1) - 1$ $[\because p(x) = 2x^3 + x^2 - 2x - 1]$

$= -2 + 1 + 2 - 1$

$\Rightarrow$ $p(-1) = 0$

Hence, $g(x)$ is a factor of $p(x)$.

(ii) The zero of $g(x) = x + 2$ is -2.

Then, $p(-2) = (-2)^3 + 3(-2)^2 + 3(-2) + 1$ $[\because p(x) = x^3 + 3x^2 + 3x + 1]$

$= -8 + 12 - 6 + 1$

$\Rightarrow$ $p(-2) = -1$

Hence, $g(x)$ is not a factor of $p(x)$.

(iii) The zero of $g(x) = x - 3$ is 3.

Then, $p(3) = 3^3 - 4(3)^2 + 3 + 6$ $[\because p(x) = x^3 - 4x^2 + x + 6]$

$= 27 - 36 + 3 + 6$

$\Rightarrow$ $p(3) = 0$

Hence, $g(x)$ is a factor of $p(x)$.

Question 3 Find the value of k, if $x - 1$ is a factor of $p(x)$ in each of the following cases.

(i) $p(x) = x^2 + x + k$ (ii) $p(x) = 2x^2 + kx + \sqrt{2}$

(iii) $p(x) = kx^2 - \sqrt{2}x + 1$ (iv) $p(x) = kx^2 - 3x + k$

Sol. The zero of $x - 1$ is 1.

(i) $\because$ $(x - 1)$ is a factor of $p(x)$, then $p(1) = 0$. (By Factor theorem)

$\Rightarrow$ $1^2 + 1 + k = 0$ $[\because p(x) = x^2 + x + k]$

$\Rightarrow$ $2 + k = 0$

$\Rightarrow$ $k = -2$

(ii) $\because$ $(x-1)$ is a factor of $p(x)$, then $p(1)=0$ (By Factor theorem)

$\Rightarrow \quad 2(1)^2 + k(1) + \sqrt{2} = 0 \quad [\because p(x) = 2x^2 + kx + \sqrt{2}]$

$\Rightarrow \quad 2 + k + \sqrt{2} = 0$

$\Rightarrow \quad k = -(2+\sqrt{2})$

(iii) $\because$ $(x-1)$ is a factor of $p(x)$, then $p(1)=0$ (By Factor theorem)

$\Rightarrow \quad k(1)^2 - \sqrt{2}(1) + 1 = 0 \quad [\because p(x) = kx^2 - \sqrt{2}x + 1]$

$\Rightarrow \quad k - \sqrt{2} + 1 = 0$

$\Rightarrow \quad k = (\sqrt{2} - 1)$

(iv) $\because$ $(x-1)$ is a factor of $p(x)$, then $p(1)=0$ (By Factor theorem)

$\Rightarrow \quad k(1)^2 - 3(1) + k = 0 \quad [\because p(x) = kx^2 - 3x + k]$

$\Rightarrow \quad k - 3 + k = 0$

$\Rightarrow \quad 2k - 3 = 0$

$\Rightarrow \quad k = \frac{3}{2}$

Question 4 Factorise

(i) $12x^2 - 7x + 1$ (ii) $2x^2 + 7x + 3$

(iii) $6x^2 + 5x - 6$ (iv) $3x^2 - x - 4$

Sol. (i) We have, $12x^2 - 7x + 1 = 12x^2 - 4x - 3x + 1$

(By splitting the middle term)

$= 4x(3x-1) - 1(3x-1)$

$= (3x-1)(4x-1)$

(ii) We have, $2x^2 + 7x + 3 = 2x^2 + 6x + x + 3$

(By splitting the middle term)

$= 2x(x+3) + 1(x+3) = (x+3)(2x+1)$

(iii) We have, $6x^2 + 5x - 6 = 6x^2 + 9x - 4x - 6$

(By splitting the middle term)

$= 3x(2x+3) - 2(2x+3) = (2x+3)(3x-2)$

(iv) We have, $3x^2 - x - 4 = 3x^2 - 4x + 3x - 4$

(By splitting the middle term)

$= x(3x-4) + 1(3x-4) = (3x-4)(x+1)$

Question 5 Factorise

(i) $x^3 - 2x^2 - x + 2$ (ii) $x^3 - 3x^2 - 9x - 5$

(iii) $x^3 + 13x^2 + 32x + 20$ (iv) $2y^3 + y^2 - 2y - 1$

Sol. (i) Let $p(x) = x^3 - 2x^2 - x + 2$, constant term of $p(x)$ is 2.

$\therefore$ Factors of 2 are ± 1 and ± 2.

Now, $p(1) = 1^3 - 2(1)^2 - 1 + 2 = 1 - 2 - 1 + 2$

$\Rightarrow \quad p(1) = 0$

By trial, we find that $p(1) = 0$, so $(x - 1)$ is a factor of $p(x)$.

So, $x^3 - 2x^2 - x + 2 = x^3 - x^2 - x^2 + x - 2x + 2$

$= x^2(x - 1) - x(x - 1) - 2(x - 1)$

$= (x - 1)(x^2 - x - 2)$

$= (x - 1)(x^2 - 2x + x - 2)$ (By splitting the middle term)

$= (x - 1)[x(x - 2) + 1(x - 2)]$

$= (x - 1)(x - 2)(x + 1)$

(ii) Let $p(x) = x^3 - 3x^2 - 9x - 5$

By trial, we find that $p(5) = (5)^3 - 3(5)^2 - 9(5) - 5$

$= 125 - 75 - 45 - 5 = 0$

So, $(x - 5)$ is a factor of $p(x)$.

So, $x^3 - 3x^2 - 9x - 5 = x^3 - 5x^2 + 2x^2 - 10x + x - 5$

$= x^2(x - 5) + 2x(x - 5) + 1(x - 5)$

$= (x - 5)(x^2 + 2x + 1)$

$= (x - 5)(x^2 + x + x + 1)$ (By splitting the middle term)

$= (x - 5)[x(x + 1) + 1(x + 1)]$

$= (x - 5)(x + 1)(x + 1)$

(iii) Let $p(x) = x^3 + 13x^2 + 32x + 20$

By trial, we find that $p(-1) = (-1)^3 + 13(-1)^2 + 32(-1) + 20$

$= -1 + 13 - 32 + 20 = -33 + 33 = 0$

So $(x + 1)$ is a factor of $p(x)$.

So, $x^3 + 13x^2 + 32x + 20 = x^3 + x^2 + 12x^2 + 12x + 20x + 20$

$= x^2(x + 1) + 12x(x + 1) + 20(x + 1)$

$= (x + 1)(x^2 + 12x + 20)$

$= (x + 1)(x^2 + 10x + 2x + 20)$ (By splitting the middle term)

$= (x + 1)[x(x + 10) + 2(x + 10)]$

$= (x + 1)(x + 10)(x + 2)$

(iv) Let $p(y) = 2y^3 + y^2 - 2y - 1$

By trial we find that $p(1) = 2(1)^3 + (1)^2 - 2(1) - 1 = 2 + 1 - 2 - 1 = 0$

So $(y - 1)$ is a factor of $p(y)$.

So, $2y^3 + y^2 - 2y - 1 = 2y^3 - 2y^2 + 3y^2 - 3y + y - 1$

$= 2y^2(y - 1) + 3y(y - 1) + 1(y - 1)$

$= (y - 1)[2y^2 + 3y + 1]$

$= (y - 1)(2y^2 + 2y + y + 1)$ (By splitting the middle term)

$= (y - 1)[2y(y + 1) + 1(y + 1)]$

$= (y - 1)(y + 1)(2y + 1)$

Exercise 2.4

Question 1 Use suitable identities to find the following products.

(i) $(x+4)(x+10)$ (ii) $(x+8)(x-10)$

(iii) $(3x+4)(3x-5)$ (iv) $\left(y^2+\frac{3}{2}\right)\left(y^2-\frac{3}{2}\right)$

(v) $(3-2x)(3+2x)$

Sol. (i) We have, $(x+4)(x+10)$

Using identity $(x+a)(x+b)=x^2+(a+b)x+ab$

$\therefore (x+4)(x+10)=x^2+(4+10)x+(4\times 10)$ $(\because a=4, b=10)$

$=x^2+14x+40$

(ii) We have, $(x+8)(x-10)$

Using identity $(x+a)(x+b)=x^2+(a+b)x+ab$

$(x+8)(x-10)=x^2+[8+(-10)]x+(8)(-10)$ $(\because a=8, b=-10)$

$=x^2-2x-80$

(iii) We have, $(3x+4)(3x-5)$

Using identity $(x+a)(x+b)=x^2+(a+b)x+ab$

$\therefore (3x+4)(3x-5)=(3x)^2+(4-5)3x+(4)(-5)$ $(\because a=4, b=-5)$

$=9x^2-3x-20$

(iv) We have, $\left(y^2+\frac{3}{2}\right)\left(y^2-\frac{3}{2}\right)$

Using identity $(x+y)(x-y)=x^2-y^2$

$\therefore \left(y^2+\frac{3}{2}\right)\left(y^2-\frac{3}{2}\right)=(y^2)^2-\left(\frac{3}{2}\right)^2=y^4-\frac{9}{4}$

(v) We have, $(3-2x)(3+2x)$

Using identity $(x+y)(x-y)=x^2-y^2$

$\therefore$ $(3-2x)(3+2x)=3^2-(2x)^2=9-4x^2$

Question 2 Evaluate the following products without multiplying directly.

(i) 103×107 (ii) 95×96

(iii) 104×96

◎ ***Thinking Process*** First adjust the given numbers into two numbers such that one is a multiple of 10 and use the proper identity.

Sol. (i) We have, $103\times 107=(100+3)(100+7)$

$=100\times 100+(3+7)(100)+(3\times 7)$

$[\because (x+a)(x+b)=x^2+(a+b)x+ab]$

$=10000+1000+21=11021$

(ii) We have, $95 \times 96 = (100-5)(100-4)$

$= 100 \times 100 + [(-5)+(-4)]\,100 + [-5 \times (-4)]$

$[\because (x+a)(x+b) = x^2 + (a+b)x + ab]$

$= 10000 - 900 + 20 = 9120$ $\quad [\because a = -5, b = -4]$

(iii) We have, $104 \times 96 = (100+4)(100-4)$

$= (100)^2 - 4^2$ $\quad [\because (x+y)(x-y) = x^2 - y^2]$

$= 10000 - 16 = 9984$

Question 3 Factorise the following using appropriate identities.

(i) $9x^2 + 6xy + y^2$ (ii) $4y^2 - 4y + 1$

(iii) $x^2 - \dfrac{y^2}{100}$

Sol. (i) We have, $9x^2 + 6xy + y^2 = (3x)^2 + 2 \times 3x \times y + (y)^2$

$= (3x+y)^2$ $\quad [\because x^2 + 2xy + y^2 = (x+y)^2]$

(ii) We have, $4y^2 - 4y + 1 = (2y)^2 - 2(2y)(1) + (1)^2$

$= (2y-1)^2$ $\quad [\because x^2 - 2xy + y^2 = (x-y)^2]$

(iii) We have, $x^2 - \dfrac{y^2}{100} = x^2 - \left(\dfrac{y}{10}\right)^2 = \left(x + \dfrac{y}{10}\right)\left(x - \dfrac{y}{10}\right)$

$[\because x^2 - y^2 = (x+y)(x-y)]$

Question 4 Expand each of the following, using suitable identities.

(i) $(x+2y+4z)^2$ (ii) $(2x-y+z)^2$

(iii) $(-2x+3y+2z)^2$ (iv) $(3a-7b-c)^2$

(v) $(-2x+5y-3z)^2$ (vi) $\left(\dfrac{1}{4}a - \dfrac{1}{2}b + 1\right)^2$

Sol. (i) We have, $(x+2y+4z)^2 = x^2 + (2y)^2 + (4z)^2 + 2(x)(2y)$

$+ 2(2y)(4z) + 2(4z)(x)$ $[\because (x+y+z)^2 = x^2 + y^2 + z^2 + 2xy + 2yz + 2zx]$

$= x^2 + 4y^2 + 16z^2 + 4xy + 16yz + 8zx$

(ii) We have, $(2x-y+z)^2 = (2x)^2 + (-y)^2 + z^2 + 2(2x)(-y)$

$+ 2(-y)(z) + 2(z)(2x)$

$[\because (x+y+z)^2 = x^2 + y^2 + z^2 + 2xy + 2yz + 2zx]$

$= 4x^2 + y^2 + z^2 - 4xy - 2yz + 4zx$

(iii) We have, $(-2x+3y+2z)^2 = (-2x)^2 + (3y)^2 + (2z)^2 + 2(-2x)(3y)$

$+ 2(3y)(2z) + 2(2z)(-2x)$

$[\because (x+y+z)^2 = x^2 + y^2 + z^2 + 2xy + 2yz + 2zx]$

$= 4x^2 + 9y^2 + 4z^2 - 12xy + 12yz - 8zx$

(iv) We have, $(3a-7b-c)^2 = (3a)^2 + (-7b)^2 + (-c)^2 + 2(3a)(-7b)$
$+ 2(-7b)(-c) + 2(-c)(3a)$
$[\because (x+y+z)^2 = x^2 + y^2 + z^2 + 2xy + 2yz + 2zx]$
$= 9a^2 + 49b^2 + c^2 - 42ab + 14bc - 6ac$

(v) We have, $(-2x+5y-3z)^2 = (-2x)^2 + (5y)^2 + (-3z)^2 + 2(-2x)(5y)$
$+ 2(5y)(-3z) + 2(-3z)(-2x)$
$[\because (x+y+z)^2 = x^2 + y^2 + z^2 + 2xy + 2yz + 2zx]$
$= 4x^2 + 25y^2 + 9z^2 - 20xy - 30yz + 12zx$

(vi) We have, $\left(\frac{1}{4}a - \frac{1}{2}b + 1\right)^2 = \left(\frac{1}{4}a\right)^2 + \left(-\frac{1}{2}b\right)^2 + 1^2 + 2\left(\frac{1}{4}a\right)\left(-\frac{1}{2}b\right)$
$+ 2\left(-\frac{1}{2}b\right)(1) + 2(1)\left(\frac{1}{4}a\right)$
$= \frac{1}{16}a^2 + \frac{1}{4}b^2 + 1 - \frac{ab}{4} - b + \frac{1}{2}a$
$[\because (x+y+z)^2 = x^2 + y^2 + z^2 + 2xy + 2yz + 2zx]$

Question 5 Factorise

(i) $4x^2 + 9y^2 + 16z^2 + 12xy - 24yz - 16xz$

(ii) $2x^2 + y^2 + 8z^2 - 2\sqrt{2}xy + 4\sqrt{2}yz - 8xz$

Sol. (i) We have, $4x^2 + 9y^2 + 16z^2 + 12xy - 24yz - 16xz$
$= (2x)^2 + (3y)^2 + (-4z)^2 + 2(2x)(3y) + 2(3y)(-4z) + 2(-4z)(2x)$
$= (2x+3y-4z)^2 = (2x+3y-4z)(2x+3y-4z)$
$[(x+y+z)^2 = x^2 + y^2 + z^2 + 2xy + 2yz + 2zx]$

(ii) We have, $2x^2 + y^2 + 8z^2 - 2\sqrt{2}xy + 4\sqrt{2}yz - 8xz$
$= (-\sqrt{2}x)^2 + (y)^2 + (2\sqrt{2}z)^2 + 2(-\sqrt{2}x)(y) + 2(y)(2\sqrt{2}z)$
$+ 2(2\sqrt{2}z)(-\sqrt{2}x)$
$= (-\sqrt{2}x + y + 2\sqrt{2}z)^2$ $[\because (x+y+z)^2 = x^2 + y^2 + z^2 + 2xy + 2yz + 2zx]$
$= (-\sqrt{2}x + y + 2\sqrt{2}z)(-\sqrt{2}x + y + 2\sqrt{2}z)$

Question 6 Write the following cubes in expanded form

(i) $(2x+1)^3$ (ii) $(2a-3b)^3$

(iii) $\left(\frac{3}{2}x+1\right)^3$ (iv) $\left(x-\frac{2}{3}y\right)^3$

Sol. (i) We have, $(2x+1)^3 = (2x)^3 + 1^3 + 3(2x)(1)(2x+1)$
[Using identity $(x+y)^3 = x^3 + y^3 + 3xy(x+y)$]
$= 8x^3 + 1 + 6x(2x+1)$
$= 8x^3 + 1 + 12x^2 + 6x = 8x^3 + 12x^2 + 6x + 1$

(ii) We have, $(2a-3b)^3=(2a)^3-(3b)^3-3(2a)(3b)(2a-3b)$

[Using identity $(x-y)^3=x^3-y^3-3xy(x-y)$]

$=8a^3-27b^3-18ab(2a-3b)$

$=8a^3-27b^3-36a^2b+54ab^2$

$=8a^3-36a^2b+54ab^2-27b^3$

(iii) We have, $\left(\frac{3}{2}x+1\right)^3=\left(\frac{3}{2}x\right)^3+1^3+3\left(\frac{3}{2}x\right)(1)\left(\frac{3}{2}x+1\right)$

[Using identity $(x+y)^3=x^3+y^3+3xy(x+y)$]

$=\frac{27}{8}x^3+1+\frac{9}{2}x\left(\frac{3}{2}x+1\right)$

$=\frac{27}{8}x^3+1+\frac{27}{4}x^2+\frac{9}{2}x=\frac{27}{8}x^3+\frac{27}{4}x^2+\frac{9}{2}x+1$

(iv) We have, $\left(x-\frac{2}{3}y\right)^3=x^3-\left(\frac{2}{3}y\right)^3-3x\left(\frac{2}{3}y\right)\left(x-\frac{2}{3}y\right)$

[Using identity $(x-y)^3=x^3-y^3-3xy(x-y)$]

$=x^3-\frac{8}{27}y^3-2xy\left(x-\frac{2}{3}y\right)=x^3-\frac{8}{27}y^3-2x^2y+\frac{4}{3}xy^2$

$=x^3-2x^2y+\frac{4}{3}xy^2-\frac{8}{27}y^3$

Mistake Alert Students may incorrectly apply the identinty as $(x-y)^3=x^3-y^3-3xy(x+y)$ instead of $(x-y)^3=x^3-y^3-3xy(x-y)$.

Question 7 Evaluate the following using suitable identities

(i) $(99)^3$ (ii) $(102)^3$ (iii) $(998)^3$

Thinking Process Use the identities $(x-y)^3=x^3-y^3-3xy(x-y)$ and $(x+y)^3=x^3+y^3+3xy(x+y)$ to find the cubes of the given numbers.

Sol. (i) $(99)^3=(100-1)^3=100^3-(1)^3-3\times100\times1(100-1)$

[Using identity $(x-y)^3=x^3-y^3-3xy(x-y)$]

$=1000000-1-300(100-1)$

$=1000000-1-30000+300=970299$

(ii) $(102)^3=(100+2)^3=100^3+2^3+3\times100\times2(100+2)$

[Using identity $(x+y)^3=x^3+y^3+3xy(x+y)$]

$=1000000+8+600(100+2)$

$=1000000+8+60000+1200=1061208$

(iii) $(998)^3=(1000-2)^3=1000^3-2^3-3\times1000\times2(1000-2)$

[Using identity $(x-y)^3=x^3-y^3-3xy(x-y)$]

$=1000000000-8-6000(1000-2)$

$=1000000000-8-6000000+12000$

$=994011992$

Question 8 Factorise each of the following

(i) $8a^3+b^3+12a^2b+6ab^2$ (ii) $8a^3-b^3-12a^2b+6ab^2$

(iii) $27-125a^3-135a+225a^2$ (iv) $64a^3-27b^3-144a^2b+108ab^2$

(v) $27p^3-\frac{1}{216}-\frac{9}{2}p^2+\frac{1}{4}p$

◎ *Thinking Process* Use identity $(x-y)^3=x^3-y^3-3xy(x-y)$

Sol. (i) We have, $8a^3+b^3+12a^2b+6ab^2=(2a)^3+b^3+6ab(2a+b)$

$=(2a)^3+b^3+3\times2a\times b(2a+b)$

$=(2a+b)^3=(2a+b)(2a+b)(2a+b)$ $[\because x^3+y^3+3xy(x+y)=(x+y)^3]$

(ii) We have, $8a^3-b^3-12a^2b+6ab^2=(2a)^3-(b)^3-6ab(2a-b)$

$=(2a)^3-(b)^3-3\times2a\times b(2a-b)$

$=(2a-b)^3=(2a-b)(2a-b)(2a-b)$ $[\because x^3-y^3-3xy(x-y)=(x-y)^3]$

(iii) We have, $27-125a^3-135a+225a^2=(3)^3-(5a)^3-45a(3-5a)$

$=(3)^3-(5a)^3-3\times3\times5a(3-5a)$

$=(3-5a)^3=(3-5a)(3-5a)(3-5a)$

$[\because x^3-y^3-3xy(x-y)=(x-y)^3]$

(iv) We have, $64a^3-27b^3-144a^2b+108ab^2$

$=(4a)^3-(3b)^3-36ab(4a-3b)$

$=(4a)^3-(3b)^3-3\times4a\times3b(4a-3b)$

$=(4a-3b)^3=(4a-3b)(4a-3b)(4a-3b)$

$[\because x^3-y^3-3xy(x-y)=(x-y)^3]$

(v) We have, $27p^3-\frac{1}{216}-\frac{9}{2}p^2+\frac{1}{4}p=(3p)^3-\left(\frac{1}{6}\right)^3-\frac{9p}{6}\left(3p-\frac{1}{6}\right)$

$=(3p)^3-\frac{1}{6^3}-3\times3p\times\frac{1}{6}\left(3p-\frac{1}{6}\right)$

$=\left(3p-\frac{1}{6}\right)^3=\left(3p-\frac{1}{6}\right)\left(3p-\frac{1}{6}\right)\left(3p-\frac{1}{6}\right)$

$[\because x^3-y^3-3xy(x-y)=(x-y)^3]$

Question 9 Verify

(i) $x^3+y^3=(x+y)(x^2-xy+y^2)$

(ii) $x^3-y^3=(x-y)(x^2+xy+y^2)$

Sol. (i) We know that,

$(x+y)^3=x^3+y^3+3xy(x+y)$

$\Rightarrow x^3+y^3=(x+y)^3-3xy(x+y)$

$=(x+y)[(x+y)^2-3xy]$

$=(x+y)[x^2+y^2+2xy-3xy]$

$=(x+y)[x^2+y^2-xy]$ **Hence Verified.**

(ii) We know that,

$$(x-y)^3 = x^3 - y^3 - 3xy(x-y)$$

$$\Rightarrow \quad x^3 - y^3 = (x-y)^3 + 3xy(x-y)$$

$$= (x-y)[(x-y)^2 + 3xy]$$

$$= (x-y)[x^2 + y^2 + 2xy + 3xy]$$

$$= (x-y)[x^2 + y^2 + xy]$$

Hence Verified.

Question 10 Factorise each of the following:

(i) $27y^3 + 125z^3$ (ii) $64m^3 - 343n^3$

Sol. (i) We have, $27y^3 + 125z^3 = (3y)^3 + (5z)^3$

$$= (3y+5z)[(3y)^2 - (3y)(5z) + (5z)^2]$$

[Using identify $x^3 + y^3 = (x+y)(x^2 + y^2 - xy)$]

$$= (3y+5z)(9y^2 - 15yz + 25z^2)$$

(ii) We have, $64\,m^3 - 343\,n^3 = (4m)^3 - (7n)^3$

$$= (4m - 7n)[(4m)^2 + (4m)(7n) + (7n)^2]$$

[Using identify $x^3 - y^3 = (x-y)(x^2 + y^2 + xy)$]

$$= (4m - 7n)(16m^2 + 28mn + 49n^2)$$

Mistake Alert Students may incorrectly apply the identity as $a^3 - b^3 = (a-b)(a^2 - ab + b^2)$ instead of $a^3 - b^3 = (a-b)(a^2 + ab + b^2)$ and $a^3 + b^3 = (a+b)(a^2 + ab + b^2)$ instead of $a^3 + b^3 = (a+b)(a^2 - ab + b^2)$.

Question 11 Factorise: $27x^3 + y^3 + z^3 - 9xyz$.

Sol. $27x^3 + y^3 + z^3 - 9xyz = (3x)^3 + y^3 + z^3 - 3 \times 3x \times y \times z$

$$= (3x+y+z)[(3x)^2 + y^2 + z^2 - 3xy - yz - z(3x)]$$

[$\because x^3 + y^3 + z^3 - 3xyz = (x+y+z)[(x^2 + y^2 + z^2 - xy - yz - zx)]$]

$$= (3x+y+z)(9x^2 + y^2 + z^2 - 3xy - yz - 3zx)$$

Question 12 Verify that

$$x^3 + y^3 + z^3 - 3xyz = \frac{1}{2}(x+y+z)[(x-y)^2 + (y-z)^2 + (z-x)^2]$$

Sol. We have, $x^3 + y^3 + z^3 - 3xyz = (x+y+z)[x^2 + y^2 + z^2 - xy - yz - zx]$

$$= \frac{1}{2}(x+y+z)[2x^2 + 2y^2 + 2z^2 - 2xy - 2yz - 2zx]$$

$$= \frac{1}{2}(x+y+z)[x^2 + x^2 + y^2 + y^2 + z^2 + z^2 - 2xy - 2yz - 2zx]$$

$$= \frac{1}{2}(x+y+z)[x^2 + y^2 - 2xy + y^2 + z^2 - 2yz + z^2 + x^2 - 2zx]$$

$$= \frac{1}{2}(x+y+z)[(x-y)^2 + (y-z)^2 + (z-x)^2]$$

[Using identify $(a-b)^2 = a^2 + b^2 - 2ab$] **Hence Verified.**

Question 13 If $x + y + z = 0$, show that $x^3 + y^3 + z^3 = 3xyz$

Sol. We know that,

$$x^3 + y^3 + z^3 - 3xyz = (x + y + z)(x^2 + y^2 + z^2 - xy - yz - zx)$$
$$= 0(x^2 + y^2 + z^2 - xy - yz - zx)$$

$(\because x + y + z = 0 \text{ given})$

$$= 0$$

$\Rightarrow \quad x^3 + y^3 + z^3 = 3xyz$ **Hence Proved.**

Question 14 Without actually calculating the cubes, find the value of each of the following

(i) $(-12)^3 + (7)^3 + (5)^3$ (ii) $(28)^3 + (-15)^3 + (-13)^3$

◎ ***Thinking Process*** If $x + y + z = 0$, then $x^3 + y^3 + z^3 = 3xyz$.

Sol. We know that, $x^3 + y^3 + z^3 - 3xyz$

$$= (x + y + z)(x^2 + y^2 + z^2 - xy - yz - zx)$$

If $x + y + z = 0$, then $x^3 + y^3 + z^3 - 3xyz = 0$

or $\quad x^3 + y^3 + z^3 = 3xyz$

(i) We have to find the value of $(-12)^3 + (7)^3 + (5)^3$.

Here, $\quad -12 + 7 + 5 = 0$

So, $\quad (-12)^3 + (7)^3 + (5)^3 = 3 \times (-12)(7)(5)$

$= -1260$

(ii) We have to find the value of $(28)^3 + (-15)^3 + (-13)^3$.

Here, $\quad 28 + (-15) + (-13) = 28 - 15 - 13 = 0$

So, $\quad (28)^3 + (-15)^3 + (-13)^3 = 3 \times (28)(-15)(-13) = 16380$

Question 15 Give possible expressions for the length and breadth of each of the following rectangles, in which their areas are given

(i) Area : $25a^2 - 35a + 12$

(ii) Area : $35y^2 + 13y - 12$

◎ ***Thinking Process*** The factors of the given expression are the length and breadth of the rectangle.

Sol. (i) We have, area of rectangle

$= 25a^2 - 35a + 12$

$= 25a^2 - 20a - 15a + 12$ [By splitting the middle term]

$= 5a(5a - 4) - 3(5a - 4) = (5a - 4)(5a - 3)$

Possible expression for length $= 5a - 3$

and breadth $= 5a - 4$

(ii) We have, area of rectangle $= 35y^2 + 13y - 12 = 35y^2 - 15y + 28y - 12$

[By splitting the middle team]

$= 5y(7y-3) + 4(7y-3) = (7y-3)(5y+4)$

Possible expression for length $= 7y - 3$

and breadth $= 5y + 4$

Question 16 What are the possible expressions for the dimensions of the cuboids whose volumes are given below?

(i) Volume : $3x^2 - 12x$ (ii) Volume : $12ky^2 + 8ky - 20k$

Sol. (i) We have, volume of cuboid $= 3x^2 - 12x = 3x(x-4)$

[$\because$ Volume of cuboid $= l \times b \times h$]

So, possible expressions for the dimensions of the cuboid are 3, x and $x - 4$.

(ii) We have, volume of cuboid $= 12ky^2 + 8ky - 20k$

$= 12ky^2 + 20ky - 12ky - 20k$

[By splitting the middle term]

$= 4ky(3y+5) - 4k(3y+5)$

$= (3y+5)(4ky - 4k)$

$= (3y+5)4k(y-1)$

So, possible expressions for the dimensions of the cuboid are $4k$, $3y+5$ and $y-1$.

DIKSHA APP Questions

Multiple Choice Questions

Q.1 The coefficient of x in the expansion $(x+3)^3$ is

(a) 27 (b) 21 (c) 4 (d) 2

Sol. (a) We have, $a(x+3)^3 = (x)^3 + (3)^3 + 3 \times x \times 3(x+3)$

[using identity $(x+y)^3 = x^3 + y^3 + 3xy(x+y)$]

$= x^3 + 27 + 9x(x+3)$

$= x^3 + 27 + 9x^2 + 27x = x^3 + 9x^2 + 27x + 27$

Hence, the coefficient of x in the expansion $(x+3)^3$ is 27.

Q.2 Zeroes of polynomial $x^2 - 2x$ are ……, ……

(a) 0, −2 (b) 2, 0

(c) 0, 0 (d) 3, 5

Sol. (b) We have, $p(x) = x^2 - 2x$

Now, $p(x) = 0$

$\Rightarrow \quad x^2 - 2x = 0$

$\Rightarrow \quad x(x-2) = 0$

$\Rightarrow \quad x = 0 \Rightarrow x = 2$

So, the zeroes of polynomial $x^2 - 2x$ are 0 and 2.

Q.3 The value of k for which $x + k$ is the factor of $x^3 + kx^2 - 2x + k + 4$ is

(a) 2 (b) 5 (c) $-\frac{4}{3}$ (d) 6

◎ ***Thinking Process*** First find the zero of $x + k$, then put $p(-k) = 0$ to find the required value.

Sol. (c) Let $p(x) = x^3 + kx^2 - 2x + k + 4$

Since, $x + k$ is a factor of $p(x)$.

Then, $p(-k) = 0$ [By factor theorem]

$\Rightarrow (-k)^3 + k(-k)^2 - 2(-k) + k + 4 = 0$

$\Rightarrow \quad -k^3 + k^3 + 2k + k + 4 = 0$

$\Rightarrow \quad 3k + 4 = 0$

$\Rightarrow \quad 3k = -4$

$\Rightarrow \quad k = \frac{-4}{3}$

Q.4 The value of the polynomial $5x - 4x^2 + 3$ at $x = -1$ is

(a) –6 (b) 4 (c) 5 (d) 0

Sol. (a) Let $p(x) = 5x - 4x^2 + 3$

$\therefore \quad p(-1) = 5 \times -1 - 4(-1)^2 + 3 = -5 - 4 + 3$

$= -9 + 3$

$\Rightarrow \quad p(-1) = -6$

Q.5 $\sqrt{5}$ is a polynomial of degree

(a) 1 (b) 2 (c) 0 (d) $\frac{1}{2}$

Sol. (c) In a polynomial $\sqrt{5}$, the highest power of variable is 0, hence the degree of polynomial is 0.

☐ Subjective Type Questions

Q.1 If $x + y + z = 0$, then calculate $x^3 + y^3 + z^3$.

Sol. We know that,

$$x^3 + y^3 + z^3 - 3xyz = (x + y + z)(x^2 + y^2 + z^2 - xy - yz - zx)$$
$$= 0(x^2 + y^2 + z^2 - xy - yz - zx) \quad (\because x + y + z = 0 \text{ given})$$
$$\Rightarrow \quad x^3 + y^3 + z^3 - 3xyz = 0$$
$$\Rightarrow \quad x^3 + y^3 + z^3 = 3xyz$$

Q.2 Simplify $x^2 - y^2$.

Sol. We have, $x^2 - y^2 = (x + y)(x - y)$

Q.3 If 2 and –2 are zeroes of the polynomial $p(x)$, then write the polynomial $p(x)$.

Sol. Since, 2 and –2 are the zeroes of the polynomial $p(x)$, then $(x - 2)$ and $(x + 2)$ are the factors of polynomial $p(x)$.

$\therefore \quad p(x) = (x - 2)(x + 2) = (x)^2 - (2)^2$

[Using identity $(a + b)(a - b) = a^2 - b^2$]

$= x^2 - 4$

Q.4 Factorise $15 - 26xy + 8x^2y^2$.

Sol. We have, $8x^2y^2 - 26xy + 15$

$= 8x^2y^2 - (20 + 6)xy + 15$ [Splitting the middle term]

$= 8x^2y^2 - 20xy - 6xy + 15$

$= 4xy(2xy - 5) - 3(2xy - 5)$

$= (2xy - 5)(4xy - 3)$

Q.5 Verify whether $\sqrt{3}t^2 + \sqrt{7}t + 5$ is a polynomial or not explain why?

Sol. Yes, it is a polynomial in one variable t because each exponent of t is a whole number.

Q.6 If $(x - 3)$ is a factor of $p(x) = x^3 - mx^2 + (m+1)x - 12$, then find the value of m.

Sol. The zero of $x - 3$ is 3.

Let $p(x) = x^3 - mx^2 + (m + 1)x - 12$

Since, $(x-3)$ is a factor of $p(x)$

$\therefore \quad p(3) = 0$

$\Rightarrow \quad (3)^3 - m(3)^2 + (m+1)3 - 12 = 0$

$27 - 9m + 3m + 3 - 12 = 0 \Rightarrow 18 - 6m = 0$

$\Rightarrow \quad 6m = 18$

$\Rightarrow \quad m = 3.$

Mistake Alert Students may incorrectly apply the factor theorem by thinking that, if $(x-a)$ is a factor of a polynomial, then 'a' must also be a factor of the polynomial.

Q.7 Find k, if $x-1$ is a factor $kx^2 - \sqrt{2}x + 1$.

Sol. The zero of $x - 1$ is 1.

Let $\quad p(x) = kx^2 - \sqrt{2}x + 1$

Since, $(x-1)$ is a factor of $p(x)$.

Then, $\quad p(1) = 0$

$\Rightarrow \quad k(1)^2 - \sqrt{2}(1) + 1 = 0$

$\Rightarrow \quad k - \sqrt{2} + 1 = 0$

$\Rightarrow \quad k = \sqrt{2} - 1$

Q.8 Use factor theorem to determine whether $(x+1)$ is a factor of $8x^4 + 12x^3 - 18x + 14$.

Sol. The zero of $x + 1$ is -1.

Let $\quad p(x) = 8x^4 + 12x^3 - 18x + 14$

$\therefore \quad p(-1) = 8(-1)^4 + 12(-1)^3 - 18(-1) + 14$

$= 8 - 12 + 18 + 14 = 40 - 12 = 28 \neq 0$

So, by factor theorem $(x+1)$ is not a factor of $8x^4 + 12x^3 - 18x + 14$.

Q.9 Evaluate 197×203.

Sol. We have, $197 \times 203 = (200-3)(200+3)$

$= (200)^2 - (3)^2 \qquad$ [Using identity $(a+b)(a-b) = a^2 - b^2$]

$= 40000 - 9 = 39991$

Q.10 Use suitable identies to find the product $(x+9)(x+7)$.

Sol. We have, $(x+9)(x+7)$

Using identity, $(x+a)(x+b) = x^2 + (a+b)x + ab$

$\therefore \quad (x+9)(x+7) = x^2 + (9+7)x + (9 \times 7)$

$= x^2 + 16x + 63$

Q.11 Factorise $7x^2 - 3x - 4$.

Sol. We have, $7x^2 - 3x - 4 = 7x^2 - (7 - 4)x - 4$ [Splitting the middle term]

$$= 7x^2 - 7x + 4x - 4$$
$$= 7x(x - 1) + 4(x - 1)$$
$$= (x - 1)(7x + 4)$$

Q.12 Factorise $18x^2 - 3x - 1$.

Sol. We have, $18x^2 - 3x - 1 = 18x^2 - (6 - 3)x - 1$ [Splitting the middle term]

$$= 18x^2 - 6x + 3x - 1$$
$$= 6x(3x - 1) + 1(3x - 1)$$
$$= (3x - 1)(6x + 1)$$

Q.13 Find the value of t, if $x + 1$ is a factor of $p(x)$.
Here $p(x) = 2x^2 + 5x + t$.

◎ ***Thinking Process*** If $(x + a)$ is a factor of $p(x)$, then $p(-a) = 0$.

Sol. The zero of $x + 1$ is -1.

Here, $p(x) = 2x^2 + 5x + t$

Since, $(x + 1)$ is a factor of $p(x)$.

Then, $p(-1) = 0$

$\Rightarrow$ $2(-1)^2 + 5 \times -1 + t = 0$

$\Rightarrow$ $2 - 5 + t = 0$

$\Rightarrow$ $-3 + t = 0$

$\Rightarrow$ $t = 3$

Q.14 Use factor theorem to check whether $g(x)$ is a factor of $p(x)$ or not. Here, $g(x) = 3x + 7$ and $p(x) = 12x^3 + 49x^2 + 55x + 14$

◎ ***Thinking Process***

- First find zero of $g(x)$, then put the value of x in $p(x)$ and simplify it.
- If $p(x) = 0$, then $g(x)$ is a factor of $p(x)$ and if $p(x) \neq 0$, then $g(x)$ is not a factor of $p(x)$.

Sol. The zero of $g(x) = 3x + 7$ is $x = \frac{-7}{3}$

Then, $p\left(\frac{-7}{3}\right) = 12 \times \left(\frac{-7}{3}\right)^3 + 49\left(\frac{-7}{3}\right)^2 + 55\left(\frac{-7}{3}\right) + 14$

$$= 12 \times \left(\frac{-343}{27}\right) + 49\left(\frac{49}{9}\right) - \frac{385}{3} + 14 = \frac{-4116}{27} + \frac{2401}{9} - \frac{385}{3} + 14$$

$$= \frac{-4116 + 7203 - 3465 + 378}{27} = \frac{0}{27} = 0$$

Hence, by the factor theorem $g(x)$ is a factor of $p(x)$.

Q.15 Check whether $2x + 9$ is factor of $4x^3 + 20x^2 + 13x + 18$.

Sol. The zero of $2x + 9$ is $x = \frac{-9}{2}$

Let $p(x) = 4x^3 + 20x^2 + 13x + 18$

Then, $p\left(\frac{-9}{2}\right) = 4 \times \left(\frac{-9}{2}\right)^3 + 20 \times \left(\frac{-9}{2}\right)^2 + 13 \times \left(\frac{-9}{2}\right) + 18$

$$= 4 \times \left(\frac{-729}{8}\right) + 20 \times \left(\frac{81}{4}\right) - \frac{117}{2} + 18 = \frac{-729}{2} + 405 - \frac{117}{2} + 18$$

$$= \frac{-846}{2} + 423 = -423 + 423 = 0$$

Therefore, by the factor theorem $2x + 9$ is a factor of

$$p(x) = 4x^3 + 20x^2 + 13x + 18.$$

Q.16 Find zeroes of $x^2 + 7x + 12$

Sol. We have, $x^2 + 7x + 12 = x^2 + (4 + 3)\,x + 12$ [Splitting the middle term]

$$= x^2 + 4x + 3x + 12 = x(x + 4) + 3(x + 4)$$

$$= (x + 4)(x + 3)$$

Now, $(x + 4)(x + 3) = 0 \Rightarrow x + 4 = 0, x + 3 = 0$

$\Rightarrow$ $x = -4, x = -3$

Therefore, the zeroes of $x^2 + 7x + 12$ are $x = -3$ and $x = -4$.

Q.17 Write the following cube in expanded form $(7x^2 + 3)^3$.

Sol. We have, $(7x^2 + 3)^3 = (7x^2)^3 + (3)^3 + 3 \times 7x^2 \times 3\,(7x^2 + 3)$

[Using identity $(a + b)^3 = a^3 + b^3 + 3ab\,(a + b)$]

$$= 343x^6 + 27 + 63x^2(7x^2 + 3)$$

$$= 343x^6 + 27 + 441x^4 + 189x^2$$

$$= 343x^6 + 441x^4 + 189x^2 + 27$$

Q.18 Factorise $2197a^3 - 1$.

Thinking Process First adjust the given terms in the form of $a^3 - b^3$, then use the identity $a^3 - b^3 = (a-b)(a^2 + ab + b^2)$ to get the required factor.

Sol. $2197a^3 - 1 = (13a)^3 - (1)^3$

$$= (13a - 1)[(13a)^2 + 13a \times 1 + (1)^2]$$

[Using identity $a^3 - b^3 = (a - b)(a^2 + ab + b^2)$]

$$= (13a - 1)(169a^2 + 13a + 1)$$

Q.19 What is polynomial?

Sol. An algebraic expression in which the variables involved have only non-negative integrals powers is called polynomial.

Q.20 Verify whether $\sqrt{2}\, t^2 + 7t + \sqrt{9}$ is a polynomial or not explain. Explain why?

Sol. Yes, it is a polynomial because, we have t as the only variable and the powers of t in each term are whole numbers.

Q.21 Given an example of trinomial polynomial of degree 7.

Sol. The trinomial of degree 7 is $t^7 + 2t + 9$.

Q.22 Given an example of binomial polynomial of degree 9.

Sol. The binomial of degree 9 is $t^9 + 2t$.

Q.23 What is the difference between zero polynomial and zero of polynomial.

Sol. **Zero polynomial** A polynomial consisting of one term, namely zero only is called zero polynomial.

Zero of a polynomial Let $p(x)$ be a polynomial and 'a' be a real number. If $p(a) = 0$, then we say that 'a' is a zero of polynomial $p(x)$.

Q.24 Find the value of $p(3)$ where, $p(t) = 3t^2 - 9t + 7$.

Sol. We have, $p(t) = 3t^2 - 9t + 7$

$\therefore \quad p(3) = 3(3)^2 - 9(3) + 7 = 27 - 27 + 7$

$\Rightarrow \quad p(3) = 7$

Hence, the value of $p(3)$ is 7.

Q.25 Find zero of $x+7$.

Sol. Let $p(x) = x + 7$. We need to find $p(x) = 0$

$\Rightarrow \quad x + 7 = 0$

$\Rightarrow \quad x = -7$

Therefore, $x = -7$ is a zero of $p(x)$ polynomial.

Q.26 Factorise $x^2 - 1 - 2a - a^2$.

Sol. We have, $x^2 - 1 - 2a - a^2 = x^2 - (1 + 2a + a^2) = (x)^2 - (a + 1)^2$

[Using identity $(a + b)^2 = a^2 + 2ab + b^2$]

$= (x + a + 1)(x - a - 1)$ [Using identity $a^2 - b^2 = (a + b)(a - b)$]

Mistake Alert Student may incorrectly apply the identity as $a^2 - 2ab + b^2 = (a+b)^2$ instead of $a^2 + 2ab + b^2 = (a+b)^2$.

Q.27 If $a+b+c=9$ and $a^2+b^2+c^2=35$, then find $a^3+b^3+c^3-3abc$.

Thinking Process First find the value of $ab + bc + ca$ by using the formula $(a+b+c)^2 = a^2+b^2+c^2+2ab+2bc+2ca$, then find the required value by using the formula $a^3+b^3+c^3-3abc = (a+b+c)$ $(a^2+b^2+c^2-ab-bc-ca)$.

Sol. We know that

$a^3 + b^3 + c^3 - 3abc = (a + b + c)\ (a^2 + b^2 + c^2 - ab - bc - ac)$

Now, $\quad (a + b + c)^2 = a^2 + b^2 + c^2 + 2ab + 2bc + 2ca$

$9^2 = 35 + 2(ab + bc + ca)$

$\Rightarrow \quad 81 = 35 + 2(ab + bc + ca)$

$\Rightarrow \quad 81 - 35 = 2(ab + bc + ca)$

$\Rightarrow \quad 46 = 2(ab + bc + ca)$

$\Rightarrow \quad ab + bc + ca = 23$

Now, $a^3 + b^3 + c^3 - 3abc = (a + b + c)\,[(a^2 + b^2 + c^2) - (ab + bc + ca)]$

$= 9\,(35 - 23)$

$- 9(12) - 108$

Q.28 If $x+y=8$ and $xy=15$, then find x^3+y^3.

Sol. Given, $x + y = 8$ and $xy = 15$ we know that

$(x + y)^3 = x^3 + y^3 + 3xy\,(x + y)$

$\Rightarrow \quad (8)^3 = x^3 + y^3 + 3 \times 15\,(8)$

$\Rightarrow \quad 512 = x^3 + y^3 + 360$

$\Rightarrow \quad x^3 + y^3 = 512 - 360 = 152$

Q.29 If $(x+1)$ and $(x-2)$ are the factors of mx^3+x^2-2x+n, then find m and n.

Sol. Let $p(x) = mx^3 + x^2 - 2x + n$

Since, $(x+1)$ is a factor of $p(x)$, then $p(-1) = 0$

$\Rightarrow \quad m(-1)^3 + (-1)^2 - 2(-1) + n = 0$

$\Rightarrow \quad -m + 1 + 2 + n = 0$

$\Rightarrow \quad -m + n = -3 \quad \ldots(i)$

and $(x-2)$ is a factor of $p(x)$, then $p(2) = 0$

$\Rightarrow \quad m(2)^3 + (2)^2 - 2(2) + n = 0$

$\Rightarrow \quad 8m + 4 - 4 + n = 0$

$\Rightarrow \quad 8m + n = 0$

$\Rightarrow \quad -8m - n = 0 \quad \ldots(ii)$

On adding Eqs. (i) and (ii), we get $-9m = -3 \Rightarrow m = \frac{1}{3}$

On putting value of m in Eq. (ii), we get

$$-8\left(\frac{1}{3}\right) - n = 0 \Rightarrow n = \frac{-8}{3}$$

$$\therefore \quad m = \frac{1}{3} \text{ and } n = \frac{-8}{3}$$

Q.30 Evaluate using the identity $55^3 - 25^3 - 30^3$.

Sol. We have, $55^3 - 25^3 - 30^3 = (55)^3 + (-25)^3 + (-30)^3$

Here, $55 - 25 - 30 = 0$

So, $(55)^3 + (-25)^3 + (-30)^3 = 3 \times (55)(-25)(-30) = 123750$

[$\because$ If $x + y + z = 0$, then $x^3 + y^3 + z^3 = 3xyz$]

Coordinate Geometry

CHAPTER 03

Important Points

01 **Cartesian System** The system used to describe the position of a point in a plane is called Cartesian System.

In cartesian system, there are two mutually perpendicular lines XX' and YY' which intersect each other at point 'O'. The horizontal line XOX' is called X-axis and vertical line YOY' is called Y-axis.

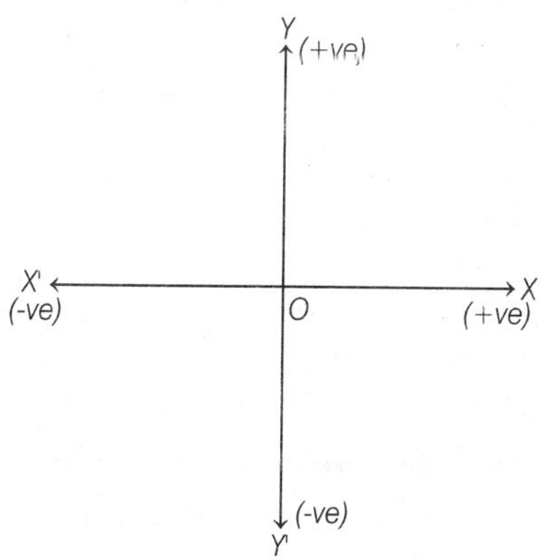

The point where XOX' and YOY', lines intersect each other is called origin and is denoted by 'O'. OX and OY are called positive directions while OX' and OY' are called negative directions.

These axes divide the plane into four parts. These four parts are called the quadrant (one-fourth part) and these are numbered I, II, III and IV in anti-clockwise from OX. So, the plane that consists of these axes and these quadrants is called the cartesian plane or the coördinate plane or the XY-plane. These axes are called the coordinate axes.

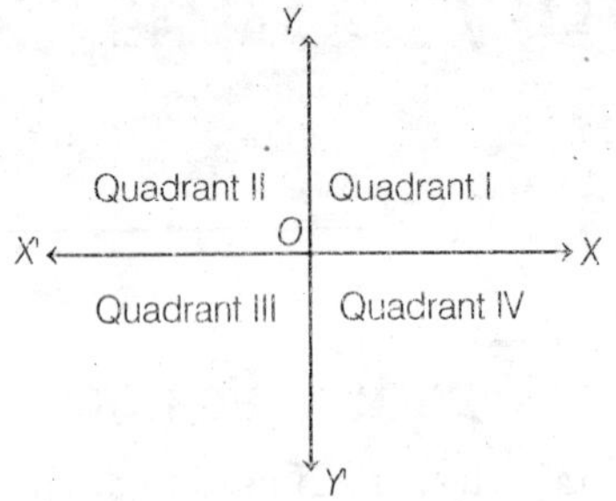

The coordinates of a point are written by using the following conventions:

(i) The x-coordinate of a point is its perpendicular distance from the Y-axis measured along the X-axis (positive along the positive direction of the X-axis and negative along the negative direction of the X-axis). The x-coordinate is also called the abscissa.

(ii) The y-coordinate of a point is its perpendicular distance from the X-axis measured along the Y-axis (positive along the positive direction of the Y-axis and negative along the negative direction of the Y-axis). The y-coordinate is also called the ordinate.

(iii) In stating the coordinates of a point in the coordinate plane, the x-coordinate comes first and then the y-coordinate. We place the coordinates in brackets denoted as (x, y).

02 Sign Conventions of Coordinates in various quadrants

(i) If a point is in the Ist quadrant, then the point will be in the form (+, +), since the Ist quadrant is enclosed by the positive X-axis and the positive Y-axis.

(ii) If a point is in the IInd quadrant, then the point will be in the form $(-, +)$, since the IInd quadrant is enclosed by the negative X-axis and the positive Y-axis.

(iii) If a point is in the IIIrd quadrant, then the point will be in the form (–, –), since the IIIrd quadrant is enclosed by the negative X-axis and the negative Y-axis.

(iv) If a point is in the IVth quadrant, then the point will be in the form (+, –), since the IVth quadrant is enclosed by the positive X-axis and the negative Y-axis (see figure).

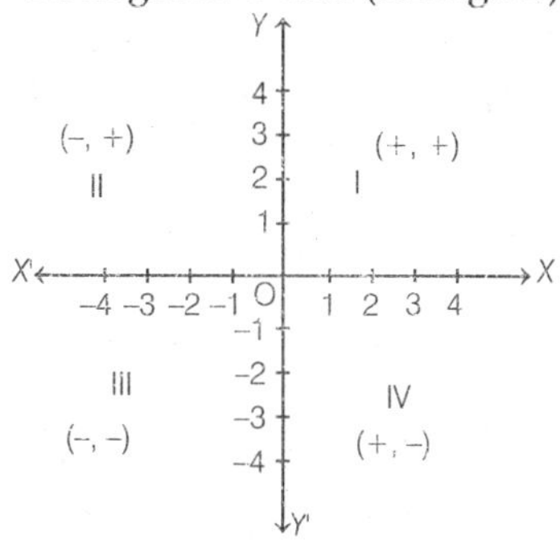

Note • The abscissa of every point on Y-axis is zero.

- The ordinates of every point on X-axis is zero.
- Coordinates of a point on Y-axis are of the form $(0, y)$.
- Coordinate of a point on X-axis are of the form $(x, 0)$.
- If $x \neq y$, the $(x, y) \neq (y, x)$ and $(x, y) = (y, x)$ if $x = y$.
- The coordinates of origin 'O' is $(0, 0)$.

Exercise 3.1

Question 1 How will you describe the position of a table lamp on your study table to another person?

Sol. Let us consider the lamp as a point A and table as a plane.

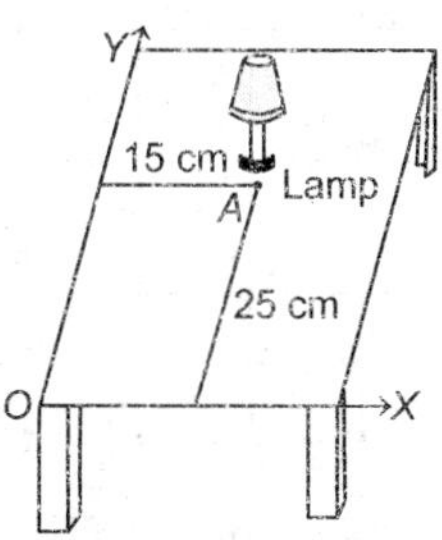

Take any two perpendicular edges of the table, say OX and OY. Measure the distance of the lamp A from the shorter edge OX, let it be 25 cm. Again, measure the distance of the lamp A from the longer edge OY, let it be 15 cm. Therefore, the position of the lamp A to the edges OX and OY is (15, 25).

Question 2 (Street Plan) A city has two main roads which cross each other at the centre of the city. These two roads are along the North-South direction and East-West direction. All the other streets of the city run parallel to these roads and are 200 m apart. There are 5 streets in each direction. Using 1 cm = 200 m, draw a model of the city on your notebook. Represent the roads/streets by single lines. There are many cross-streets in your model. A particular cross-street is made by two streets, one running in the North-South direction and another in the East-West direction. Each cross-street is referred to in the following manner : If the 2nd street running in the North-South direction and 5th in the East-West direction meet at some crossing, then we will call this cross-street (2, 5). Using this convention, find:

(i) how many cross-streets can be referred to as (4, 3).

(ii) how many cross-streets can be referred to as (3, 4).

Sol. The street plan is shown by the following figure.

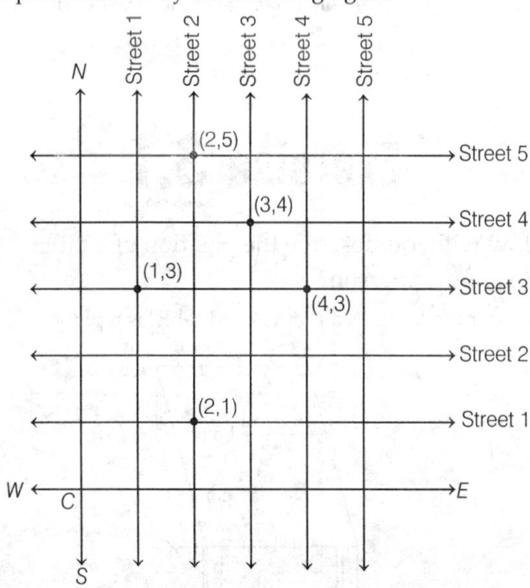

(i) There is only one cross-street which can be referred as (4, 3).

(ii) There is only one cross-street which can be referred as (3, 4).

Exercise 3.2

Question 1 Write the answer of each of the following questions

(i) What is the name of horizontal and the vertical lines drawn to determine the position of any point in the Cartesian plane?

(ii) What is the name of each part of the plane formed by these two lines?

(iii) Write the name of the point where these two lines intersect.

Sol. (i) Horizontal line is known as X-axis and vertical line is known as Y-axis.

(ii) Each part of the plane formed by horizontal and vertical lines is known as quadrant.

(iii) The name of the point where these two lines intersect is the origin.

Question 2 See figure, and write the following

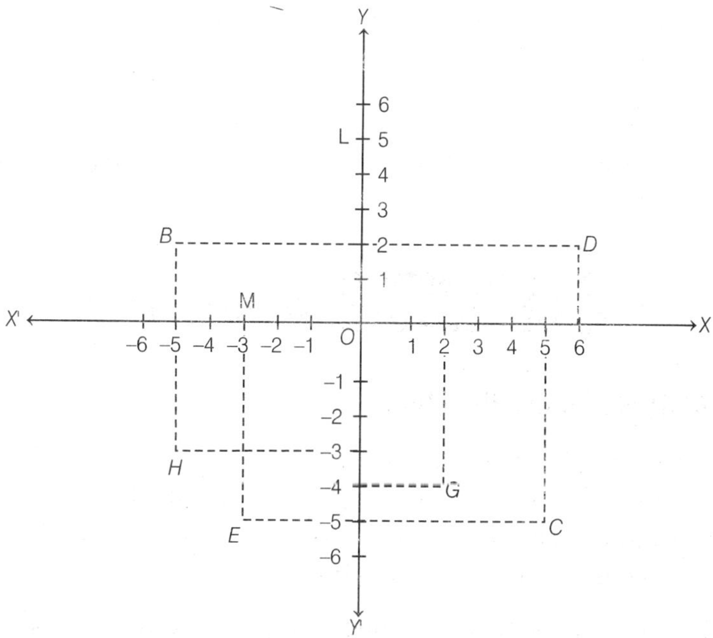

(i) The coordinates of *B*.

(ii) The coordinates of *C*.

(iii) The point identified by the coordinates $(-3, -5)$.

(iv) The point identified by the coordinates $(2, -4)$.
(v) The abscissa of the point D.
(vi) The ordinate of the point H.
(vii) The coordinates of the point L.
(viii) The coordinates of the point M.

Thinking Process The coordinates of any point on the cartesian plane are (x, y), where x is abscissa and y is ordinate of that point.

Then, x = perpendicular distance from Y-axis and Y = perpendicular distance from X-axis.

Sol. (i) $\because$ The point B lies in IInd quadrant.

The distance of point B from Y-axis (Abscissa) = –5

and the distance of point B from X-axis (ordinate) = 2

So, the coordinates of point B is $(-5, 2)$.

(ii) The coordinates of $C = (5, -5)$. ($\because$ Abscissa = 5, ordinate = –5)

(iii) The point identified by the coordinates $(-3, -5)$ is E.

(iv) The point identified by the coordinates $(2, -4)$ is G.

(v) The abscissa of the point $D = 6$

(vi) The ordinate of the point $H = -3$

(vii) The coordinates of the point $L = (0, 5)$ (Lies on Y-axis)

(viii) The coordinates of the point $M = (-3, 0)$ (Lies on X-axis)

DIKSHA APP Questions

Multiple Choice Questions

Q.1 Abscissa of all points on of Y-axis is

(a) 1 (b) 0 (c) 2 (d) –1

Sol. (b) Abscissa is the x-coordinate and on Y-axis, x-coordinate is 0.

So, abscissa of all points on Y-axis is '0'

Q.2 P and Q are points $(-2,7)$ and $(-3, 4)$, respectively. Value of abscissa of P) - (abscissa of Q) is

(a) 1 (b) –1 (c) 2 (d) –21

Sol. (a) Abscissa of P is -2 and abscissa of Q is -3.

Now, (abscissa of P) $-$ (abscissa of Q) $= -2-(-3) = -2+3 = 1$

Q.3 The point whose ordinate is 3 and which lies on Y-axis is

(a) (3, 0) (b) (0, 3)

(c) (3, 1) (d) (−23, 0)

◎ ***Thinking Process*** The coordinates of a point, which lies on Y-axis are $(0, y)$ where, y is ordinate of that point.

Sol. (b) Ordinate is 3 means y-coordinate is 3 and point lies on Y-axis.

$\therefore$ abscissa is 0.

So, the coordinates of that point are (0, 3).

Q.4 (x, y) and (y, x) represent the same point on Cartesian plane if.

(a) $x > y$

(b) $x < y$

(c) $x = y$

(d) None of the above

◎ ***Thinking Process*** If $(x, y) = (y, x)$, then $x = y$

Sol. (c) $x = y$ represent the same points on Cartesian plane.

☐ Subjective Type Questions

Q.1 A point lies on X-axis at a distance of 9 units from Y-axis. What are its coordinates? What will be the coordinates of a point if it lies on Y-axis at a distance of -9 units from X-axis?

Sol. Point lies on X-axis at a distance of 9 units from Y-axis is (9, 0).

Point lies on Y-axis at a distance of -9 units from X-axis is $(0, -9)$.

Mistake Alert Be careful about abscissa and ordinate, abscissa is distance from Y-axis and ordinate is distance from X-axis.

Q.2 Write the coordinates of the following

(i) 4 units right to the origin and 3 units below origin.

(ii) 2 units above origin and 1 unit left to the origin.

Sol. (i) 4 units right to origin means 4 units towards positive X-axis and 3 unit below origin means 3 units towards negative Y-axis.

The coordinates of that point = (4, – 3).

(ii) 2 unit above origin means 2 units towards positive Y-axis and 1 unit left to origin means 1 unit to negative X-axis.

The coordinates of point = (–1, 2)

Q.3 The distance of the point (–3, 5) from X-axis is

Sol. The distance of point (–3, 5) from X-axis is 5 unit, that is y-coordinate.

Mistake Alert Many students get confused in distance of a point from X-axis is abscissa or ordinate of that point.

Q.4 In which quadrant or on which axis each of the points lie?

A (3, –4), B (4, 0), C (0, –3), D (–4, –6), E (–2, 0)

Thinking Process Sign convention of coordinates in various quadrants

Quadrants	Sign
I	(+, +)
II	(–, +)
III	(–, –)
IV	(+, –)

The coordinates of points which lies on X-axis = $(x, 0)$ and the coordinates of points which lies on Y-axis = $(0, y)$.

Sol. Point A (3, –4) lies in IVth quadrant.

Point B (4, 0) lies on positive X-axis.

Point C (0, –3) lies on negative Y-axis.

Point D (–4, –6) lies in IIIrd quadrant.

Point E (–2, 0) lies on negative X-axis.

Q.5 The perpendicular distances of a point from X-axis and Y-axis are 3 and 2 respectively. What are its coordinates?

Sol. The perpendicular distance of a point from X-axis = 3

∴ Ordinate = 3

and the perpendicular distance of a point from Y-axis = 2

∴ Abscissa = 2

Now, the coordinates of the point = (2, 3).

Q.6 Write the coordinates of the vertices of a rectangle whose length and breadth are 5 and 3 units, respectively, one vertex at origin, the longer side on the X-axis and one of vertices in third quadrant.

Sol. Consider the graph plotted as follows

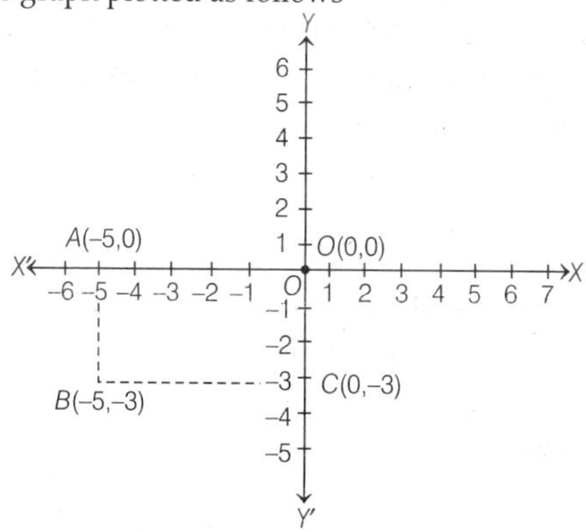

The coordinates of the vertices of a rectangle $ABCO$ are $O(0, 0)$, $A(-5, 0)$, $B(-5, -3)$, $C(0, -3)$.

Q.7 From the given figure, answer the following questions.

(i) The abscissa and ordinate of point P are ...and ...respectively.

(ii) The y-coordinate and x-coordinate of point Q are ...... and ...... respectively.

(iii) The coordinate of point R are ......

(iv) The x-coordinate and y-coordinate of point S are ...... and ...... respectively.

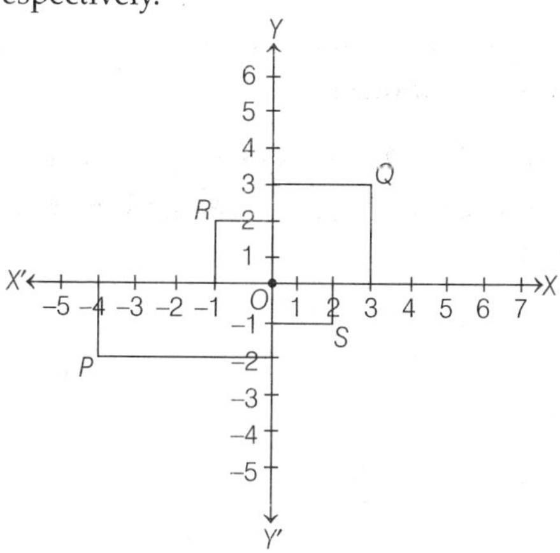

Sol. (i) The abscissa and ordinate of point P are –4 and –2 respectively.

(ii) The y-coordinate and x-coordinate of point Q are 3 and 3 respectively.

(iii) The coordinates of point R are (–1, 2).

(iv) The x-coordinate and y-coordinate of points S are 2 and –1, respectively.

Q.8 If the coordinates of point M are (–2, 9) which can also be expressed as $(1+x, y^2)$ and $y>0$, then find in which quadrant do the following points lie :

$P(y, x)$, $Q(2, x)$, $R(x^2, y-1)$, $S(2x, -3y)$

Sol. Coordinates of point $M = (-2, 9) = (1+x, y^2)$

On comparing the abscissa and ordinate on both sides, we get

$$-2 = 1 + x \text{ and } 9 = y^2$$

$\Rightarrow$ $x = -3$

and $y = \pm 3$

$\Rightarrow$ $y = 3$ $(\because y > 0)$

Point $P(y, x)$

Now, coordinates of point $P(y, x) = (3, -3)$

$\therefore$ Point $P(y, x)$ lies in IVth quadrant.

Point $Q(2, x)$

Coordinates of point $Q(2, x) = (2, -3)$

$\therefore$ Point Q lies in IVth quadrant.

Point $R(x^2, y-1)$

Coordinates of point $R(x^2, y-1) = (9, 2)$

$\therefore$ Point P lies in Ist quadrant.

Point $S(2x, -3y)$

Coordinates of point $S(2x, -3y) = (-6, -9)$

$\therefore$ Point S lies in IIIrd quadrant.

Q.9 Join the points $A(4, -4)$, $B(4, 4)$, $C(-4, 4)$, $D(-4, -4)$ on X, Y plane to get the square $ABCD$. Also, find the perimeter and area of the square.

Sol. We have, the vertices of the square $A(4, -4)$, $B(4, 4)$, $C(-4, 4)$, $D(-4, -4)$

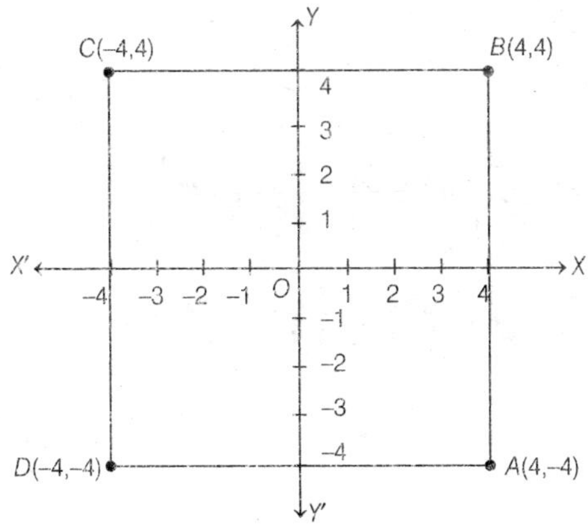

Length of $AB = (4 + 4) = 8$ units

$\therefore$ Perimeter of square $= 4 \times 8 = 32$ units [$\because$ Perimeter of square $4 \times$ Side]

and Area of square $= 8^2 = 64$ square units [$\because$ Area of square $=$ Side^2]

Q.10 Plot each of the following points by taking a co-ordinate system on a graph paper.

$A(3, 1)$, $B(2, -3)$, $C(-4, 0)$, $D(-2, -1)$, $E(-5, 2)$, $F(0, -5)$

◎ ***Thinking Process*** Abscissa of a point = distance from Y-axis and Ordinate of a point = distance from X-axis.

Sol. The point A, B, C, D, E and F plotted as in given graph.

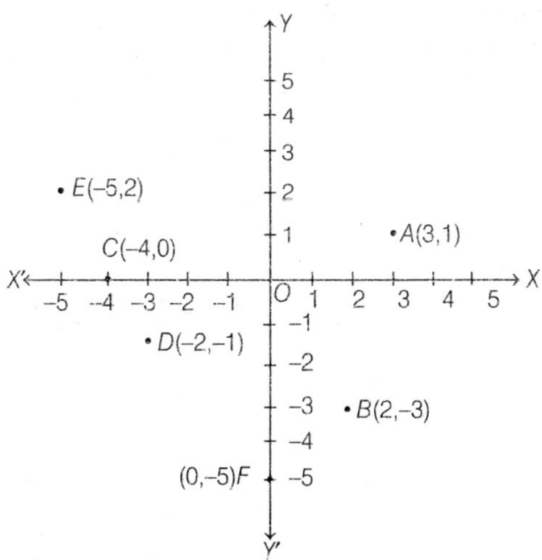

Linear Equations in Two Variables

CHAPTER 04

Important Points

01 **Linear Equations** Any equation which can be put in the form $ax + by + c = 0$, where a, b and c are real numbers and a and b are both non zero is called a linear equation in two variables.

The solution of a linear equation is not affected, when

(i) the same number is added to (or subtracted from) both the sides of the equation.

(ii) you multiply or divide both the sides of the equation by the same non-zero number.

02 A linear equation in two variables has infinitely many solutions.

Exercise 4.1

Question 1 The cost of a notebook is twice the cost of a pen. Write a linear equation in two variables to represent this statement.

(Take the cost of a notebook to be ₹ x and that of a pen to be ₹ y)

Sol. Let the cost of a notebook = ₹ x and the cost of a pen = ₹ y.

According to question,

$$\text{Cost of a notebook} = 2(\text{cost of a pen})$$

$$\therefore \quad x = 2y$$

$$\Rightarrow \quad x - 2y = 0$$

Question 2 Express the following linear equations in the form $ax + by + c = 0$ and indicate the values of a, b and c in each case.

(i) $x + 3y = 9.3\overline{5}$ (ii) $x - \frac{y}{5} - 10 = 0$

(iii) $-2x + 3y = 6$ (iv) $x = 3y$

(v) $2x = -5y$ (vi) $3x + 2 = 0$

(vii) $y - 2 = 0$ (viii) $5 = 2x$

◎ *Thinking Process* Firstly express the given linear equation in the form of standard linear equation $ax + by + c = 0$, then compare with this and find the values of a, b and c.

Sol. (i) $2x + 3y = 9.3\overline{5} \Rightarrow 2x + 3y - 9.3\overline{5} = 0$

On comparing with $ax + by + c = 0$, we get

$$a = 2, b = 3 \text{ and } c = -9.3\overline{5}$$

(ii) $$x - \frac{y}{5} - 10 = 0$$

On comparing with $ax + by + c = 0$, we get $a = 1$, $b = \frac{-1}{5}$ and $c = -10$.

(iii) $$-2x + 3y = 6$$

$$\Rightarrow \quad -2x + 3y - 6 = 0$$

On comparing with $ax + by + c = 0$, we get $a = -2$, $b = 3$ and $c = -6$.

(iv) $$x = 3y \Rightarrow x - 3y + 0 = 0$$

On comparing with $ax + by + c = 0$, we get $a = 1$, $b = -3$ and $c = 0$.

(v) $$2x = -5y$$

$$\Rightarrow \quad 2x + 5y + 0 = 0$$

On comparing with $ax + by + c = 0$, we get $a = 2$, $b = 5$ and $c = 0$.

(vi) $3x + 2 = 0$

$\Rightarrow \quad 3x + 0y + 2 = 0$

On comparing with $ax + by + c = 0$, we get the values of $a = 3$, $b = 0$ and $c = 2$.

(vii) $y - 2 = 0$

$\Rightarrow \quad 0x + y - 2 = 0$

On comparing with $ax + by + c = 0$, we get the values of $a = 0$, $b = 1$ and $c = -2$.

(viii) $5 = 2x \Rightarrow 2x + 0y - 5 = 0$

On comparing with $ax + by + c = 0$, we get the values of $a = 2$, $b = 0$ and $c = -5$.

Exercise 4.2

Question 1 Which one of the following options is true and why?
$y = 3x + 5$ has

(i) a unique solution (ii) only two solutions

(iii) infinitely many solutions

Sol. (iii) A linear equation in two variables has infinitely many solutions because for every value of x, there will be value of y which satisfies the given equation and *vice-versa*.

Question 2 Write four solutions for each of the following equations

(i) $2x + y = 7$ (ii) $\pi x + y = 9$

(iii) $x = 4y$

Sol. (i) $2x + y = 7$

By inspection, $x = 2$ and $y = 3$ is a solution because for $x = 2$, $y = 3$,

$$2x + y = 2 \times 2 + 3 = 4 + 3 = 7$$

Now, let us choose $x = 0$ with this value of x, the given equation reduces to $y = 7$. So, $x = 0$, $y = 7$ is also a solution of $2x + y = 7$. Similarly, taking $y = 0$, the given equation reduces to $2x = 7$ which has the unique solution $x = \frac{7}{2}$. So, $x = \frac{7}{2}$, $y = 0$ is a solution of $2x + y = 7$. Finally, let us take $x = 1$. The given equation now reduces to $2 + y = 7$ whose solution is given by $y = 5$. Therefore, (1, 5) is also a solution of the given equation. So, four of the infinitely many solutions of the given equation are (2, 3), (0, 7), $\left(\frac{7}{2}, O\right)$ and (1, 5).

(ii) $\pi x + y = 9$

By inspection, $x = \frac{1}{\pi}, y = 8$ is a solution because for $x = \frac{1}{\pi}$ and $y = 2$,

$$\pi x + y = \pi \times \frac{1}{\pi} + 8 = 1 + 8 = 9$$

Now, let us choose $x = 0$ with this value of x, the given equation reduces to $y = 9$ which has a unique solution $y = 9$. So, $x = 0, y = 9$ is also a solution of $\pi x + y = 9$. Similarly, taking $y = 0$, the given equation reduces to $x = \frac{9}{\pi}$. So, $x = \frac{9}{\pi}, y = 0$ is a solution of $\pi x + y = 9$ as well. Finally, let us take $x = 7$ the given equation now reduces to $\frac{22}{7}$. $7 + y = 9$ whose solution is given by $y = -13$. Therefore, $(7, -13)$ is also a solution of the given equation. So, four of the infinitely many solutions of the given equation are

$$\left(\frac{1}{\pi}, 8\right), (0, 9), \left(\frac{9}{\pi}, 0\right) \text{ and } (7, -13)$$

or $\left(\frac{7}{22}, 8\right), (0, 9), \left(\frac{63}{22}, 0\right)$ and $(7, -13)$ $\left(\because \pi = \frac{22}{7}\right)$

(iii) $x = 4y \Rightarrow x - 4y = 0$

By inspection, $x = 0, y = 0$ is a solution because for $x = y = 0$, $0 - 4 \times 0 = 0 - 0 = 0$, it satisfies.

Now, let us choose $x = 4$ with this value of x, the given equation reduces to $y = 1$ which has a unique solution $y = 1$. So, $x = 4, y = 1$ is also a solution of $x - 4y = 0$. Similarly, taking $y = \frac{1}{2}$, the given equation reduces to $x = 2$. So, $x = 2, y = \frac{1}{2}$ is a solution $x - 4y = 0$ as well. Finally, let us take $x = 1$, the given equation now reduces to $1 - 4y = 0$ whose solution is given by $y = \frac{1}{4}$. Therefore, $(1, 1/4)$ is also a solution of the given equation. So, four of the infinitely many solutions of the given equation are $(0, 0), (4, 1), \left(2, \frac{1}{2}\right)$ and $\left(1, \frac{1}{4}\right)$.

Question 3 Check which of the following are solution of the equation $x - 2y = 4$ and which are not

(i) $(0, 2)$ (ii) $(2, 0)$ (iii) $(4, 0)$ (iv) $(\sqrt{2}, 4\sqrt{2})$

(v) $(1, 1)$

Sol. (i) Take $x - 2y$ and put $x = 0, y = 2$, we get

$$0 - 2 \times 2 = 0 - 4 = -4 \neq 4$$

Hence, $(0, 2)$ is not a solution of $x - 2y = 4$.

(ii) Take $x - 2y$ and put $x = 2, y = 0$, we get

$$2 - 2 \times 0 = 2 - 0 = 2 \neq 4$$

Hence, $(2, 0)$ is not a solution of $x - 2y = 4$.

(iii) Take $x - 2y$ and put $x = 4$, $y = 0$, we get

$$4 - 2 \times 0 = 4 - 0 = 4$$

Hence, (4, 0) is a solution of $x - 2y = 4$.

(iv) Take $x - 2y$ and put $x = \sqrt{2}$, $y = 4\sqrt{2}$, we get

$$\sqrt{2} - 2 \times 4\sqrt{2} = \sqrt{2} - 8\sqrt{2} = -7\sqrt{2} \neq 4$$

Hence, $(\sqrt{2}, 4\sqrt{2})$ is not a solution of $x - 2y = 4$.

(v) Take $x - 2y$ and put $x = 1$, $y = 1$, we get

$$1 - 2 \times 1 = 1 - 2 = -1 \neq 4$$

Hence, (1, 1) is not a solution of $x - 2y = 4$.

Note An easy way of getting a solution is to take $x = 0$ and get the corresponding value of y. Similarly, we can put $y = 0$ and obtain the corresponding value of x.

Question 4 Find the value of k, if $x = 2$, $y = 1$ is a solution of the equation $2x + 3y = k$.

◎ ***Thinking Process*** Firstly put the value of x and y in the given linear equation and find the value of k.

Sol. Given, $2x + 3y = k$ ...(i)

On substituting $x = 2$, $y = 1$, in Eq. (i) we get, $2 \times 2 + 3 \times 1 = k \Rightarrow 4 + 3 = k \Rightarrow k = 7$.
Therefore, the value of k is 7.

DIKSHA APP Questions

□ Multiple Choice Questions

Q.1 If a linear equation has solutions $(-2, 2)$, $(0, 0)$ and $(2, -2)$, then it is of the form

(a) $y - x = 0$ (b) $x + y = 0$

(c) $2y - x = 0$ (d) $y - 2x = 0$

Sol. (b) Let us consider a linear equation $ax + by + c = 0$ ...(i)

Since, (–2, 2), (0, 0) and (2, –2) are the solutions of linear equation therefore it satisfy the Eq. (i)

So, at (–2, 2), $-2a + 2b + c = 0$ ...(ii)

at (0, 0), $0 + 0 + c = 0$

$\Rightarrow$ $c = 0$ ...(iii)

and at (2, –2), $2a - 2b + c = 0$ ...(iv)

From Eqs. (ii) and (iii), we get

$$-2a + 2b = 0$$

$$\Rightarrow \quad 2a = 2b$$

$$\Rightarrow \quad a = b$$

On putting $a = b$ and $c = 0$ in Eq. (i), we get

$$bx + by + 0 = 0$$

$$\Rightarrow \quad b(x + y) = 0$$

$$\Rightarrow \quad x + y = 0 \qquad [\because b \neq 0]$$

Hence, $x + y = 0$ is the required form of the linear equation.

Q.2 If (2, 1) is the solution of the equation $gx - 2y = 10$, then the value of g is

(a) 6 (b) –6 (c) 7 (d) –7

Sol. (a) We have, $gx - 2y = 10$,

On putting $x = 2$, $y = 1$ in the given equation, we get

$$g \times 2 - 2 \times 1 = 10$$

$$\Rightarrow \quad 2g - 2 = 10$$

$$\Rightarrow \quad 2g = 12$$

$$\Rightarrow \quad g = 6$$

Q.3 A linear equation in two variable is of the form $ax + by + c = 0$, where

(a) $a \neq 0, b \neq 0$ (b) $a = 0, b \neq 0$

(c) $a \neq 0, b = 0$ (d) $a = 0, c = 0$

Sol. (a) A linear equation in two variables is of the form $ax + by + c$, where $a \neq 0$, $b \neq 0$.

Q.4 $x = 5, y = -2$ is a solution of the linear equation.

(a) $2x + y = 9$ (b) $2x - y = 12$

(c) $x + 3y = 1$ (d) $x + 3y = 0$

Sol. (b) We have, $x = 5$ and $y = -2$

For option (a)

On putting $x = 5$ and $y = -2$ in $2x + y = 9$, we get

$$2 \times 5 + (-2) = 9$$

$$\Rightarrow \quad 10 - 2 = 9$$

$\Rightarrow 8 = 9$, which is not true.

Hence, $x = 5$ and $y = -2$ is not a solution of linear equation $2x + y = 9$.

For option (b)

On putting $x = 5$ and $y = -2$ in $2x - y = 12$, we get

$$2 \times 5 - (-2) = 12$$

$\Rightarrow$ $10 + 2 = 12$

$\Rightarrow$ $12 = 12$, which is true.

Hence, $x = 5$ and $y = -2$ is a solution of linear equation $2x - y = 12$.

For option (c)

On putting $x = 5$ and $y = -2$ in $x + 3y = 1$, we get

$$5 + 3(-2) = 1$$

$\Rightarrow$ $5 - 6 = 1$

$\Rightarrow$ $-1 = 1$, which is not true.

Hence, $x = 5$ and $y = -2$ is not a solution of linear equation $x + 3y = 1$.

For option (d)

On putting $x = 5$ and $y = -2$ in $x + 3y = 0$, we get

$$5 + 3(-2) = 0$$

$\Rightarrow$ $5 - 6 = 0$

$\Rightarrow$ $-1 = 0$, which is not true.

Hence, $x = 5$ and $y = -2$ is not a solution of linear equation $x + 3y = 0$.

☐ Subjective Type Questions

Q.1 Find four solutions of $4x - 3y = 18$.

Sol. We have, $4x - 3y = 18$

On putting $x = 0$ in $4x - 3y = 18$, we get

$$4 \times 0 - 3y = 18$$

$\Rightarrow$ $3y = 18$

$\Rightarrow$ $y = -6$

On putting $x = 6$ in $4x - 3y = 18$, we get

$$4 \times 6 - 3y = 18$$

$\Rightarrow$ $24 - 3y = 18$

$\Rightarrow$ $-3y = 18 - 24$

$\Rightarrow$ $-3y = -6$

$\Rightarrow$ $y = 2$

On putting $x = 9$ in $4x - 3y = 18$, we get

$$4 \times 9 - 3y = 18$$

$\Rightarrow$ $36 - 3y = 18$

$\Rightarrow \quad -3y = 18 - 36$

$\Rightarrow \quad -3y = -18$

$\Rightarrow \quad y = 6$

On putting $y = 0$ in $4x - 3y = 18$, we get

$4x - 3 \times 0 = 18$

$\Rightarrow \quad 4x - 0 = 18$

$\Rightarrow \quad 4x = 18$

$\Rightarrow \quad x = \frac{18}{4}$

$\Rightarrow \quad x = \frac{9}{2}$

Hence, the required solutions are

x	0	6	9	9/2
y	–6	2	6	0

Q.2 Express the linear equations $5 = 2x$ in the form $ax + by + c = 0$ and indicate the values of a, b and c.

Sol. We have, $\quad 5 = 2x$

$\Rightarrow \quad 2x + 0y - 5 = 0$

On compaing with $ax + by + c$, we get $a = 2$, $b = 0$ and $c = -5$

Mistake Alert Students may incorrectly take the standard form of linear equation $ax + by = c$ instead of $ax + by + c = 0$.

Q.3 Solve the equation $2y + 1 = 3y - 5$ and represent the solution on the number line.

Sol. We have, $\quad 2y + 1 = 3y - 5$

$\Rightarrow \quad 2y - 3y = -5 - 1$

$\Rightarrow \quad y = -6$

$\Rightarrow \quad y = 6$

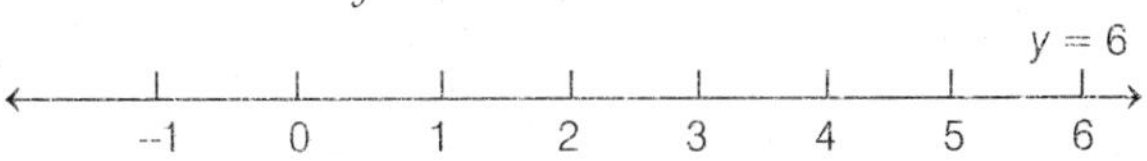

Q.4 Write four solutions of $x + 3y - 8 = 0$.

Sol. We have, $x + 3y - 8 = 0$

On putting $y = 0$ in $x + 3y - 8 = 0$, we get

$x + 3 \times 0 - 8 = 0$

$\Rightarrow \quad x = 8$

On putting $y = 1$ in $x + 3y - 8 = 0$, we get

$$x + 3 \times 1 - 8 = 0$$

$\Rightarrow \quad x + 3 = 8$

$\Rightarrow \quad x = 5$

On putting $y = 2$ in $x + 3y - 8 = 0$, we get

$$x + 3 \times 2 - 8 = 0$$

$\Rightarrow \quad x + 6 = 8$

$\Rightarrow \quad x = 2$

On putting $y = 3$ in $x + 3y - 8 = 0$, we get

$$x + 3 \times 3 - 8 = 0$$

$\Rightarrow \quad x + 9 = 8$

$\Rightarrow \quad x = -1$

Hence, the required solutions are

x	8	5	2	−1
y	0	1	2	3

Q.5 Find the value of a if $(-1, 1)$ is a solution of the equation $5x - ay = 7$.

Sol. Given $(-1, 1)$ is a solution of the equation $5x - ay = 7$

$\therefore \quad 5 \times (-1) - a(1) = 7$

$\Rightarrow \quad -5 - a = 7$

$\Rightarrow \quad -a = 7 + 5$

$\Rightarrow \quad a = -12$

Hence, the value of $a = -12$.

Introduction to Euclid's Geometry

CHAPTER 05

Important Points

01 Axioms or Postulates Axioms or postulates are the assumptions which are obvious universal truths. They are not proved.

Mainly postulates are used for specially geometry and axioms are used for specially algebra.

02 Theorems Theorems are statements which are proved using definitions, axioms, previously proved statements and deductive reasoning.

03 Euclid's Definitions, Axioms or Postulates

(i) A point is that which has no part.

(ii) A line is breadthless length.

(iii) The ends of a line are points.

(iv) A straight line is a line which lies evenly with the points on itself.

(v) A surface is that which has length and breadth only.

(vi) The edges of a surface are lines.

(vii) A plane surface is a surface which lies evenly with the straight lines on itself.

04 Undefined Terms There are some terms like point etc which have no definitions, these terms are called undefined terms.

In geometry, a point, a line and a plane (in Euclid's words, a plane surface) are undefined terms.

05 Euclid's Axioms

(i) Things which are equal to the same thing are equal to one another.

(ii) If equals are added to equals, the wholes are equal.

(iii) If equals are subtracted from equals, the remainders are equal.

(iv) Things which coincide with one another are equal to one another.

(v) The whole is greater than the part.

(vi) Things which are double of the same things are equal to one another.

(vii) Things which are halves of the same things are equal to one another.

06 Euclid's Five Postulates Euclid's five postulates are given below

Postulate 1 A straight line may be drawn from any one point to any other point.

Axiom Given two distinct points, there is a unique line that passes through them.

Postulate 2 A terminated line can be produced indefinitely. Euclid's terminated line is called a line segment. So, according to the present day terms, 'A line segment can be extended on either side to form a line'.

Postulate 3 A circle can be drawn with any centre and any radius.

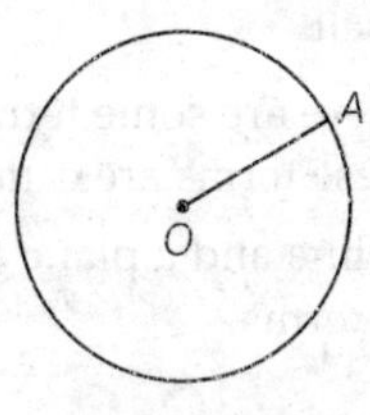

Postulate 4 All right angles are equal to one another.

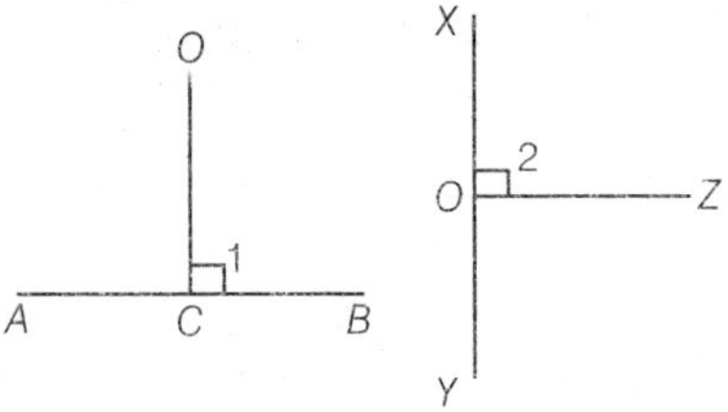

If $\angle 1 = 90°$ and $\angle 2 = 90°$

Then, $\angle 1 = \angle 2$

Postulate 5 If a straight line falling on two straight lines makes the interior angles on the same side of it taken together less than two right angles, then the two straight lines, if produced indefinitely, meet on that side on which the sum of angles is less than two right angles.

e.g., The line PQ falls on lines AB and CD such that the sum of the interior angles 1 and 2 is less than 180° on the left side of PQ. Therefore, the lines AB and CD will eventually intersect on the left side of PQ.

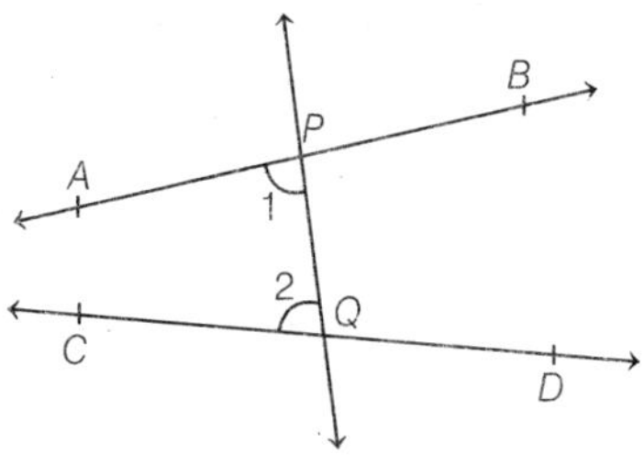

Note Two distinct lines cannot have more than one point in common.

07 Mid-point of a Line Segment For a given line segment AB, a point M is said to be the mid-point of AB if M is an interior or point on AB and $AM = MB$.

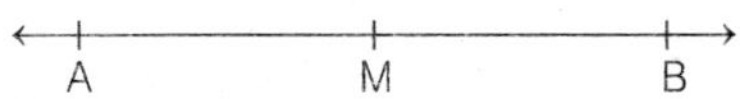

08 Betweenness Point B is said to lie between the two points A and C if

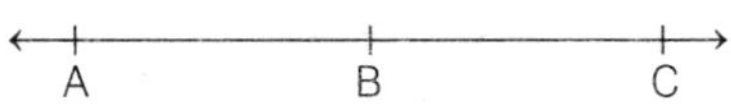

(i) point A, B and C are collinear

(ii) $AB + BC = AC$

Exercise 5.1

Question 1 Which of the following statements are true and which are false? Give reasons for your answers.

(i) Only one line can pass through a single point.

(ii) There are an infinite number of lines which pass through two distinct points.

(iii) A terminated line can be produced indefinitely on both the sides.

(iv) If two circles are equal, then their radii are equal.

(v) In figure, if $AB = PQ$ and $PQ = XY$, then $AB = XY$.

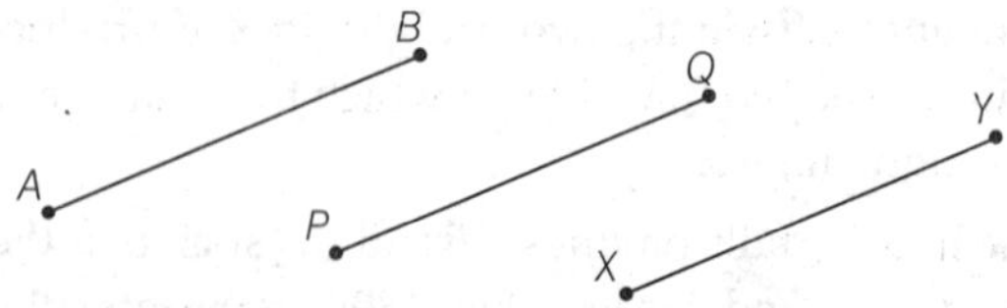

Sol. (i) False. In a single point, infinite number of lines can pass through it.

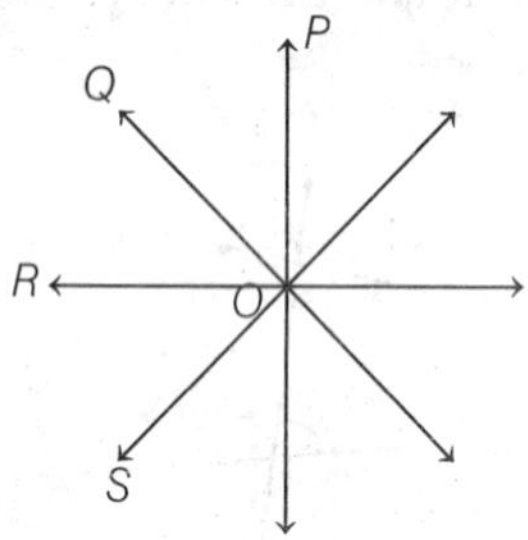

(ii) False. Through two distinct points, only one straight line can be pass.

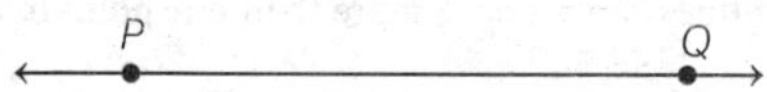

(iii) True. Since line segment is a part of line.

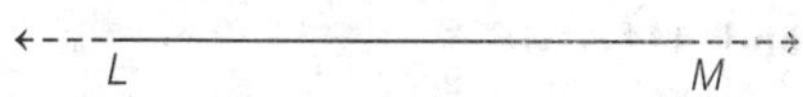

(iv) True. [∵ Radii of congruent (equal) circles are always equal]

(v) True. According to Euclid's 1 axiom, "Things which are equal to the same thing are also equal to one another.

Given, $AB = PQ$ ...(i)

$PQ = XY$ ...(ii)

From Eqs. (i) and (ii), we get $AB = XY$

Question 2 Give a definition for each of the following terms. Are there other terms that need to be defined first? What are they and how might you define them?

(i) Parallel lines (ii) Perpendicular lines
(iii) Line segment (iv) Radius of a circle
(v) Square

Sol. Yes, there are other terms which need to be defined first. They are as follows.

Point A point is that which has no part.

Line A collection of points that has only length and no breadth is known as a line. It can be extended in both direction.

Plane Surface A plane surface is a surface which lies evenly with straight lines on it.

(i) **Parallel lines** Two lines in a plane are said to be parallel, if they have no point in common.

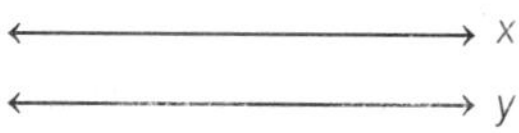

In figure, x and y are said to be parallel because they have no point in common and we write, $x \parallel y$.

We have to define point and straight line first

(ii) **Perpendicular lines** Two lines in a plane are said to be perpendicular, if they intersect each other at a right angle.

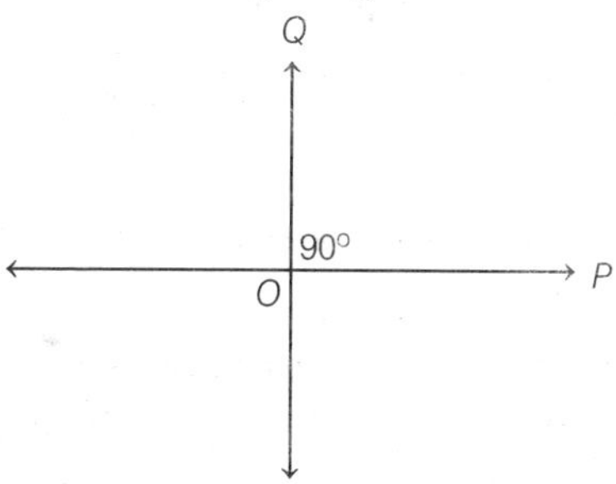

In figure, P and Q are said to be perpendicular lines because they intersect each other at 90° and we write $Q \perp P$.

(iii) **Line segment** The definite length between two points is called the line segment.

In figure, the definite length between A and B is line segment and represented by $\overline{AB}$. A line segment has 2 end points.

(iv) **Radius of a circle** The distance from the centre to a point on the circle is called the radius of the circle.

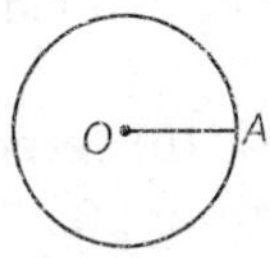

In the adjoining figure OA is the radius.

(v) **Square** A square is a closed two-dimensional shape with four sides of equal length and four right angles intirior angles.

Question 3 Consider two 'postulates' given below

(i) Given any two distinct points A and B, there exists a third point C which is in between A and B.

(ii) There exist atleast three points that are not on the same line. Do these postulates contain any undefined terms? Are these postulates consistent? Do they follow from Euclid's postulates? Explain.

Sol. Yes these postulates contain undefined terms. There are so many undefined words which should be knowledge.

They are consistent because they deal with two different situations that is

(i) if two points A and B are given, then there exists a third point C which is in between A and B.

(ii) if two points A and B are given, then we can take a point C which don't lie on the line passes through the point A and B.

These postulates don't follow Euclid's postulates. However, they follow axiom Euclid's postulate 1 stated as through two distinct points, there is a unique line that passes through them.

Mistake Alert Not forget to assumed that there is a unique line passing through two points.

Question 4 If a point C lies between two points A and B such that $AC = BC$, then prove that $AC = \frac{1}{2} AB$, explain by drawing the figure.

Thinking Process Euclid's Asiom says that things which coincide with one another are equal to one another. If AB coincides with $AC + CB$, therefore we can say $AC + CB = AB$.

Sol. Line AB is drawn by joining A and B with a point C taken between them. Such that $AC = BC$

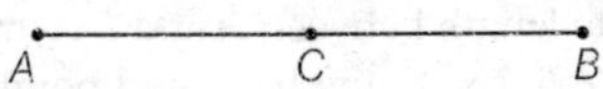

Given, $AC = BC$

$\because$ Equals are added on both sides

$$AC + AC = BC + AC \quad \text{...(i)}$$

Here, $BC + AC$ coincides with AB. Since things which coincide with one another are equal to one another.

$$\therefore \quad BC + AC = AB \quad \text{...(ii)}$$

Since things which are equal to the same thing are equal to one another

$\therefore$ by Eqs. (i) and (ii), we get

$$AC + AC = AB \Rightarrow 2AC = AB$$

$$\Rightarrow \quad AC = \frac{1}{2}AB$$

Question 5 In question 4, point C is called a mid-point of line segment AB. Prove that every line segment has one and only one mid-point.

Sol. Here, C is the mid-point of line segment AB, such that $AC = BC$

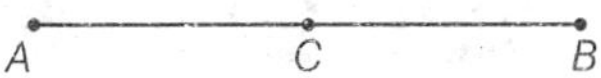

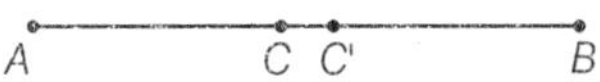

Let there are two mid-points C and C' of AB.

$$\Rightarrow \quad AC = \frac{1}{2}AB \quad \text{...(i)}$$

and

$$AC' = \frac{1}{2}AB \quad \text{...(ii)}$$

$\because$ Things which are equal to the same things are equal to one another.

$\therefore$ From Eqs. (i) and (ii), we get

$$\Rightarrow \quad AC = AC'$$

which is only possible when C and C' coincide.

$\Rightarrow$ Point C' lies on C.

Hence, every line segment has one and only one mid-point.

Question 6 In figure, if $AC = BD$, then prove that $AB = CD$.

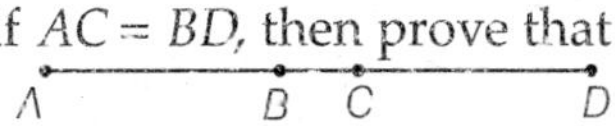

Sol. We have,

$$AC = BD \quad \text{...(i)}$$

$$AC = AB + BC \quad \text{...(ii)}$$

$$BD = BC + CD \quad \text{...(iii)}$$

$\because$ If equals are added to equals the wholes are equal.

From Eqs. (i), (ii) and (iii), we get

$$AB + BC = BC + CD$$

Therefore, $AB = CD$

Question 7 Why is axiom 5, in the list of Euclid's axioms, considered a 'universal truth'?

Sol. According to Euclid's Axiom 5, we have
"The whole is greater than a part, which is a universal truth".
Let a line segment $PQ = 8$ cm. Consider a point R in its interior, such that $PR = 5$ cm.

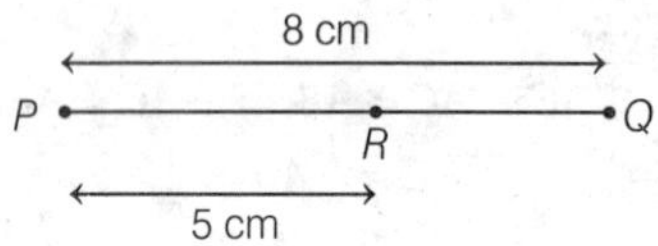

Clearly, PR is a part of the line segment PQ and R lies in its interior.
$\Rightarrow PR$ is smaller than PQ.
Hence, the whole is greater than its part.

DIKSHA APP Questions

☐ Multiple Choice Questions

Q.1 Euclid divided his famous treatise 'the Elements' into how many chapter?

(a) 11 (b) 12
(c) 13 (d) 14

Sol. (c) 13

Q.2 Euclid stated that all right angles are equal to each other in the form of

(a) postulate (b) axiom
(c) definition (d) proof

Sol. (a) Euclid stated that all right angles are equal to each other in the form of postulate.

Q.3 Euclid belongs to which country?

(a) India (b) Babylon
(c) Greece (d) Egypt

Sol. (c) Greece

Q.4 Lines are parallel, if they do not intersect is stated in the form of

(a) postulate (b) axiom

(c) definition (d) proof

Sol. (a) Postulate

Q.5 Which of the following needs a proof?

(a) Axiom (b) Theorem

(c) Definition (d) Postulate

Sol. (b) Theorem

☐ Subjective Type Questions

Q.1 What is a consistent system of axioms?

Sol. A system of axioms is called consistent, if it is impossible to deduce from these axioms a statement that contradicts any axioms or previously proved statement.

Q.2 Given two distinct points, how many lines can passes through them?

Sol. Only one unique line passes through two distinct points.

Q.3 Pythagoras was a student of ......

Sol. Thales.

Q.4 What are the boundaries of a solid called as?

Sol. Surfaces.

Q.5 What is the number of dimensions, a solid has?

Sol. Three.

Q.6 In the given figure $AC = BD$. Prove that $AD - BC$ state the Euclid's postulate/axiom used for the same.

Sol. Therefore,

Given $AC = BD$ and $AD = BC$

Since, Euclid's Axiom, if equals are added to equals, the wholes are equal.

$$AC + AD = BC + BD$$

$\Rightarrow$ $AC + AD = BC + AC$ ...(i) ($\because AC = BD$)

Now, we know by Euclid's Axiom 3, "If equals are subtracted from equals, then remainders are equal".

Therefore, from Eq. (i), we get $AD = BC$ **Hence Proved.**

Q.7 By which axiom we can say that area of sector of circle is always less than the area of the circle?

Sol. By Euclid's Axioms 5 "The whole is greater than parts". We can say that area of sector of circls is always less than the area of circle.

Q.8 If $AB = PQ$ and $PQ = XY$, then by which Euclid's axiom we can show that $AB = XY$?

Sol. Things which are equal to the same things are equal to one another.

Q.9 Write any four Euclid's axioms.

Sol. (a) Things which are equal to the same things are equal to one another.

(b) If equals are added to equals, the wholes are equal.

(c) If equals are subtracted from equals, the remainders are equal.

(d) The whole is greater than the part.

Q.10 Prove that two distinct lines cannot have more than one point in common.

Sol. Two distinct lines l and m intersect at a point P.

Let us suppose they will intersect at another point, say Q (different from P).

It means two lines l and m passing through two distinct points P and Q.

But it is contrary to axiom, which states that "Given two distinct points, there exists one and only one line pass through them".

So, our supposition is wrong.

Hence, two distinct lines cannot have more than one point in common.

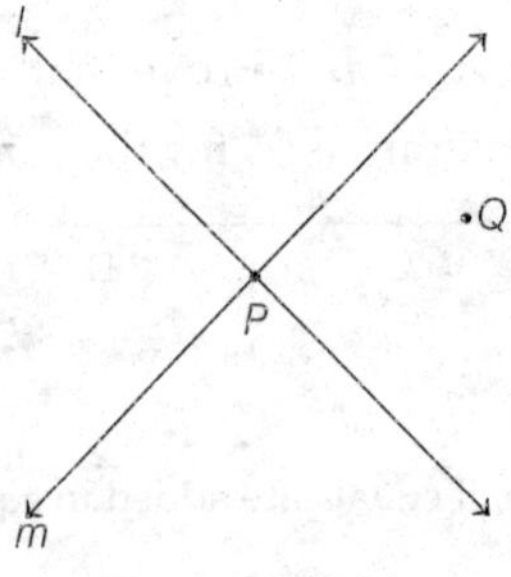

Q.11 If l and m are intersecting lines, $l \parallel p$ and $m \parallel q$, find the relation between p and q.

Sol. $P \parallel L$ and $Q \parallel M$

$L \times M$, Lets assume that P and Q don't intersect, so $P \parallel Q$. ...(i)

But $P \parallel L$ and $Q \parallel M$ ...(ii)

Therefore, Eqs. (i) and (ii), we get

$L \parallel M$, But we are given that L intersect M.

Therefore, our assumption is contradicted.

Hence, P intersects Q.

Q.13 An industrialist wants to setup a factory to give employment to villagers. He requirear (ADQ) from the land $ABPQ$ for the factory but in lieu of this area he gives equal ar (BPC) to villagers. Can we say that ar $(ABCD)$ is same area which villagers will get in lieu of ar $(ABPQ)$? Explain using Euclid's axiom.

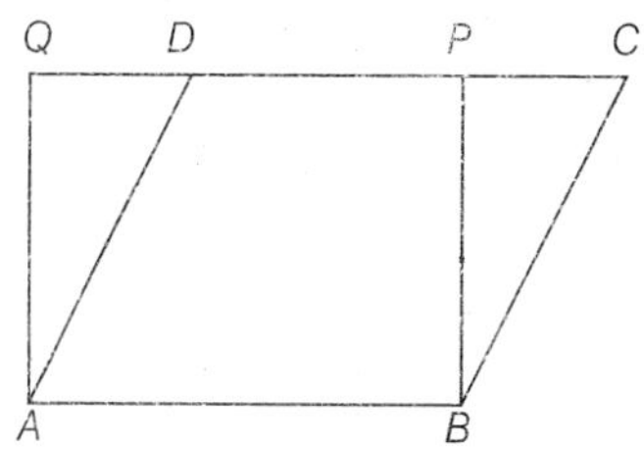

◎ ***Thinking Process*** Euclid axiom says, "Things which are equal to the same thing are equal to one another". In question, an industrialist requirear (ADQ) from the land $ABPQ$ for the factory, in lieu for this area he gives equal ar (BPC) to villagers.

So, above axiom can be equal.

Sol. Area of land $ABPQ = [\text{Area}(AQD) + \text{Area of land } ABPD]$

Since, by Euclid's axiom, we know that "Things which are equal to the same thing are equal to one another".

$\therefore$ Area of land $ABPQ = \text{Area}(BPC) + \text{Area of land } ABPD$

$[\because \text{Area of } AQD = \text{Area of } BPC]$

$= \text{area of land } ABCD$

Hence, we can say that ar $(ABCD)$ is same area which villagers will get in lieu of ar $(ABPQ)$.

Lines and Angles

CHAPTER 06

Important Points

01 Basic Terms and Definitions

(i) **Line** A line is a one-dimensional figure, which has length but no width and made of a set of points which is extended in opposite directions infinitely.

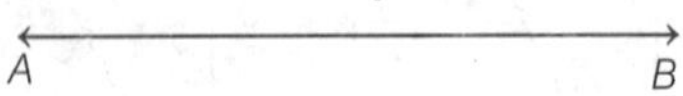

Line AB is denoted by $\overleftrightarrow{AB}$.

(ii) **Line segment** A part of a line with two end points is called a line segment.

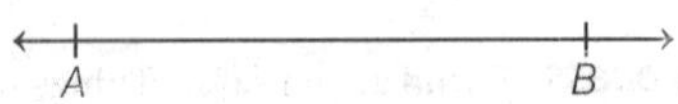

Line segment AB is denoted by $\overline{AB}$.

(iii) **Ray** A part of a line with one end point is called a ray.

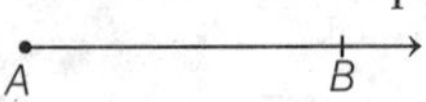

The ray AB is denoted by $\overrightarrow{AB}$.

(iv) **Collinear Points and Non-collinear Points** If three or more than three points lie on the same line, then they are called collinear points, otherwise they are non-collinear points.

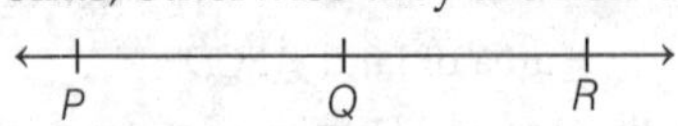

P, Q and R are collinear points.

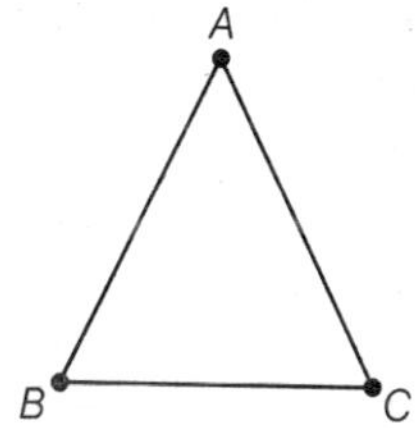

A, *B* and *C* are non-collinear points.

02 Angle An angle is formed when two rays originate from the same end point.

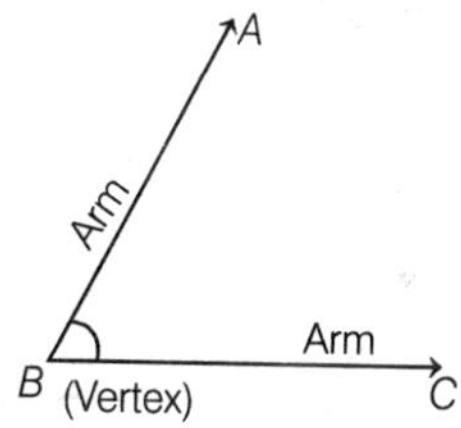

Angle *ABC* is denoted as $\angle ABC$.

The rays ($\overrightarrow{BA}$ and $\overrightarrow{BC}$) making an angle are called the arms of $\angle ABC$ and the end point (*B*) is called the vertex of $\angle ABC$.

03 Types of Angles There are different types of angles such as acute angle, right angle, obtuse angle, straight angle and reflex angle.

(i) **Acute angle** An acute angle is an angle which is less than 90°.

Acute angle $0° < x < 90°$.

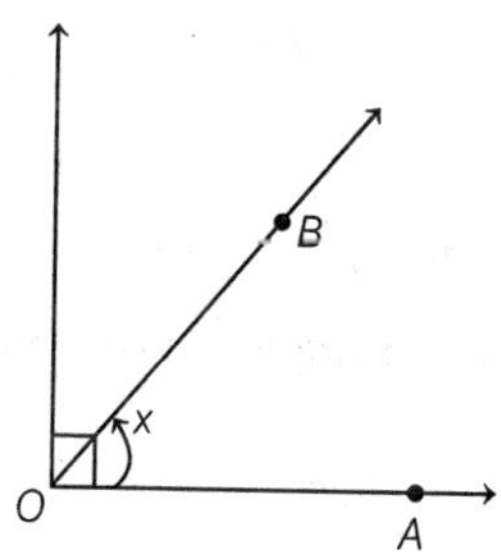

(ii) **Right angle** A right angle is an angle which is equal to 90°.

Right angle $y = 90°$

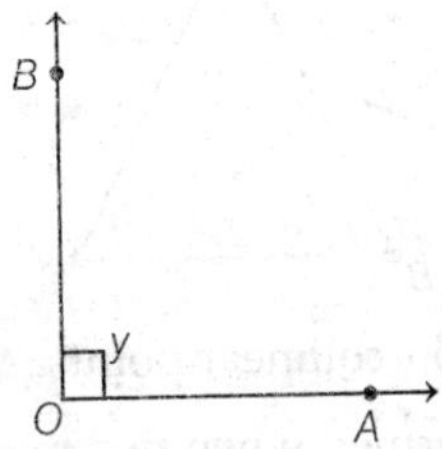

(iii) **Obtuse angle** An obtuse angle is an angle which is more than 90° and less than 180°.

Obtuse angle $90° < z < 180°$

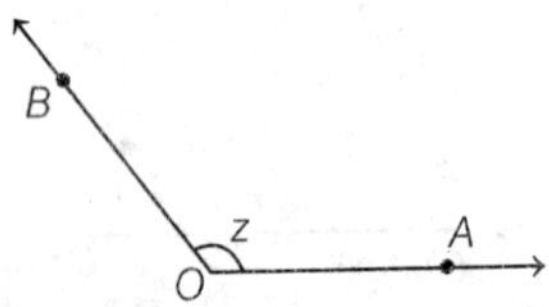

(iv) **Straight angle** A straight angle is an angle which is equal to 180°.

Straight angle $s = 180°$

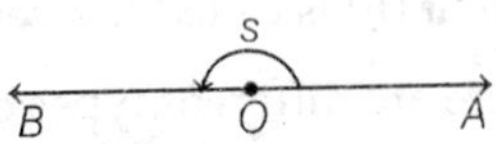

(v) **Reflex angle** A reflex angle is an angle, which is more than 180° and less than 360°.

Reflex angle $180° < t < 360°$

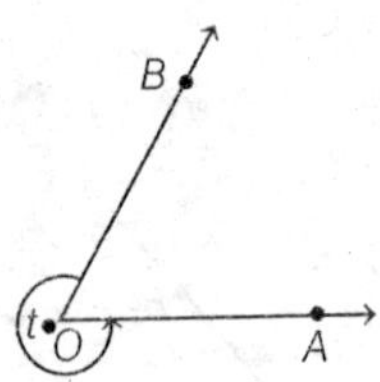

(vi) **Complete angle** An angle whose measure is 360° is called complete angle.

Complete angle $x = 360°$

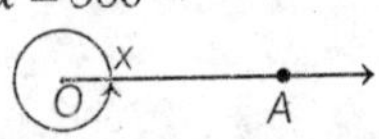

04 Complementary Angles Two angles whose sum is 90° are called complementary angles.

e.g., → Complement of 30° angle is 60° angle.

05 **Supplementary Angles** Two angles whose sum is 180° are called supplementary angles.

e.g., → Supplement of 70° angle is 110° angle.

06 **Adjacent Angles** Two angles are adjacent, if they have a common vertex, a common arm and their non-common arms are on different sides of common arm.

$\angle ABD$ and $\angle DBC$ are adjacent angle. Ray BD is their common arm and point B is their common vertex. Ray BA and ray BC are non-common arms.

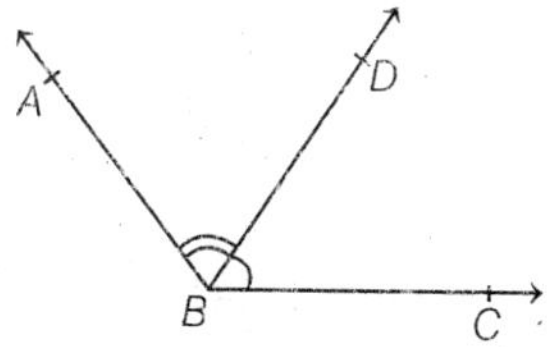

Note $\angle ABC = \angle ABD + \angle DBC$

07 **Vertically Opposite Angles** The vertically opposite angles formed when two lines intersect each other at a point.

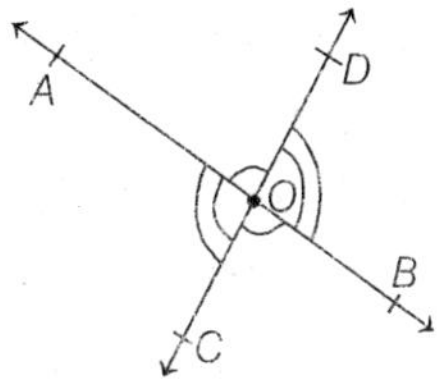

Two lines AB and CD intersect each other at point O, then there are two pairs of vertically opposite angles. One pair is $\angle AOD$ and $\angle BOC$ and another pair is $\angle AOC$ and $\angle BOD$.

08 **Intersecting Lines and Non-intersecting Lines**

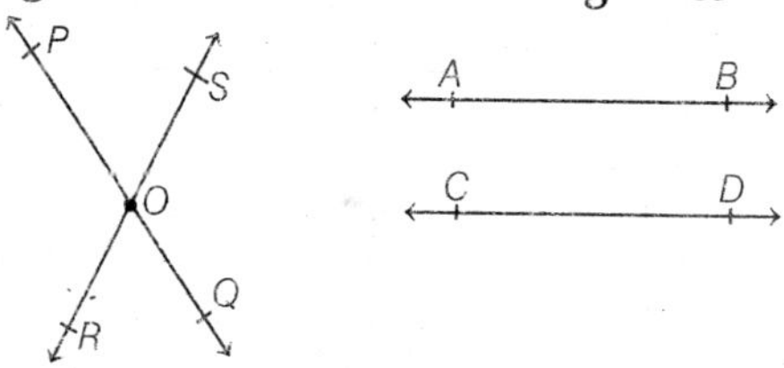

Lines PQ and RS are intersecting lines because they are intersecting each other at O.

Lines AB and CD are non-intersecting (parallel) lines.

Note The lengths of the common perpendicular at different points on these parallel lines are same. This equal length is called the distance between two parallel lines.

09 Linear Pair of Angles When the sum of two adjacent angles is 180°, then they are called a linear pair of angles.

(i) If a ray stands on a line, then the sum of two adjacent angles so formed is 180°.

(ii) If the sum of two adjacent angles is 180°, then the non-common arms of the angles form a line.

$$\angle AOC + \angle BOC = 180°$$

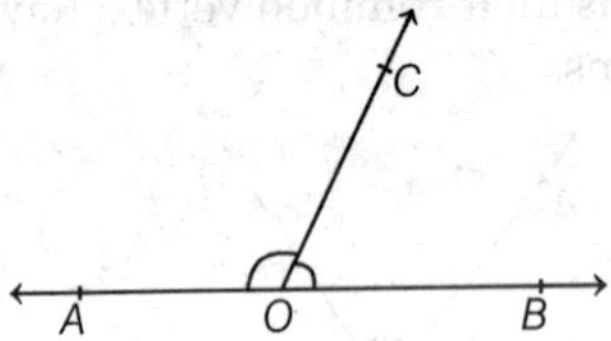

Property If two lines intersect each other, then the vertically opposite angles are equal.

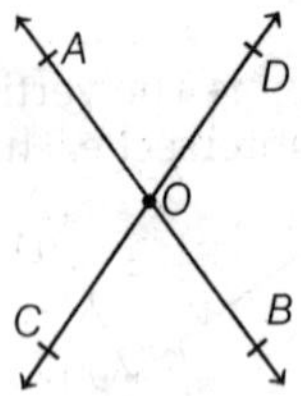

$$\angle AOD = \angle BOC$$
$$\angle COA = \angle DOB$$

10 Lines Parallel to the Same Line If two lines are parallel to the same line, then they are also parallel to each other.

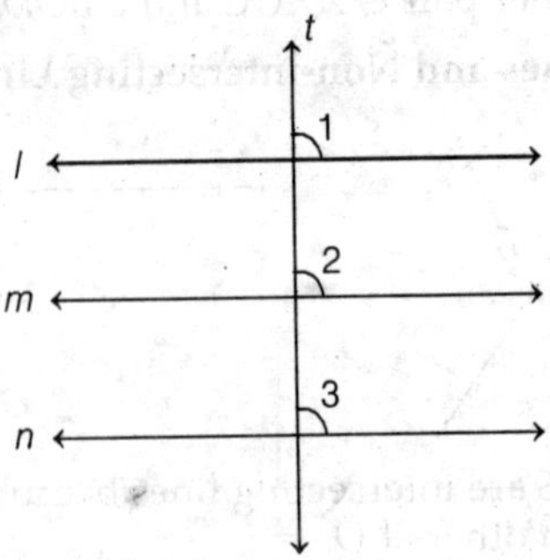

Here, line *m* parallel to line *l* and line *n* parallel to line *l*.

Hence, line *m* parallel to line *n*.

Exercise 6.1

Question 1 In figure, lines AB and CD intersect at O.
If $\angle AOC + \angle BOE = 70°$ and $\angle BOD = 40°$, find $\angle BOE$ and reflex $\angle COE$.

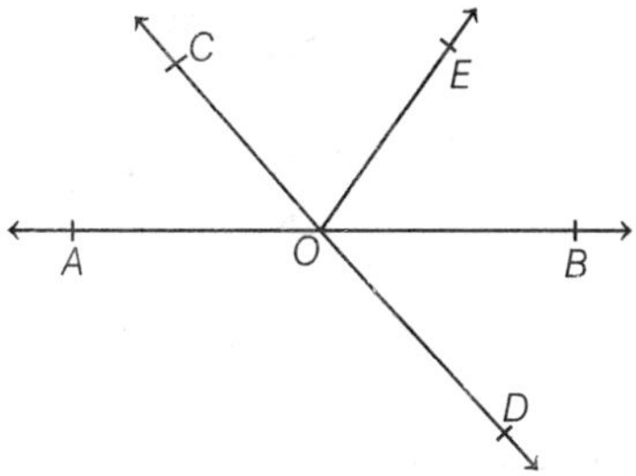

Sol. Here, $\angle AOC$ and $\angle BOD$ are vertically opposite angles.

$\therefore$ $\angle AOC = \angle BOD$

$\Rightarrow$ $\angle AOC = 40°$ [$\because \angle BOD = 40°$ (Given)] ...(i)

We have, $\angle AOC + \angle BOE = 70°$ (Given)

$40° + \angle BOE = 70°$ [From Eq. (i)]

$\Rightarrow$ $\angle BOE = 30°$ ...(ii)

Also, $\angle AOC + \angle COE + \angle BOE = 180°$ (Linear pair axiom)

$\Rightarrow$ $40° + \angle COE + 30° = 180°$ [From Eq. (i) and (ii)]

$\Rightarrow$ $\angle COE = 110°$ ...(iii)

Now, $\angle COE + \text{reflex } \angle COE = 360°$ (Angles at a point)

$110° + \text{reflex } \angle COE = 360°$ [From Eq. (iii)]

$\Rightarrow$ Reflex $\angle COE = 250°$

Question 2 In figure, lines XY and MN intersect at O. If $\angle POY = 90°$ and $a : b = 2 : 3$. find c.

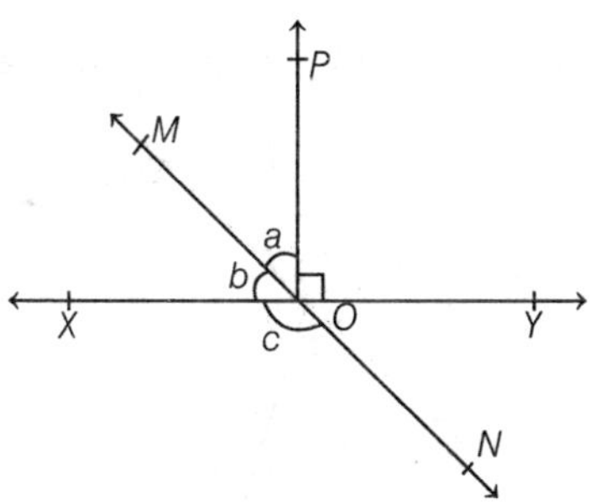

Sol. We have, $\angle POY = 90^\circ$

Now, $\angle POY + \angle POX = 180^\circ$ (Linear pair axiom)

$90^\circ + \angle POX = 180^\circ$

$\Rightarrow \angle POX = 90^\circ$

$\Rightarrow a + b = 90^\circ$ $[\because \angle POX = \angle POM + \angle MOX]$ ...(i)

Also, $a : b = 2 : 3$ (Given)

Let $a = 2k, b = 3k$

Now, from Eq. (i), we get

$2k + 3k = 90^\circ$

$\Rightarrow 5k = 90^\circ$

$\Rightarrow k = 18^\circ$

$\therefore a = 2 \times 18^\circ = 36^\circ$

and $b = 3 \times 18^\circ = 54^\circ$

Now, $\angle MOX + \angle XON = 180^\circ$ (Linear pair axiom)

$b + c = 180^\circ$

$\Rightarrow 54^\circ + c = 180^\circ \Rightarrow c = 126^\circ$

Question 3 In figure, $\angle PQR = \angle PRQ$, then prove that $\angle PQS = \angle PRT$.

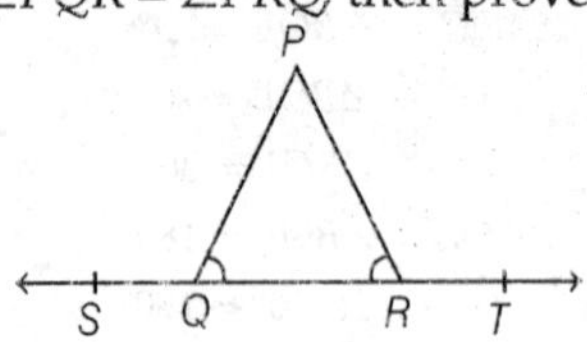

Sol. Since, ST is a straight line

$\because \angle PQS + \angle PQR = 180^\circ$ (Linear pair axiom) ...(i)

and $\angle PRT + \angle PRQ = 180^\circ$ (Linear pair axiom)...(ii)

From Eqs. (i) and (ii), we get

$\angle PQS + \angle PQR = \angle PRT + \angle PRQ$

$\Rightarrow \angle PQS + \angle PRQ = \angle PRT + \angle PRQ$ [Given, $\angle PQR = \angle PRQ$]

$\Rightarrow \angle PQS = \angle PRT$ **Hence Proved.**

Question 4 In figure, if $x + y = w + z$, then prove that AOB is a line.

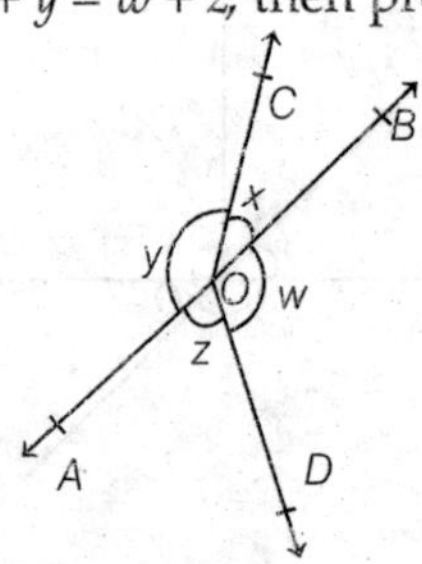

Sol. Given, $x + y = w + z$ ...(i)

$\because$ $x + y + w + z = 360°$ (Angle at a point)

$\therefore$ $x + y + x + y = 360°$ [From Eq. (i)]

$\Rightarrow$ $2(x + y) = 360° \Rightarrow x + y = 180°$ (Linear pair axiom)

Hence, AOB is a straight line.

Question 5 In figure, POQ is a line. Ray OR is perpendicular to line PQ, OS is another ray lying between rays OP and OR. Prove that

$$\angle ROS = \frac{1}{2}(\angle QOS - \angle POS)$$

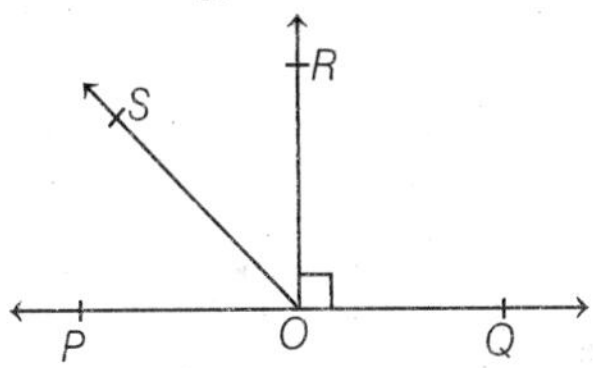

Sol. We have,

$$\angle POR = \angle ROQ = 90°$$

($\because$ Given that, OR is perpendicular to PQ)

$\therefore$ $\angle POS + \angle ROS = 90°$

$\Rightarrow$ $\angle ROS = 90° - \angle POS$

On adding $\angle ROS$ both sides, we get

$$2\angle ROS = 90° - \angle POS + \angle ROS$$

$\Rightarrow$ $2\angle ROS = (90° + \angle ROS) - \angle POS$

$\Rightarrow$ $2\angle ROS = \angle QOS - \angle POS$

($\because \angle QOS = \angle ROQ + \angle ROS = 90° + \angle ROS$)

$\Rightarrow$ $\angle ROS = \frac{1}{2}(\angle QOS - \angle POS)$ **Hence Proved.**

Quick Solution

We know that $\angle POR = \angle QOR$

$\Rightarrow$ $\angle POS + \angle ROS = \angle QOR$

$\Rightarrow$ $\angle POS + \angle ROS = \angle QOS - \angle SOR$

$\Rightarrow$ $\angle SOR + \angle ROS = \angle QOS - \angle POS$

$\Rightarrow$ $2\angle ROS = \angle QOS - \angle POS$

$\Rightarrow$ $\angle ROS = \frac{1}{2}(\angle QOS - \angle POS)$

Question 6 It is given that $\angle XYZ = 64°$ and XY is produced to point P. Draw a figure from the given information. If ray YQ bisects $\angle ZYP$, find $\angle XYQ$ and reflex $\angle QYP$.

Sol. Here, YQ bisects $\angle ZYP$.

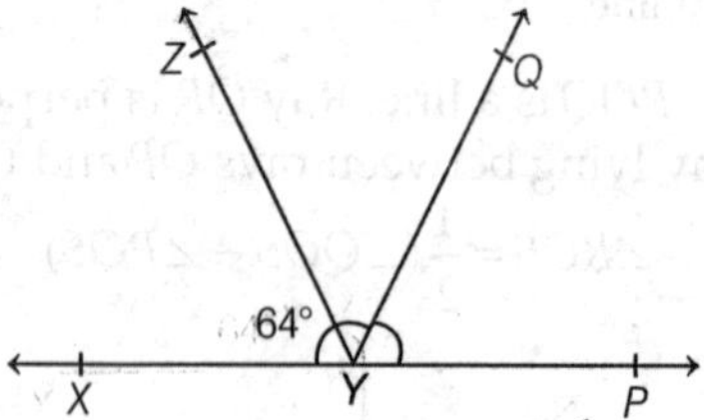

$\therefore$ $$\angle ZYQ = \angle QYP = \frac{1}{2}\angle ZYP \quad \text{...(i)}$$

Given, $$\angle XYZ = 64° \quad \text{...(ii)}$$

$\because$ $$\angle XYZ + \angle ZYQ + \angle QYP = 180° \quad \text{(Linear pair axiom)}$$

$\Rightarrow$ $$64° + \angle ZYQ + \angle ZYQ = 180° \quad \text{[From Eqs. (i) and (ii)]}$$

$\Rightarrow$ $$2\angle ZYQ = 180° - 64°$$

$\Rightarrow$ $$\angle ZYQ = \frac{1}{2} \times 116°$$

$\Rightarrow$ $$\angle ZYQ = 58°$$

$\therefore$ $$\angle XYQ = \angle XYZ + \angle ZYQ = 64° + 58° = 122°$$

Now, $$\angle QYP + \text{reflex } \angle QYP = 360° \quad \text{(Angles at a point)}$$

$\Rightarrow$ $$58° + \text{reflex } \angle QYP = 360°$$

$\Rightarrow$ $$\text{reflex } \angle QYP = 302°$$

Exercise 6.2

Question 1 In figure, if $AB \parallel CD$, $CD \parallel EF$ and $y : z = 3 : 7$, find x.

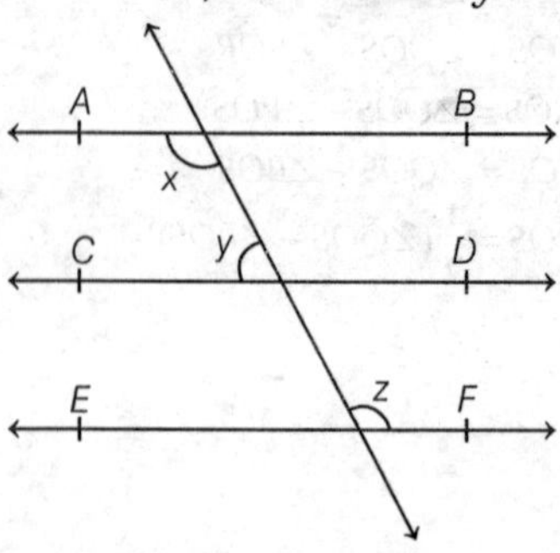

Sol. Given, $y : z = 3 : 7$

Let $y = 3k$ and $z = 7k$

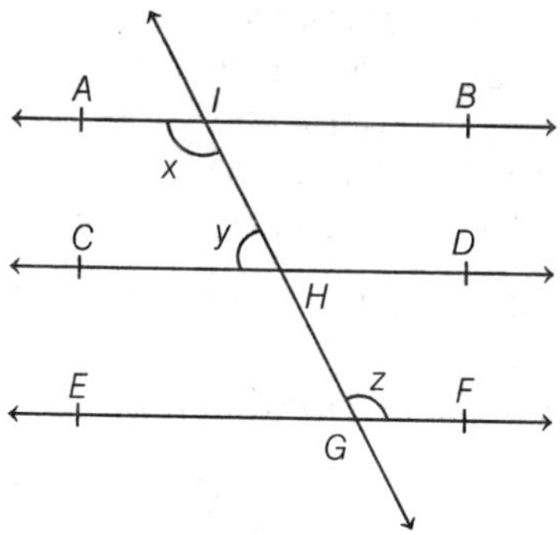

Here, $x = \angle CHG$ (Corresponding angles)...(i)

and $\angle CHG = z$ (Alternate angles)...(ii)

From Eqs. (i) and (ii), we get

$x = z$ ...(iii)

Now, $x + y = 180°$

(Internal angles on the same side of the transversal)

$\Rightarrow$ $z + y = 180°$ [From Eq. (iii)]

$\Rightarrow$ $7k + 3k = 180°$

$\Rightarrow$ $10k = 180°$

$\Rightarrow$ $k = 18$

$\therefore$ $y = 3 \times 18° = 54°$,

$z = 7 \times 18° = 126°$

and $x = z$ [$\because$ Eq. (iii)]

$\Rightarrow$ $x = 126°$

Question 2 In figure, if $AB \parallel CD$, $EF \perp CD$ and $\angle GED = 126°$, find $\angle AGE$, $\angle GEF$ and $\angle FGE$.

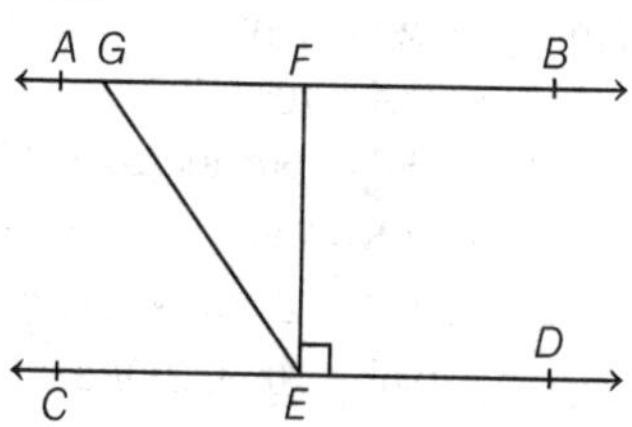

Sol. If $AB \parallel CD$ and GE is the transversal

Then, $\angle AGE = \angle GED$ (Alternate interior angles)

But $\angle GED = 126°$ (Given)

$\Rightarrow$ $\angle AGE = 126°$ $(\because \angle AGE = \angle GED)$...(i)

Now, $\angle GED = 126°$

$\Rightarrow$ $\angle GEF + \angle FED = 126°$

$\Rightarrow$ $\angle GEF + 90° = 126°$ $(\because EF \perp CD)$

$\Rightarrow$ $\angle GEF = 36°$

Also, $\angle AGE + \angle FGE = 180°$ (Linear pair axiom)

$\Rightarrow$ $126° + \angle FGE = 180° \Rightarrow \angle FGE = 54°$

Question 3 In figure, if $PQ \parallel ST$, $\angle PQR = 110°$ and $\angle RST = 130°$, find $\angle QRS$.

[**Hint** Draw a line parallel to ST through R]

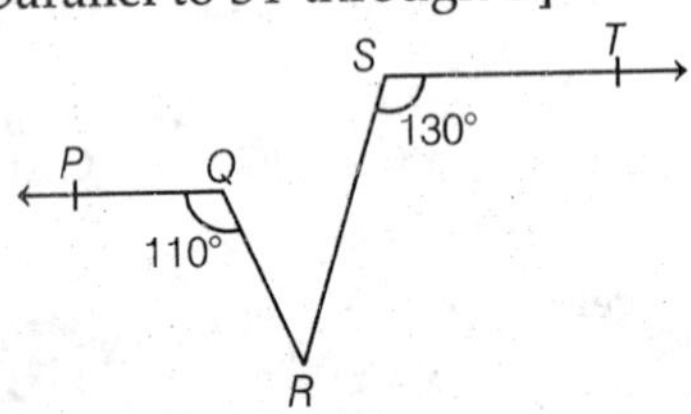

Sol. Drawing a line parallel to ST through R.

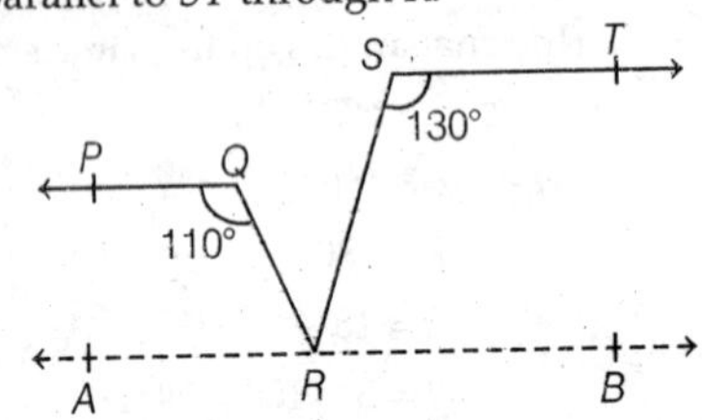

Given, $PQ \parallel ST$ ...(i)

Let $AB \parallel ST$ ...(ii)

From Eqs (i) and (iii), we get

$AB \parallel PQ \parallel ST$

$\because$ $\angle PQR + \angle QRA = 180°$

(Interior angles on the same side of a transversal)

$\Rightarrow$ $110° + \angle QRA = 180°$ $(\because PQR = 110°)$

$\Rightarrow$ $\angle QRA = 70°$ ...(iii)

$\because$ $\angle TSR = 130°$ and $ST \parallel AB$

$\therefore$ $\angle ARS = 130°$ (Alternate interior angle)

$\because$ $\angle ARS = \angle ARQ + \angle QRS$

$\Rightarrow$ $130° = 70° + \angle QRS$ [From Eq. (iii)]

$\Rightarrow$ $\angle QRS = 130° - 70° = 60°$

$\Rightarrow$ $\angle QRS = 60°$

Question 4 In figure, if $AB \parallel CD$, $\angle APQ = 50°$ and $\angle PRD = 127°$, find x and y.

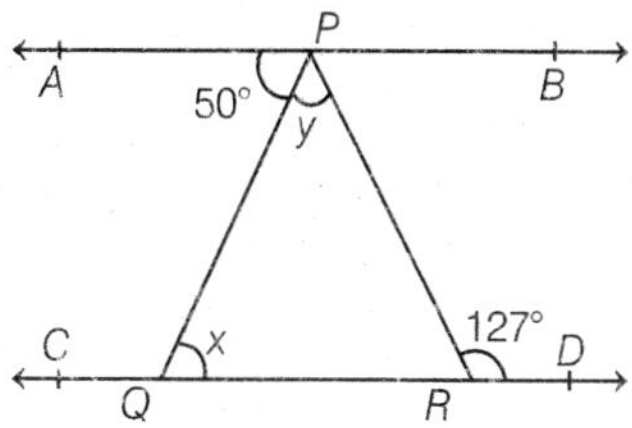

Sol. We have, $AB \parallel CD$

$\therefore$ $\angle APQ = \angle PQR$ (Alternate interior angles)

$\Rightarrow$ $50° = x \Rightarrow x = 50°$

and $\angle APR = \angle PRD$ (Alternate interior angles)

$\Rightarrow$ $50° + y = 127°$

$\Rightarrow$ $y = 77°$

Question 5 In figure, PQ and RS are two mirrors placed parallel to each other. An incident ray AB strikes the mirror PQ at B, the reflected ray moves along the path BC and strikes the mirror RS at C and again reflects back along CD. Prove that $AB \parallel CD$.

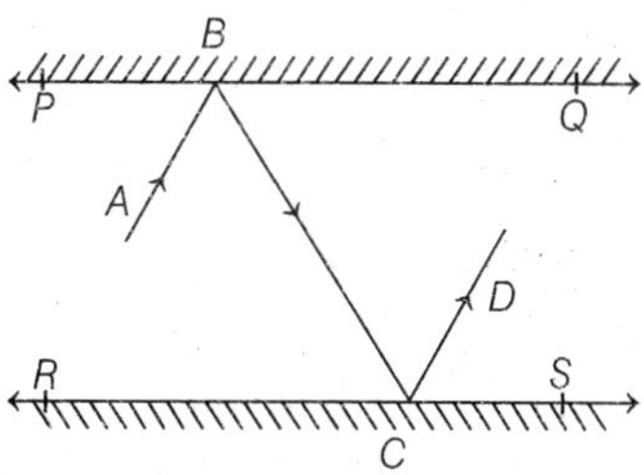

Sol. Draw $BE \perp PQ$ and $CF \perp RS$.

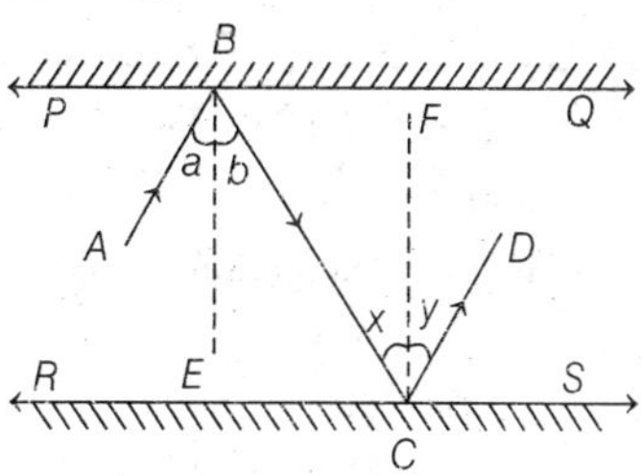

As $PQ \parallel RS$

So, $BE \parallel FC$

[$\because$ Perpendiculars drawn on two parallel lines are parallel to each other.]

Also, $\angle a = \angle b$ ...(i)

$\angle x = \angle y$ ...(ii)

($\because$ Angle of incidence = angle of reflection)

Now, $\angle b = \angle x$ (Alternate interior angles)

$\Rightarrow$ $2\angle b = 2\angle x$

$\Rightarrow$ $\angle b + \angle b = \angle x + \angle x$

$\Rightarrow$ $\angle a + \angle b = \angle x + \angle y$ [From Eq. (i) and (ii)]

$\Rightarrow$ $\angle ABC = \angle DCB$

$\Rightarrow$ $AB \parallel CD$ ($\because$ Alternate interior angles axiom)

Hence Proved.

DIKSHA APP Questions

☐ Multiple Choice Questions

Q.1 Two supplementary angles which are in the ratio 4 : 5 are

(a) 70°, 110° (b) 80°, 100° (c) 60°, 120° (d) 50°, 130°

Sol. (b) Let the angles are $4x$ and $5x$.

We know that sum of two supplementary angles is 180°.

$\therefore$ $4x + 5x = 180°$

$\Rightarrow$ $9x = 180°$

$\Rightarrow$ $x = 20°$

So, the angles are $4x = 4 \times 20 = 80°$

and $5x = 5 \times 20 = 100°$

Mistake Alert Sometimes students confuse in finding the complement and supplement of an angle. So, always remember that the sum of two complementary angles is 90° and sum of two supplementary angles is 180°.

Q.2 Two complementary angles are in the ratio 2 : 3. The angles are

(a) 25°, 65° (b) 35°, 55° (c) 15°, 75° (d) 36°, 54°

Sol. (d) Let the angles are $2x$ and $3x$

We know that sum of two complementary angles is 90°.

$\therefore$ $2x + 3x = 90°$

$\Rightarrow$ $5x = 90°$

$\Rightarrow$ $x = 18°$

So, the angles are $2x = 2 \times 18 = 36°$

and $3x = 3 \times 18 = 54°$

□ Subjective Type Questions

Q.1 In the given figure, $x = 30°$, calculate the value of y.

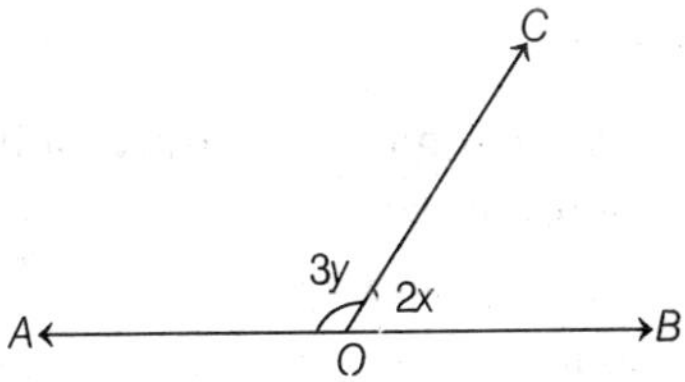

◎ *Thinking Process* If a ray stands on a line, then the sum of two adjacent angles, so formed is 180°.

Sol. Given, $x = 30°$

Now, $\angle COB = 2x = 2 \times 30° = 60°$ [Linear pair axiom]

and $\angle AOC + \angle BOC = 180°$ [Linear pair axiom]

$\Rightarrow \quad 3y + 60° = 180°$

$\Rightarrow \quad 3y = 120°$

$\Rightarrow \quad y = 40°$

Hence, the value of y is 40°.

Q.2 Calculate the complement of an angle 'p'.

Sol. Let the required angle be x.

We know that sum of two complementary angle is 90°.

$\therefore \quad x + P = 90°$

$\Rightarrow \quad x = 90° - P$

Hence, the complement of an angle 'P' is $90° - P$.

Q.3 Two lines AB and CD intersect at O. If $\angle AOC = 85°$, then measure of $\angle AOD$.

Sol. Given, two lines AB and CD intesect at O and $\angle AOC = 85°$

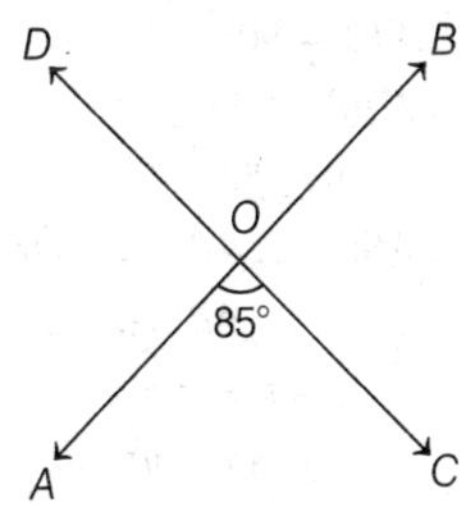

From the figure, we have $\angle AOC + \angle AOD = 180°$ [Linear pair axiom]

$\Rightarrow \quad 85° + \angle AOD = 180°$

$\Rightarrow \quad \angle AOD = 95°$

Hence, the measure of $\angle AOD = 95°$

Q.4 The supplement of an angle is one third of itself. Determine the angle and its supplement.

Sol. Let the measure of the required angle be $x°$.

Then, the measure of its supplementary angle is $(180 - x)°$.

From the given condition, we have

$$180° - x = \frac{1}{3}x$$

$\Rightarrow \quad 3(180° - x) = x$

$\Rightarrow \quad 540° - 3x = x$

$\Rightarrow \quad 4x = 540°$

$\Rightarrow \quad x = 135°$

$\therefore$ Supplementary angle $= 180° - 135° = 45°$

Thus, the measure of the angle is 135° and its supplement is 45°.

Q.5 If the bisectors of the adjacent angles are perpendicular to each other, then prove that their outer arms are in the same straight line.

Sol. Let $\angle ABD$ and $\angle DBC$ are adjacent angles BE and BF are their bisectors, respectively.

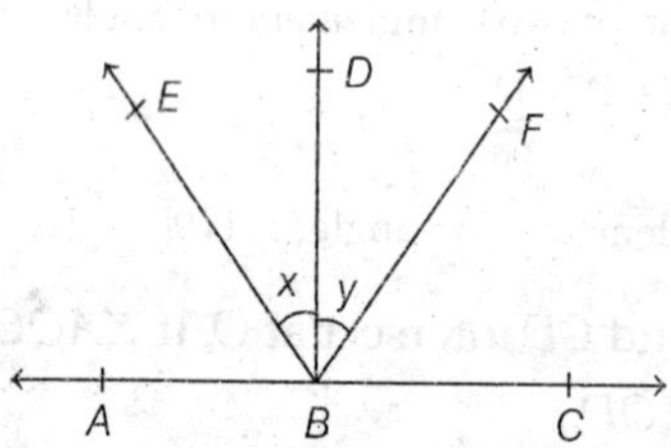

Given, the bisectors of the adjacent angle are perpendicular to each other.

$\therefore \quad \angle EBF = 90°$

$\Rightarrow \quad \angle EBD + \angle DBF = 90°$

$\Rightarrow \quad x + y = 90° \quad$ ...(i)

Now, $\quad \angle ABC = \angle ABD + \angle DBC$

$= \angle ABE + \angle EBD + \angle DBF + \angle FBC$

$= x + x + y + y = 2x + 2y$

$= 2(x + y)$

$= 2 \times 90° = 180°$ [From Eq. (i)]

Hence, outer arms of the adjaast angles are in same straight line.

Q.6 In the adjoining figure, $m \parallel n$ and $P \parallel q$. If $\angle 1 = 75°$, prove that $\angle 2 = \angle 1 + \frac{1}{3}$ of right angle.

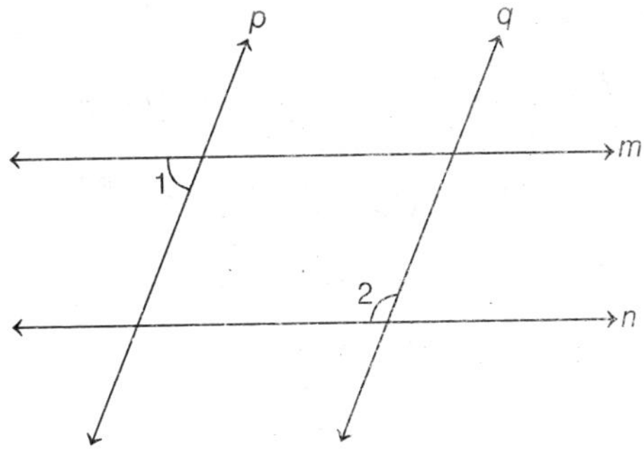

Sol. Given, $m \parallel n$, $p \parallel q$ and $\angle 1 = 75°$

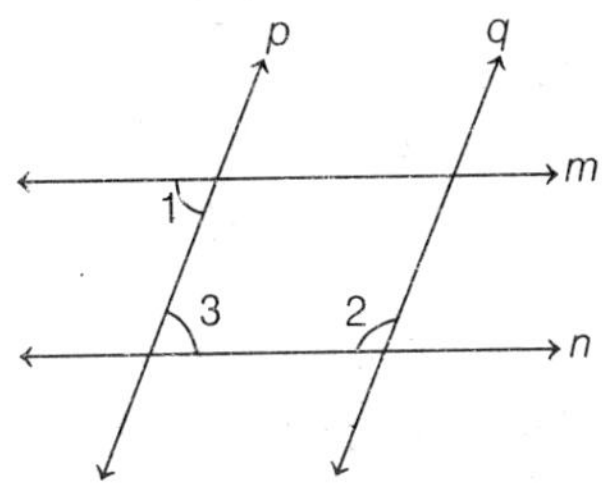

Now, $\angle 1 = \angle 3 = 75°$ (Corresponding angles)

and $\angle 2 + \angle 3 = 180°$ (Angles on the same side of a transversal)

$\Rightarrow \angle 2 + 75° = 180°$

$\Rightarrow \angle 2 = 180° - 75°$

$\Rightarrow \angle 2 = 105°$ ...(i)

Now, we have to prove that $\angle 2 = \angle 1 + \frac{1}{3}$ of right angle

$$\text{RHS} = \angle 1 + \frac{1}{3} \text{ of right angle}$$

$$= 75° + \frac{1}{3} \times 90°$$

$$= 75° + 30°$$

$$= 105° = \angle 2 = \text{LHS}$$

[From Eq. (i)] Hence Proved.

Q.7 Let OA, OB, OC and OD be the rays in the anticlockwise direction starting from OA, such that $\angle AOB = \angle COD = 100°$, $\angle AOD = \angle BOC = 80°$. Is it true that AOC and BOD are straight lines?

Thinking Process If AOC and BOD are straight lines, then $\angle AOC = 180°$ and $\angle BOD = 180°$.

Sol. Given, OA, OB, OC and OD are the range in the anticlockwise direction starting from OA and $\angle AOB = \angle COD = 100°$, $\angle AOD = \angle BOC = 80°$.

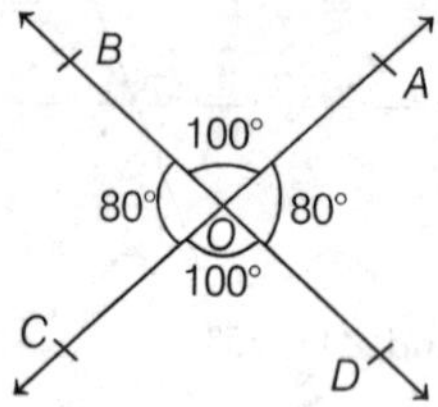

From the figure, we have

$$\angle AOC = \angle AOB + \angle BOC$$
$$= 100° + 80° = 180°$$

and

$$\angle BOD = \angle BOC + \angle COD$$
$$= 80° + 100° = 180°$$

Hence, AOC and BOD are straight lines.

Triangles

CHAPTER 07

Important Points

01 Triangle A closed figure formed by three intersecting lines is called a triangle ('Tri.' means 'three'). A triangle has three sides, three angles and three vertices.

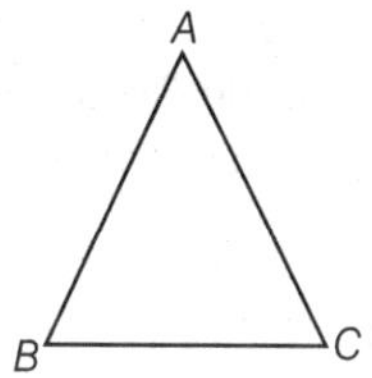

e.g., In triangle ABC, denoted as $\Delta\ ABC$; AB, BC, CA are the three sides, $\angle A, \angle B, \angle C$ are the three angles and A, B, C are three vertices.

Note In a triangle, sum of length of two sides should be greater than the length of third side.

02 Congruence of Triangles Two triangles are congruent, if the sides and angles of one triangle are equal to the corresponding sides and angles of the other triangle.

If ΔPQR is congruent to ΔABC, we write $\Delta PQR \cong \Delta ABC$ but it will not be correct to write $\Delta QRP \cong \Delta ABC$

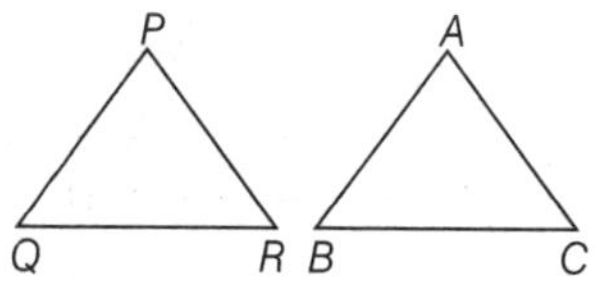

Note Congruent triangles corresponding parts are equal and we write in short 'CPCT' for Corresponding Parts of Congruent Triangles.

03 Criteria for Congruence of Triangles

(i) **SAS congruence rule** Two triangles are congruent, if two sides and the included angle of one triangle are equal to the two sides and the included angle of the other triangle.

Note SAS congruence rule holds but not ASS or SSA rule.

(ii) **ASA congruence rule** Two triangles are congruent, if two angles and the included side of one triangle are equal to two angles and the included side of other triangle.

(iii) **AAS congruence rule** Two triangles are congruent, if any two pairs of angles and one pair of corresponding sides are equal.

(iv) **SSS congruence rule** Two triangles are congruent, if three sides of one triangle are equal to the three sides of the other triangle.

(v) **RHS congruence rule** If in two right triangles, hypotenuse and one side of a triangle are equal to the hypotenuse and one side of other triangle, then the two triangles are congruent.

Note
- SAS stands for Side-Angle-Side.
- ASA stands for Angle-Side-Angle.
- AAS stands for Angle-Angle-Side.
- SSS stands for Side-Side-Side.
- RHS stands for Right angle-Hypotenuse-Side.

04 Properties of a Triangle

(i) **Isosceles triangle** A triangle in which two sides are equal is called an isosceles triangle. In the given figure ΔABC is an isosceles triangle with $AB = AC$.

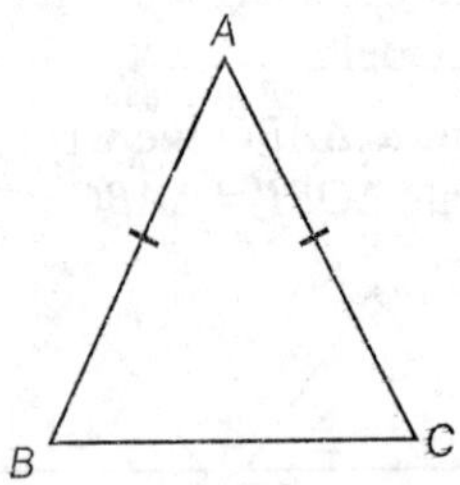

(ii) **Theorem 1** Angles opposite to equal sides of an isosceles triangle are equal.

i.e., $\angle B = \angle C$

(iii) **Theorem 2** The sides opposite to equal angles of a triangle are equal.

i.e., $AB = AC$

Exercise 7.1

Question 1 In quadrilateral $ACBD$, $AC = AD$ and AB bisects $\angle A$ (see figure). Show that $\Delta ABC \cong \Delta ABD$. What can you say about BC and BD?

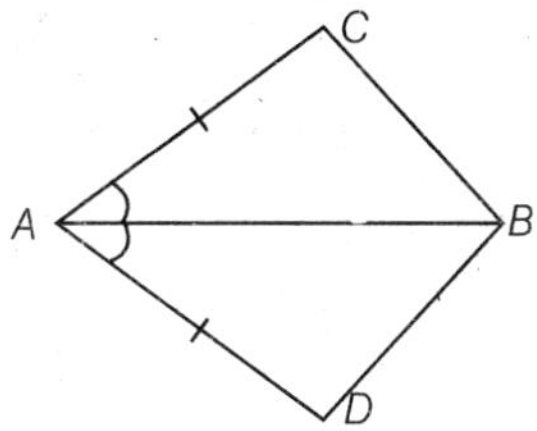

Thinking Process If two sides and the included angle of one triangle are equal to the two sides and the included angle of the other triangle, then they are congruent.

Sol. In ΔABC and ΔABD, we have

	$AC = AD$	(Given)
	$\angle CAB = \angle DAB$	($\because$ AB bisects $\angle A$)
and	$AB = AB$	(Common)
$\therefore$	$\Delta ABC \cong \Delta ABD$	(By SAS congruence axiom)
$\therefore$	$BC = BD$	(By CPCT)

Therefore, BC and BD are of equal length.

Question 2 $ABCD$ is a quadrilateral in which $AD = BC$ and $\angle DAB = \angle CBA$ (see figure). Prove that

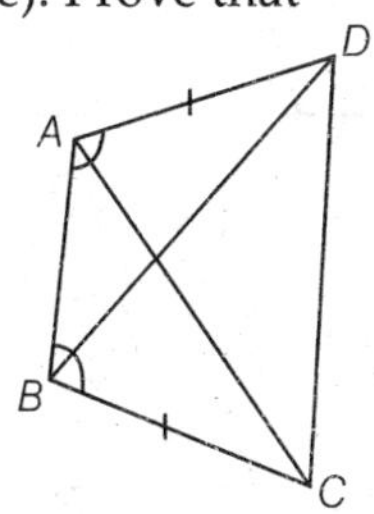

(i) $\Delta ABD \cong \Delta BAC$ (ii) $BD = AC$

(iii) $\angle ABD = \angle BAC$

Sol. In ΔABD and ΔBAC, we have

	$AD = BC$	(Given)
	$\angle DAB = \angle CBA$	(Given)
and	$AB = AB$	(Common)
$\therefore$	$\Delta ABD \cong \Delta BAC$	(By SAS congruence axiom)
Hence,	$BD = AC$	(By CPCT)
and	$\angle ABD = \angle BAC$	(By CPCT)

Question 3 AD and BC are equal perpendiculars to a line segment AB (see figure). Show that CD bisects AB.

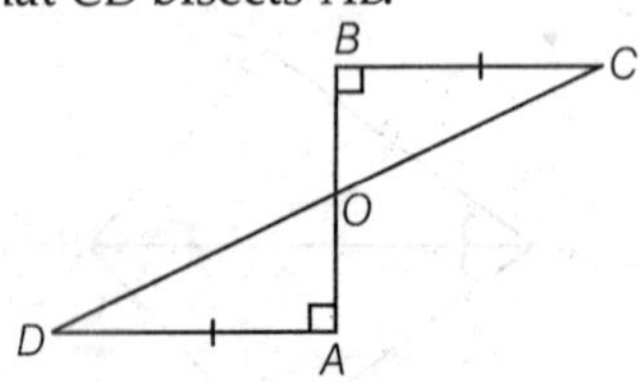

Sol. In ΔAOD and ΔBOC, we have

$$\angle AOD = \angle BOC$$

$\because$ AB and CD intersects at O.

$\therefore$ Which are vertically opposite angle

$\because$	$\angle DAO = \angle CBO = 90°$	
and	$AD = BC$	(Given)
$\therefore$	$\Delta AOD \cong \Delta BOC$	(By AAS congruence axiom)
Hence,	$OA = OB$	(By CPCT)

$\Rightarrow$ O is the mid-pont of AB.

Hence, CD bisects AB.

Question 4 l and m are two parallel lines intersected by another pair of parallel lines p and q (see figure). Show that $\Delta ABC \cong \Delta CDA$.

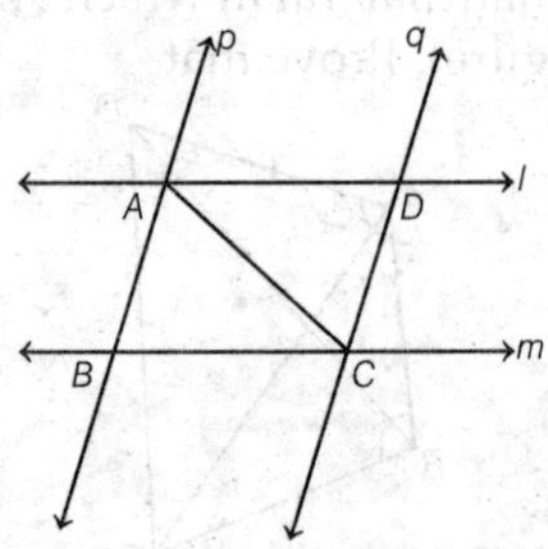

Sol. From figure, we have

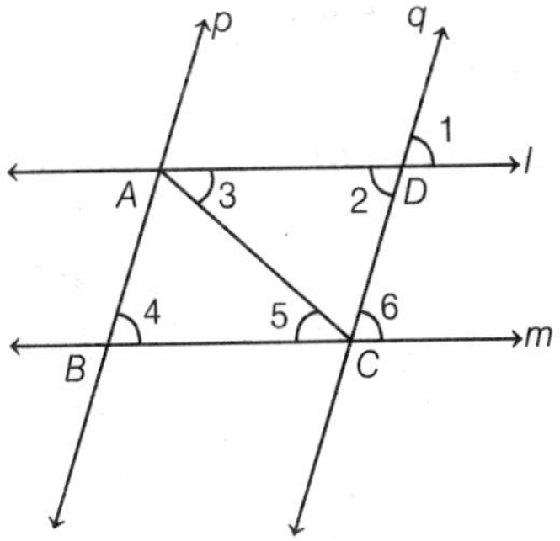

$\angle 1 = \angle 2$ (Vertically opposite angles)...(i)

$\angle 1 = \angle 6$ (Corresponding angles)...(ii)

$\angle 6 = \angle 4$ (Corresponding angles) ...(iii)

From Eqs. (i), (ii) and (iii), we have

$\angle 1 = \angle 4$

and $\angle 2 = \angle 4$ ...(iv)

In Δ ABC and Δ CDA, we have

$\angle 4 = \angle 2$ [From Eq. (iv)]

$\angle 5 = \angle 3$ (Alternate interior angles)

and $AC = AC$ (Common)

$\therefore$ $\Delta\ ABC \cong \Delta\ CDA$ (By AAS congruence axiom)

Question 5 Line l is the bisector of angle $\angle A$ and B is any point on l. BP and BQ are perpendiculars from B to the arms of $\angle A$ (see figure). Show that

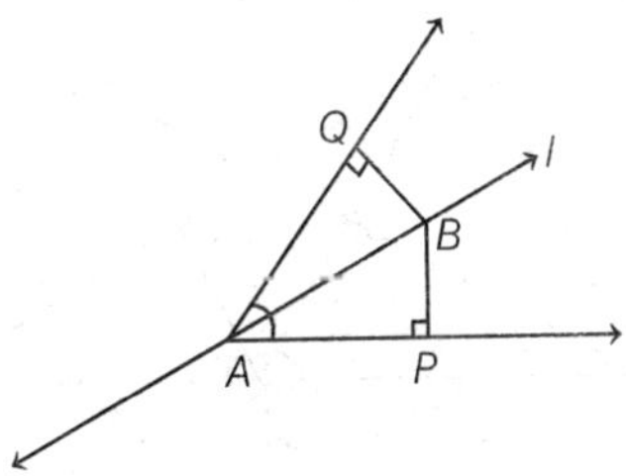

(i) $\Delta APB \cong \Delta AQB$

(ii) $BP = BQ$ or B is equidistant from the arms of $\angle A$.

Sol. In Δ APB and Δ AQB, we have

$\angle\ APB = \angle\ AQB = 90°$

$\angle\ PAB = \angle\ QAB$ ($\because$ AB bisects $\angle\ PAQ$)

and $AB = AB$ (Common)

$\therefore$ $\Delta APB \cong \Delta AQB$ (By AAS congruence axiom)

$\Rightarrow$ $BP = BQ$ (By CPCT)

$\Rightarrow B$ is equidistant from the arms of $\angle A$.

Question 6 In figure, $AC = AE$, $AB = AD$ and $\angle BAD = \angle EAC$. Show that $BC = DE$.

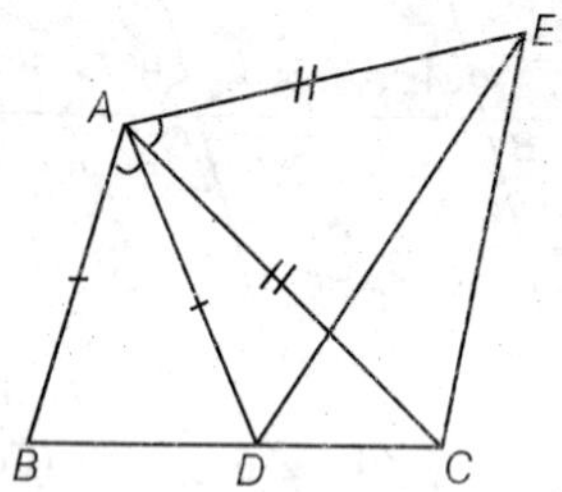

Sol. In ΔABC and ΔADE, we have

$AB = AD$ (Given)

$\angle BAD = \angle EAC$ (Given)...(i)

On adding $\angle DAC$ on both sides in Eq. (i), we get

$$\angle BAD + \angle DAC = \angle EAC + \angle DAC$$

$\Rightarrow$ $\angle BAC = \angle DAE$

and $AC = AE$ (Given)

$\therefore$ $\Delta ABC \cong \Delta ADE$ (By SAS congruence axiom)

$\Rightarrow$ $BC = DE$ (By CPCT)

Question 7 AB is a line segment and P is its mid-point. D and E are points on the same side of AB such that $\angle BAD = \angle ABE$ and $\angle EPA = \angle DPB$. (see figure). Show that

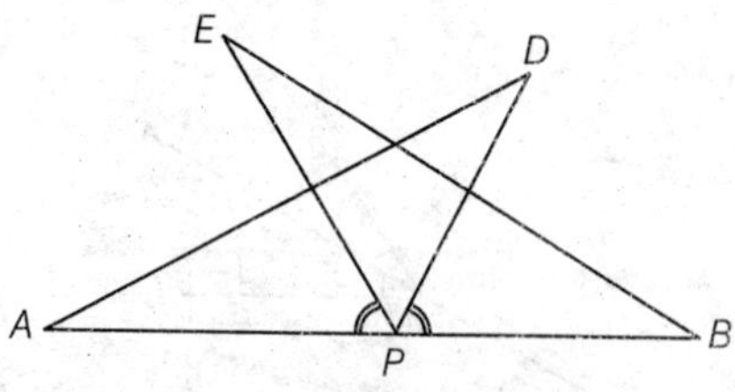

(i) $\Delta DAP \cong \Delta EBP$ (ii) $AD = BE$

Thinking Process Mid-point of a line divide always it into equal two part. Consider all equal angles and side. If two angles and the included side of one triangle are equal to two angles and the included side of other triangle, then they will be congruent.

Sol. We have,

$AP = BP$ [$\because$ P is the mid-point of AB (Given)]...(i)

$\angle EPA = \angle DPB$ (Given)...(ii)

$\angle BAD = \angle ABE$ (Given)...(iii)

On adding $\angle EPD$ on both sides in Eq. (ii), we have

$\Rightarrow \quad \angle EPA + \angle EPD = \angle DPB + \angle EPD$

$\Rightarrow \quad \angle DPA = \angle EPB$ ...(iv)

Now, In ΔDAP and ΔEBP, we have

$\angle DPA = \angle EPB$ [From Eq. (iv)]

$\angle BAD = \angle ABE$ [From Eq. (iii)]

and $AP = BP$ [From Eq. (i)]

$\therefore \quad \Delta DAP \cong \Delta EBP$ (By ASA congruence rule)

Hence, $AD = BE$ (By CPCT)

Question 8 In right triangle ABC, right angled at C, M is the mid-point of hypotenuse AB. C is joined to M and produced to a point D such that $DM = CM$. Point D is joined to point B (see figure). Show that

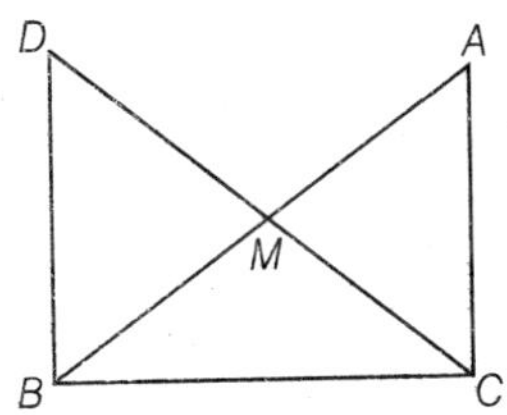

(i) $\Delta AMC \cong \Delta BMD$

(ii) $\angle DBC$ is a right angle

(iii) $\Delta DBC \cong \Delta ACB$

(iv) $CM = \frac{1}{2} AB$

Sol. Given, ΔACB in which $\angle C = 90°$ and M is the mid-point of AB.

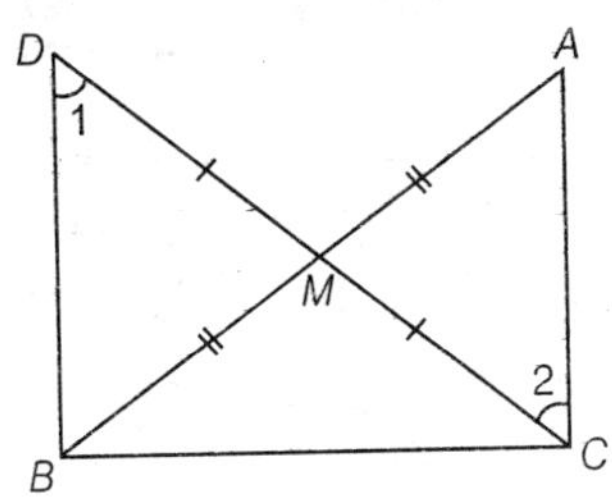

To prove (i) $\Delta\ AMC \cong \Delta\ BMD$ (ii) $\angle DBC$ is a right angle
(iii) $\Delta\ DBC \cong \Delta\ ACB$ (iv) $CM = \frac{1}{2}\ AB$

Proof In $\Delta\ AMC$ and $\Delta\ BMD$, we have

$AM = BM$ (M is the mid-point of AB)
$CM = DM$ (Given)
and $\angle AMC = \angle BMD$ (Vertically opposite angles)
$\therefore$ $\Delta\ AMC \cong \Delta\ BMD$ [which is part (i)] (by SAS congruence axiom)
$\Rightarrow$ $AC = DB$ (By CPCT) ...(i)
and $\angle 1 = \angle 2$ (By CPCT)
Which are alternate angles
$\therefore$ $BD \parallel CA$
Now, $BD \parallel CA$ and BC is transversal
$\therefore$ $\angle\ ACB + \angle\ CBD = 180°$ (Interior angles on the same side of transversal)
$\Rightarrow$ $90° + \angle\ CBD = 180°$ [given $\angle ACB = 90°$]
$\Rightarrow$ $\angle\ CBD = 90°$
$\Rightarrow$ $\angle\ DBC = 90°$ [Which is part (ii)]
In $\Delta\ DBC$ and $\Delta\ ACB$, we have
$CB = BC$ (Common)
$DB = AC$ [Using Eq. (i)]
and $\angle\ CBD = \angle\ BCA$ (Each 90°)
$\therefore$ $\Delta\ DBC \cong \Delta ACB$ (by SAS congruence axiom) [Which is part (iii)]
$\Rightarrow$ $DC = AB$ (by CPCT)
$\Rightarrow$ $\frac{1}{2}\ DC = \frac{1}{2}\ AB$ [dividing by 2 on both sides]
$\Rightarrow$ $CM = \frac{1}{2}\ AB$ ($\because CM = \frac{1}{2}\ DC$) [Which is part (iv)]

Exercise 7.2

Question 1 In an isosceles triangle ABC, with $AB = AC$, the bisectors of $\angle B$ and $\angle C$ intersect each other at O. Join A to O. Show that
(i) $OB = OC$ (ii) AO bisects $\angle A$

Sol. (i) In $\Delta\ ABC$, we have

$AB = AC$ (Given)
$\Rightarrow$ $\angle\ B = \angle\ C$
($\because$ Angles opposite to equal sides are equal)

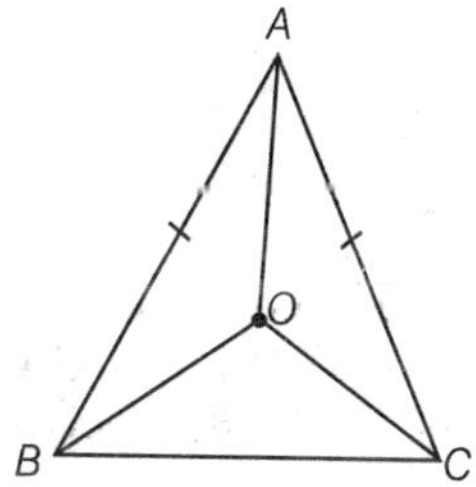

$\Rightarrow \quad \frac{1}{2}\angle B = \frac{1}{2}\angle C$ (Divide by 2 on both sides)

$\Rightarrow \quad \angle OBC = \angle OCB$ ...(i)

and $\quad \angle OBA = \angle OCA$

($\because$ OB and OC are bisectors of $\angle B$ and $\angle C$ respectively).

($\because \angle OBC = \frac{1}{2}\angle B$ and $\angle OCB = \frac{1}{2}\angle C$)

$\Rightarrow \quad OB = OC$ ...(ii)

($\because$ Sides opposite to equal angles are equal)

(ii) In $\Delta\ ABO$ and $\Delta\ ACO$, we have

$AB = AC$ (Given)

$\angle OBA = \angle OCA$ [From Eq. (i)]

$\Rightarrow \quad OB = OC$ [From Eq. (ii)]

$\therefore \quad \Delta\ ABO \cong \Delta\ ACO$ (By SAS congruence axiom)

$\Rightarrow \quad \angle BAO = \angle CAO$ (By CPCT)

$\Rightarrow AO$ is the bisector of $\angle BAC$.

Mistake Alert Angles opposite to equal sides are equal i.e., in ΔABC, $AB = AC$, then $\angle B = \angle C$. Also, not forget to use $\frac{1}{2}\angle B = \frac{1}{2}\angle C$.

Question 2 In ΔABC, AD is the perpendicular bisector of BC (see figure). Show that $\Delta\ ABC$ is an isosceles triangle in which $AB = AC$.

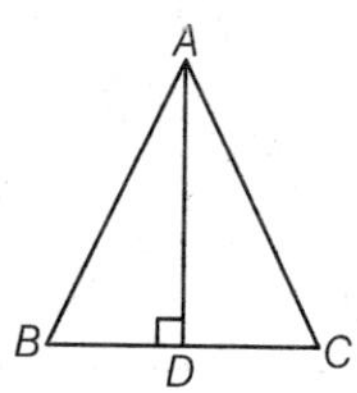

Sol. In ΔABD and ΔACD, we have

$DB = DC$ ($\because$ D bisect BC)

$\angle ADB = \angle ADC$ ($\because AD \perp BC$)

and $AD = AD$ (Common)

$\therefore$ $\Delta\ ABD \cong \Delta\ ACD$ (By SAS congruence axiom)

$\Rightarrow$ $AB = AC$ (By CPCT)

Hence, $\Delta\ ABC$ is an isosceles triangle.

Question 3 *ABC* is an isosceles triangle in which altitudes *BE* and *CF* are drawn to equal sides *AC* and *AB* respectively (see figure). Show that these altitudes are equal.

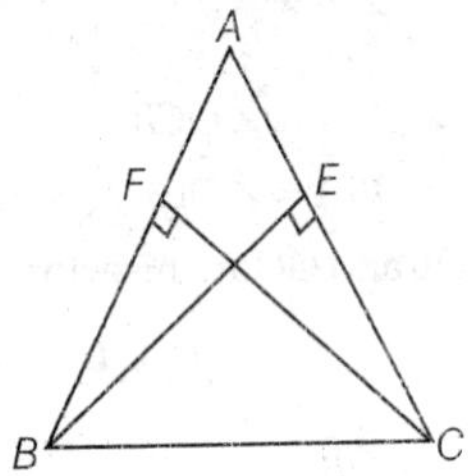

Sol. In $\Delta\ ABE$ and $\Delta\ ACF$, we have

$\angle\ AEB = \angle\ AFC$ ($BE \perp AC, CF \perp AB$, each 90°)

$\angle\ A = \angle\ A$ (Common)

and $AB = AC$ (Given)

$\therefore$ $\Delta\ ABE \cong \Delta\ ACF$ (By AAS congruence rule)

$\Rightarrow$ $BE = CF$ (By CPCT)

Mistake Alert Not confuse with AAS congruence rule and ASA congruence rule. Use carefully, AAS and ASA both are different.

Question 4 *ABC* is a triangle in which altitudes *BE* and *CF* to sides *AC* and *AB* are equal (see figure). Show that

(i) $\Delta ABE \cong \Delta ACF$

(ii) $AB = AC$ *i.e.*, *ABC* is an isosceles triangle.

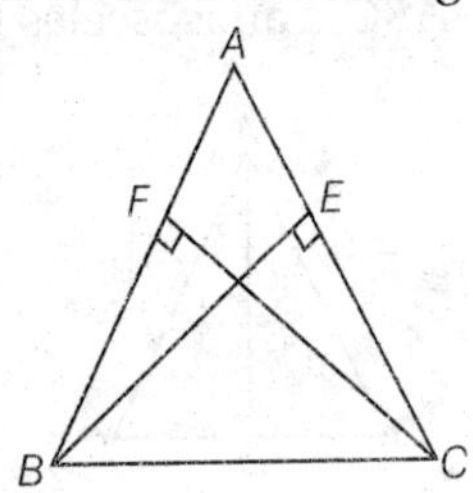

Sol. In ΔABE and ΔACF, we have

$\angle\ AEB = \angle\ AFC$ (Each 90°)

$\angle\ BAE = \angle\ CAF$ (Common)

and $BE = CF$ (Given)

$\therefore$ $\Delta\ ABE \cong \Delta\ ACF$ (By AAS congruence axiom)

Two sides of triangles are equal (By CPCT)

$\therefore$ $AB = AC$

So, $\Delta\ ABC$ is isosceles.

Question 5 ABC and DBC are isosceles triangles on the same base BC (see figure). Show that $\angle ABD = \angle ACD$.

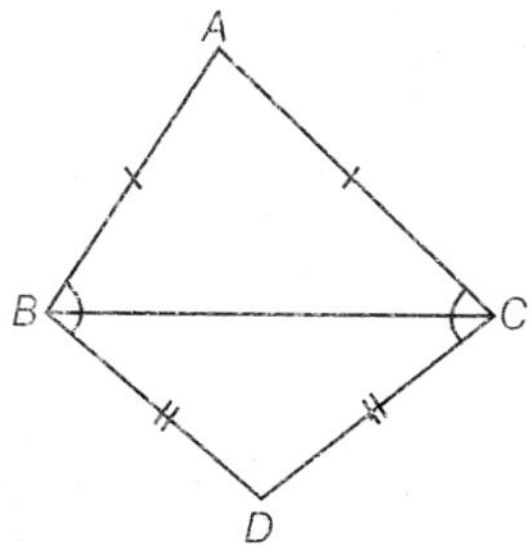

◎ *Thinking Process* In a isosceles triangle two sides are equal and angles opposite to equal sides are equal.

Sol. In $\Delta\ ABC$, we have

$AB = AC$ ($\because \Delta ABC$ is an isosceles triangle)

$\therefore$ $\angle ABC = \angle ACB$ ...(i)

($\because$ Angles opposite to equal sides are equal)

In $\Delta\ DBC$, we have

$BD = CD$ ($\because \Delta DBC$ is an isosceles triangle)

$\therefore$ $\angle DBC = \angle DCB$ ...(ii)

($\because$ Angles opposite to equal sides are equal)

On adding Eqs. (i) and (ii), we have

$$\angle ABC + \angle DBC = \angle ACB + \angle DCB$$

$\Rightarrow$ $\angle ABD = \angle ACD$ **Hence Proved.**

Question 6 ΔABC is an isosceles triangle in which $AB = AC$. Side BA is produced to D such that $AD = AB$ (see figure). Show that $\angle BCD$ is a right angle.

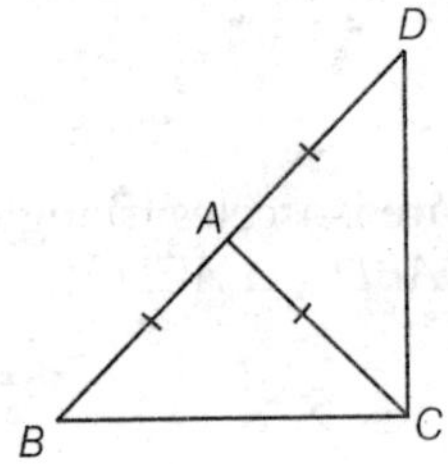

Sol. In Δ ABC, we have

$AB = AC$ (Given)

$\Rightarrow$ $\angle ACB = \angle ABC$ ...(i)

($\because$ Angles opposite to equal sides are equal)

Now, $AB = AD$ (Given)

$\therefore$ $AC = AD$ ($\because AB = AC$)

Now, In Δ ADC, we have

$AD = AC$ (From above)

$\Rightarrow$ $\angle ACD = \angle ADC$ ...(ii)

($\because$ Angles opposite to equal sides are equal)

On adding Eqs.(i) and (ii), we have

$$\angle ACB + \angle ACD = \angle ABC + \angle ADC$$

$\Rightarrow$ $\angle BCD = \angle ABC + \angle BDC$ ($\because \angle ADC = \angle BDC$)

Adding $\angle BCD$ on both sides, we have

$$\angle BCD + \angle BCD = \angle ABC + \angle BDC + \angle BCD$$

$\Rightarrow$ $2\angle BCD = 180°$ (By Δ property)

$\Rightarrow$ $\angle BCD = 90°$

Question 7 ABC is a right angled triangle in which $\angle A = 90°$ and $AB = AC$, find $\angle B$ and $\angle C$.

Sol. We have, $\angle A = 90°$ (Given)

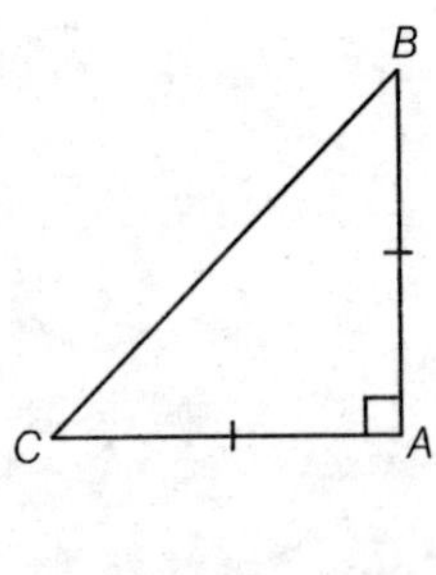

$$AB = AC \quad \text{(Given)}$$
$$\Rightarrow \quad \angle B = \angle C$$
($\because$ Angles opposite to equal sides are equal)

Now, we have

$$\angle A + \angle B + \angle C = 180° \quad \text{(By } \Delta \text{ property)}$$
$$\Rightarrow \quad 90° + \angle B + \angle B = 180° \quad (\because \angle B = \angle C)$$
$$\Rightarrow \quad 2\angle B = 90°$$
$$\Rightarrow \quad \angle B = 45°$$
$$\therefore \quad \angle B = \angle C = 45°$$

Mistake Alert Not forget in isosceles right angle triangle a angle is 90° and other both remain angles will be acute and equal to each other.

Question 8 Show that the angles of an equilateral triangle are 60° each.

Sol. Let Δ ABC be an equilateral triangle, such that

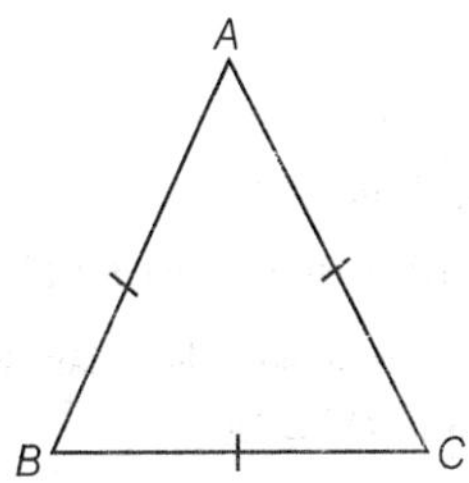

$$AB = BC = CA$$
($\because$ The length of all sides of equilateral triangle is same.)

Now, $\quad AB = AC$
$$\Rightarrow \quad \angle B = \angle C \quad \text{...(i)}$$
($\because$ Angles opposite to equal sides are equal)

Similarly, $\quad CB = CA$
$$\Rightarrow \quad \angle A = \angle B \quad \text{...(ii)}$$
($\because$ Angles opposite to equal sides are equal)

From Eqs. (i) and (ii), we have
$$\angle A = \angle B = \angle C \quad \text{...(iii)}$$
Now, $\quad \angle A + \angle B + \angle C = 180° \quad$ (Angle sum property of triangle)
$$\Rightarrow \quad \angle A + \angle A + \angle A = 180° \quad \text{[From Eq. (iii)]}$$
$$\Rightarrow \quad 3\angle A = 180°$$
$$\Rightarrow \quad \angle A = 60°$$
Hence, $\quad \angle A = \angle B = \angle C = 60°$

Therefore, the angles of an equilateral triangle are 60° each. **Hence Proved.**

Exercise 7.3

Question 1 ΔABC and ΔDBC are two isosceles triangles on the same base BC and vertices A and D are on the same side of BC (see figure). If AD is extended to intersect BC at P, show that

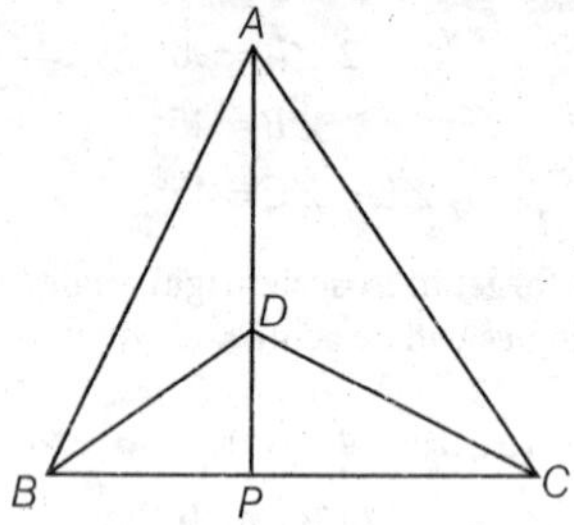

(i) $\Delta ABD \cong \Delta ACD$

(ii) $\Delta ABP \cong \Delta ACP$

(iii) AP bisects $\angle A$ as well as $\angle D$

(iv) AP is the perpendicular bisector of BC.

Sol. Given ΔABC and ΔDBC are two isosceles triangles having common base BC, such that $AB = AC$ and $DB = DC$.

To prove (i) $\Delta ABD \cong \Delta ACD$

(ii) $\Delta ABP \cong \Delta ACP$

(iii) AP bisects $\angle A$ as well as $\angle D$.

(iv) AP is the perpendicular bisector of BC.

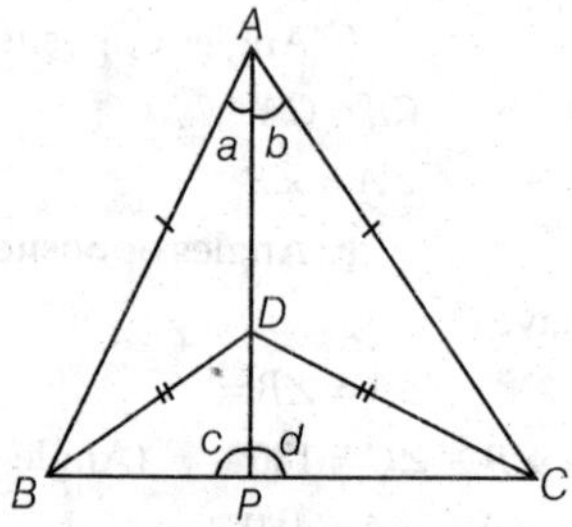

Proof (i) In ΔABD and ΔACD, we have

	$AB = AC$	(Given)
	$BD = CD$	(Given)
and	$AD = AD$	(Common)
$\therefore$	$\Delta ABD \cong \Delta ACD$	(By SSS congruence rule)

(ii) In $\Delta\ ABP$ and $\Delta\ ACP$, we have

	$AB = AC$	(Given)
	$\angle a = \angle b$	($\because \Delta\ ABD \cong ACD$)
and	$AP = AP$	(Common)
$\therefore$	$\Delta\ ABP \cong \Delta\ ACP$	(By SAS congruence axiom)

(iii) From part (ii), we have $\angle a = \angle b$ ($\because \Delta\ ABD \cong \Delta\ ACD$)

$\Rightarrow AP$ bisects $\angle A$

Now,	$\angle ADB = \angle ADC$	($\because \Delta\ ABD \cong \Delta\ ACD$)
$\Rightarrow$	$180° - \angle ADB = 180° - \angle ADC$	(By linear pair axiom)
$\Rightarrow$	$\angle BDP = \angle CDP$	

$\Rightarrow AP$ bisects $\angle D$.

(iv) $BP = CP$ ($\because \Delta\ ABP \cong \Delta\ ACP$)

and	$\angle c = \angle d$	...(i)
But	$\angle c + \angle d = 180°$	(Linear pair)
$\therefore$	$\angle c + \angle c = 180° \Rightarrow \angle c = 90°$,	[From Eq. (i)]
$\Rightarrow$	$\angle c = \angle d = 90°$	

Hence, AP is the perpendicular bisector of BC.

Question 2 AD is an altitude of an isosceles triangle ABC in which $AB = AC$. Show that

(i) AD bisects BC (ii) AD bisects $\angle A$

Sol. In $\Delta\ ABD$ and $\Delta\ ACD$, we have

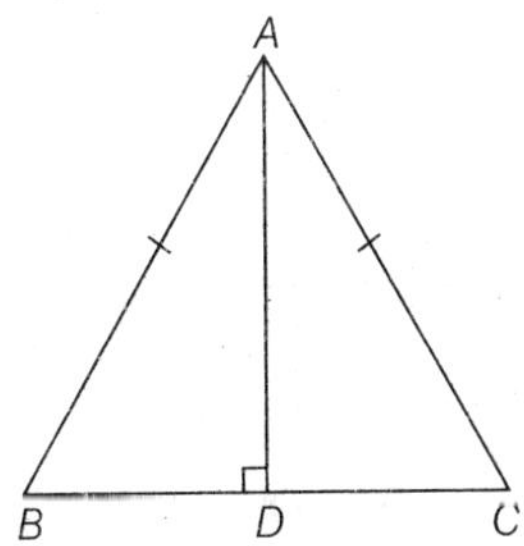

	$AB = AC$	(Given)
	$\angle ADB = \angle ADC = 90°$	($\because$ Given $AD \perp BC$)
and	$AD = AD$	(Common)
$\therefore$	$\Delta\ ABD \cong \Delta\ ACD$	(By RHS congruence rule)

So, $BD = DC$ (By CPCT)

$\Rightarrow AD$ bisects BC.

Also, $\angle BAD = \angle CAD$ (By CPCT)

$\Rightarrow AD$ bisects $\angle A$.

Question 3 Two sides AB and BC and median AM of one triangle ABC are respectively equal to sides PQ and QR and median PN of ΔPQR (see figure). Show that

(i) $\Delta ABM \cong \Delta PQN$ (ii) $\Delta ABC \cong \Delta PQR$

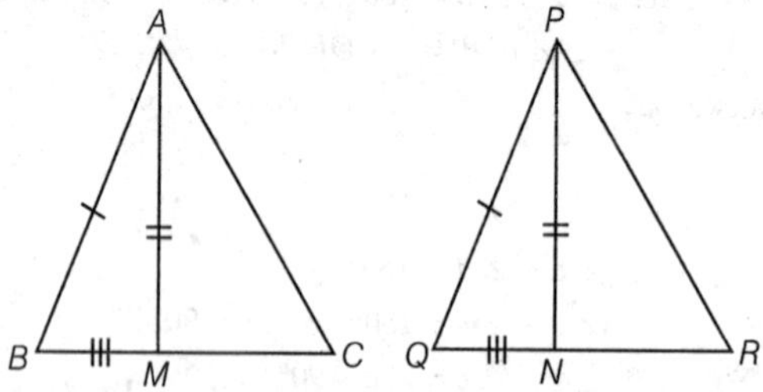

Sol. We have, AM is the median of $\Delta\ ABC$

$\Rightarrow$ $$BM = MC = \frac{1}{2} BC$$ ($\because$ M bisects BC) ...(i)

PN is the median of ΔPQR.

$\Rightarrow$ $$QN = NR = \frac{1}{2} QR$$ ($\because$ N bisects QR) ...(ii)

Now, we have

$$BC = QR$$ (Given)

$\Rightarrow$ $$\frac{1}{2} BC = \frac{1}{2} QR$$

$\therefore$ $$BM = QN$$ [From Eqs. (i) and (ii)] ...(iii)

(i) In ΔABM and ΔPQN, we have

$$AB = PQ$$ (Given)

$$AM = PN$$ (Given)

and $$BM = QN$$ [From Eq. (iii)]

$\therefore$ $$\Delta ABM \cong \Delta PQN$$ (By SSS congruence axiom)

(ii) In ΔABC and ΔPQR, we have

$$AB = PQ$$ (Given)

$$\angle B = \angle Q$$ ($\because \Delta\ ABM \cong \Delta\ PQN$)

and $$BC = QR$$ (Given)

$\therefore$ $$\Delta ABC \cong \Delta PQR$$ (By SAS congruence axiom)

Question 4 BE and CF are two equal altitudes of a triangle ABC. Using RHS congruence rule, prove that the triangle ABC is isosceles.

◎ ***Thinking Process*** If in two right triangles the hypotenuse and one side of one triangle are equal to the hypotenuse and one side of the other triangle, then the two triangles are congruent.

Sol. In ΔBEC and ΔCFB, we have

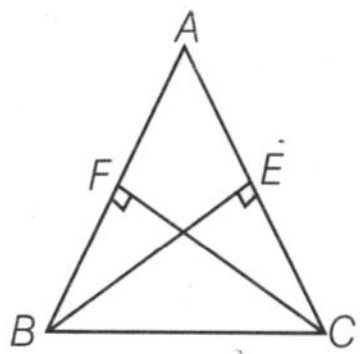

$$\angle BEC = \angle CFB = 90^\circ$$

[$\because BE \perp AC$ and $CF \perp AB$ (Given)]

$BC = BC$ (Common)

and $BE = CF$ (Given)

$\therefore$ $\Delta BEC \cong \Delta CFB$ (By RHS congruence axiom)

$\therefore$ $EC = FB$ (By CPCT)...(i)

In $\Delta\ AEB$ and $\Delta\ AFC$, we have

$\angle A = \angle A$ (Common)

$\angle AEB = \angle AFC = 90^\circ$ ($\because BE \perp AC$ and $CF \perp AB$) (Given)

and $EB = FC$ (Given)

$\therefore$ $\Delta AEB \cong \Delta AFC$ (By AAS congruence axiom)

$\therefore$ $AE = AF$ (By CPCT) ...(ii)

On adding Eqs.(i) and (ii), we have

$$EC + AE = FB + AF$$

($\because AC = EC + AE$ and $AB = FB + AF$)

$\Rightarrow$ $AC = AB$

Hence, $\Delta\ ABC$ is an isosceles triangle.

Question 5 ABC is an isosceles triangle with $AB = AC$. Draw $AP \perp BC$ to show that $\angle B = \angle C$.

Sol. In ΔABP and ΔACP, we have

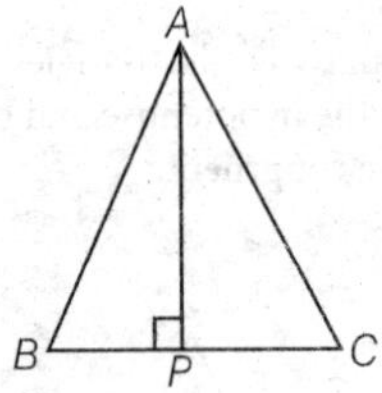

	$AB = AC$	(Given)
	$AP = AP$	(Common)
and	$\angle APB = \angle APC = 90°$	($\because AP \perp BC$)
$\therefore$	$\Delta ABP \cong \Delta ACP$	(By RHS congruence rule)
$\Rightarrow$	$\angle B = \angle C$	(By CPCT) **Hence Proved.**

DIKSHA APP Questions

☐ Multiple Choice Questions

Q.1 Following is not a congruence condition of triangles.

(a) ASA (b) AAA (c) SAS (d) SSS

Sol. (b) AAA

Q.2 In two triangles, ABC and PQR, $\angle A = 30°$, $\angle B = 70°$, $\angle P = 70°$, $\angle Q = 80°$ and $AB = RP$, then.

(a) $\Delta ABC \cong \Delta PQR$ (b) $\Delta ABC \cong \Delta QRP$

(c) $\Delta ABC \cong \Delta RPQ$ (d) $\Delta ABC \cong \Delta RQP$

Sol. (c)

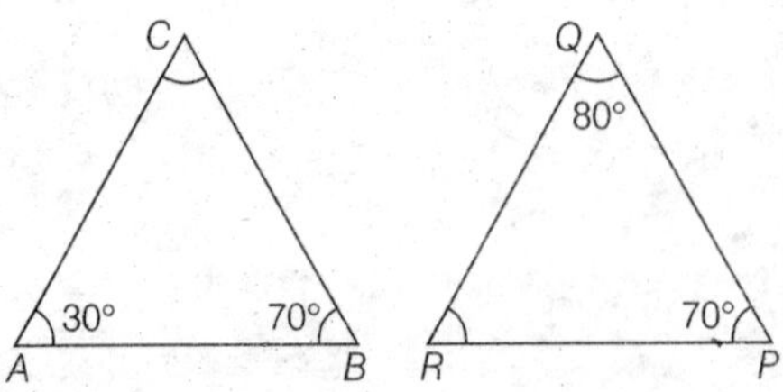

In ΔABC, we have

$$\angle A = 30°, \angle B = 70°$$

Now, $\angle A + \angle B + \angle C = 180°$ [By angle sum property of a triangle]

$\Rightarrow$ $30° + 70° + \angle C = 180°$

$\Rightarrow$ $\angle C = 80°$

In ΔPQR,

$\angle P + \angle Q + \angle R = 180°$ [By angle sum property of a triangle]

$\Rightarrow$ $70° + 80° + \angle R = 180°$

$\Rightarrow$ $\angle R = 30°$

In ΔABC and ΔPQR

$$\angle A = \angle R,\ \angle B = \angle P,\ \angle C = \angle Q$$

$AB = RP$ (Given)

$\therefore$ $\Delta ABC \cong \Delta RPQ$ (As ASA congruence rule)

Q.3 $\Delta ABC \cong \Delta DEF$, $\angle A = 30°$, $\angle E = 50°$ then the measure of $\angle C$ is

(a) 50° (b) 100° (c) 80° (d) 30°

Sol. (b)

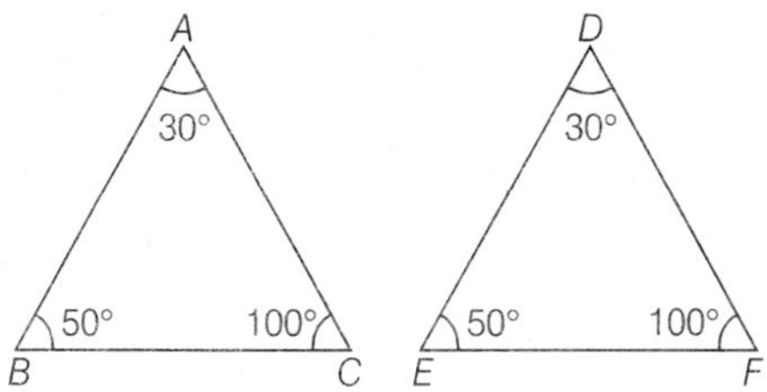

If $\Delta ABC \cong \Delta DEF$ (Given)

Then, corresponding angles are equal

$\therefore$ $\angle B = \angle E = 50°$

$\Rightarrow$ $\angle A = \angle D = 30°$

In ΔABC,

$\angle A + \angle B + \angle C = 180°$ (Angle sum property)

$\Rightarrow$ $30° + 50° + \angle C - 180°$

$\Rightarrow$ $80° + \angle C = 180°$

$\Rightarrow$ $\angle C = 100°$

Q.4 Two sides of a triangle are 5.1 cm and 1.6 cm. The length of the third side can not be

(a) 4 cm (b) 4.5 cm

(c) 3.4 cm (d) 3.8 cm

Sol. (c) We know that, in a triangle, the sum of length of any two sides should be greater than the length of third side.

Here,

From option (a)

$$1.6 \text{ cm} + 4 \text{ cm} = 5.6 \text{ cm} > 5.1 \text{ cm}$$

Hence, third side can be 4 cm.

From option (b)

$$1.6 \text{ cm} + 4.5 \text{ cm} = 6.1 \text{ cm} \not> 5.1 \text{ cm}$$

Hence, third side can be 4.5 cm.

From option (c)

$$1.6 \text{ cm} + 3.4 \text{ cm} = 5 \text{ cm} > 5.1 \text{ cm}$$

So, third side can not be 3.4 cm.

From option (d)

$$1.6 \text{ cm} + 3.8 \text{ cm} = 5.4 \text{ cm} > 5.1 \text{ cm}$$

Also, third side can be 3.8 cm.

Hence, option (c) is correct.

Q.5 If $\Delta ABC \cong \Delta PQR$ and ΔABC is not congruent to ΔRPQ, which of the following is not true?

(a) $AC = PR$ (b) $BC = PQ$

(c) $BC = QR$ (d) $AB = PQ$

Sol. (b) It is given that

$$\Delta ABC \cong \Delta PQR$$

As corresponding sides are equal

$$AB = PQ$$
$$AC = PR$$
$$BC = QR$$

Also, given ΔABC is not congruent to ΔRPQ therefore, BC is not equal to PQ.

So, $BC = PQ$ is not true for the given triangles.

☐ Subjective Type Questions

Q.1 $\Delta ABC \cong \Delta DEF$ and if $AB = DE = 3$ and $BC = EF = 4$, then what is the necessary condition for $\Delta ABC \cong (\Delta DEF)$

Sol. For $\Delta ABC \cong \Delta DEF$

$$BC = EF = 4 \quad \text{(Given)}$$
$$AB = DE = 3 \quad \text{(Given)}$$

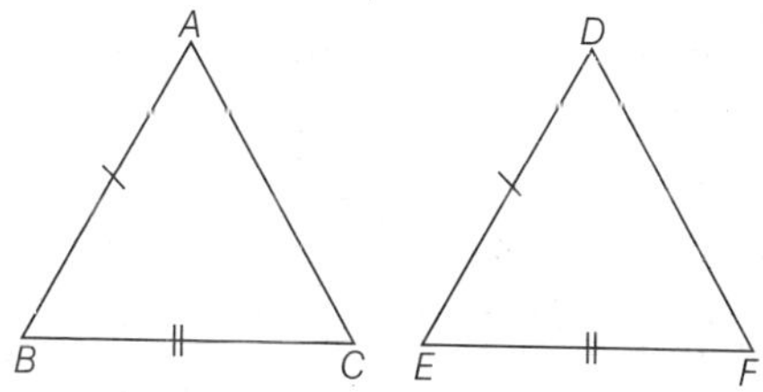

Two sides are equal, so $\angle B = \angle E$ for the SAS congruency.

So, $\angle B = \angle E$ is the necessary condition for $\Delta ABC \cong \Delta DEF$.

Q.2 In a ΔABC, if $AB = AC$ and BC is produced to D such that $\angle ACD = 100°$, then calculate $\angle A$.

Sol.

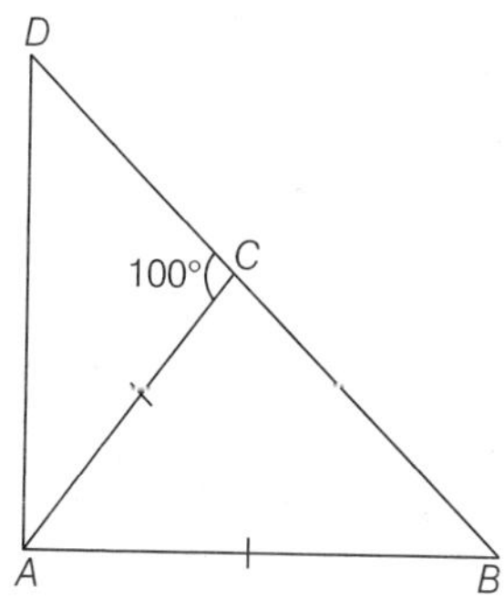

In ΔABC, we have

$$AB = AC \quad \text{(Given)}$$

$$\angle ABC = \angle ACB \quad \ldots\text{(i)}$$

[$\because$ Angles opposite to equal sides are equal]

Now, $\angle ACB + \angle ACD = 180°$ [linear pair axiom]

$\Rightarrow$ $\angle ACB + 100° = 180°$

$\Rightarrow$ $\angle ACB = 80°$

$\Rightarrow$ $\angle ABC = \angle ACB = 80°$ [By Eq. (i)]

Now, In ΔABC,

$\angle ABC + \angle ACB + \angle CAB = 180°$ [Angle sum property]

$\Rightarrow$ $80° + 80° + \angle CAB = 180°$

$\Rightarrow$ $\angle CAB + 160° = 180°$

$\Rightarrow$ $\angle CAB = 20°$

The value of $\angle A = 20°$.

Q.3 If the sides of the triangle are 4 cm, 6 cm, 10 cm, then is the triangle possible?

Sol. Let sides of triangle are

$$AB = 4 \text{ cm}, BC = 6 \text{ cm and } AC = 10 \text{ cm}$$

We know that, in a triangle, the sum of length of two sides should be greater than third side.

Now, from given sides, we see

$$4 \text{ cm} + 6 \text{ cm} = 10 \text{ cm}$$

i.e., $AB + BC = AC$

Thus, sum of AB and BC is not greater than AC.

Therefore, the triangle is not possible with given sides.

Q.4 In triangle ABC, $AB > AC$, then what is the relation between $\angle C$ and $\angle B$?

Sol. Given, in ΔABC,

$$AB > AC$$

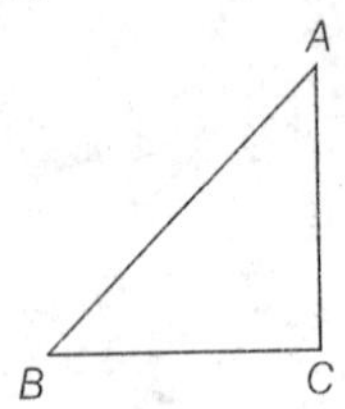

We know that, in a triangle if two sides of are unequal, then the angle opposite to the longer side is greater.

So, in ΔABC, $\angle C$ is greater than $\angle B$.

Hence, required relation between $\angle C$ and $\angle B$ is $\angle C > \angle B$.

Q.5 In triangle PQR, if $\angle R > \angle Q$, then what is the relation between PQ and PR sides?

Sol. In ΔPQR,

$$\angle R > \angle Q \qquad \text{(Given)}$$

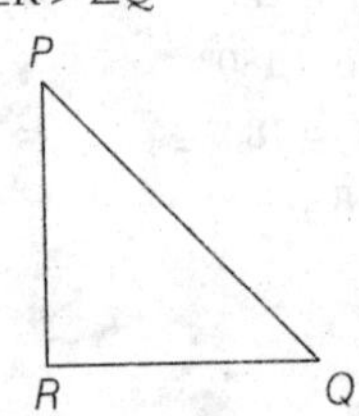

We know that, in a triangle if two sides are unequal, then the angle opposite to the longer side is greater.

So, in ΔPQR, side PQ is longer than side PR because $\angle R$ is greater than $\angle Q$.

Hence, the required relation between PQ and PR sides is $PQ > PR$.

Q.6 In ΔPQR, if $\angle P - \angle Q = 42°$ and $\angle Q - \angle R = 21°$, find $\angle P$, $\angle Q$ and $\angle R$.

Sol. In ΔPQR,

$$\angle P - \angle Q = 42° \quad \text{... (i) (Given)}$$

$$\angle Q - \angle R = 21° \quad \text{... (ii) (Given)}$$

In ΔPQR,

$$\angle P + \angle Q + \angle R = 180° \quad \text{... (iii)}$$

From Eq. (i) $\quad \angle P = 42° + \angle Q \quad$ [Angle sum property of triangle]

From Eq. (ii)

$$\angle R = \angle Q - 21°$$

On substituting the values of $\angle P$ and $\angle R$ in Eq. (iii), we get

$$42° + \angle Q + \angle Q - 21° + \angle Q = 180°$$

$\Rightarrow \quad 3\angle Q = 180° - 21°$

$\Rightarrow \quad 3\angle Q = 159°$

$\Rightarrow \quad \angle Q = 53°$

$\therefore \quad \angle P = 42° + 53° = 95°$

and $\quad \angle R = \angle Q - 21° = 53° - 21° = 32°$

The value of $\angle P = 95°$, $\angle Q = 53°$, $\angle R = 32°$.

Q.7 ABC is an equilateral triangle drawn on side BC of square $BCDE$. Prove that $AE = AD$.

Sol. Given, $BCDE$ is a square and ABC is an equilateral triangle.

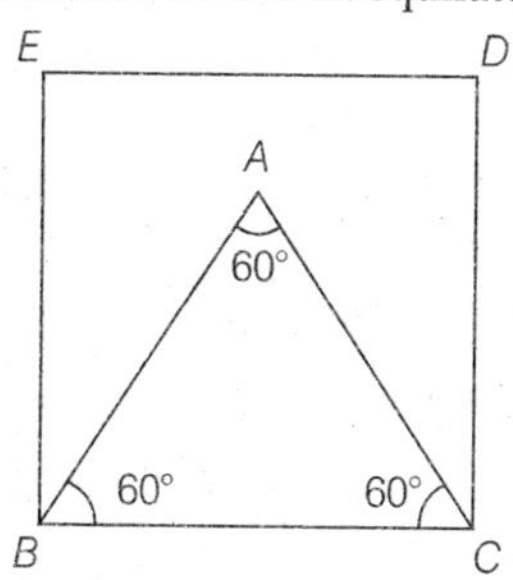

$\therefore \quad AB = BC = AC$

$\therefore \quad \angle ABC = 60°$ and $\angle ACB = 60°$

[Each angle of equilateral triangle is 60°]

Since, $BCDE$ is a square

$\therefore \quad \angle EBA = 90° - 60° = 30°$ ...(i)

and $\quad \angle DCA = 90° - 60° = 30°$ ...(ii)

In ΔABE and ΔACD,

$BE = CD$ [Sides of squares are equal]

$AB = AC$ [Sides of equilateral triangle are equal]

$\therefore \quad \angle EBA = \angle DCA = 30°$ [from Eq. (i) and (ii)]

$\therefore \quad \Delta ABE \cong \Delta ACD$ [by SAS rule]

$\therefore \quad AE = AD$

Hence Proved.

Q.8 In ΔPQR, $\angle Q = 40°$ and $PQ = PR$. Find $\angle P$ and $\angle R$.

◎ ***Thinking Process*** In a triangle having two equal sides is called isosceles triangle and angle opposite to equal sides are equal.

Sol. In ΔPQR

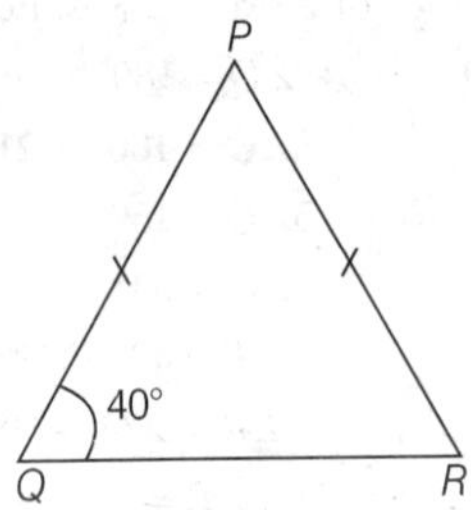

$\angle Q = 40°$ (Given)

$PQ = PR$ (Given)

$\therefore \quad \angle Q = \angle R$

[$\because$ Angle opposite to equal sides are equal]

$\therefore \quad \angle R = 40°$ ($\because \angle Q = 40°$)

In ΔPQR

$\angle P + \angle Q + \angle R = 180°$ [Angle sum property of triangle]

$\Rightarrow \quad \angle P + 40° + 40° = 180°$

$\Rightarrow \quad \angle P + 80° = 180° \Rightarrow \angle P = 100°$

The values of $\angle P = 100°$ and $\angle R = 40°$

Q.9 PQR is a triangle in which $PQ = PR$ and S is any point on the side PQ. Through S, a line is draw parallel to QR and intersecting PR at T. Prove that $PS = PT$.

Sol.

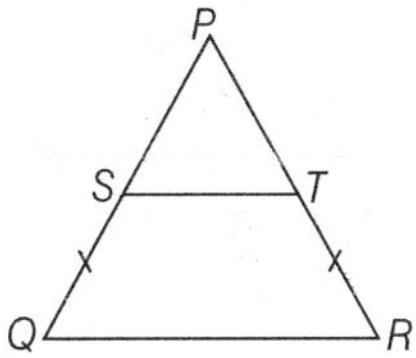

In ΔPQR, $PQ = PR$ (Given)

$\therefore$ $\angle PQR = \angle PRQ$ [$\because$ Angle apposite to equal sides are equal]

Now, $ST \parallel QR$ and PQ is the transversal.

Sol $\angle PST = \angle PQR$ [Corresponding angles]

$\angle PTS = \angle PRQ$ [Corroesponding angles]

Then, $\angle PST = \angle PTS$ [$\because \angle PQR = \angle PRQ$]

$\therefore$ $PS = PT$ [Side opposite to equal angles are equal]

Hence Proved.

Q.10 In triangle QSR side SQ and RS are produced to point T and P respectively. If $\angle TQR = 125°$ and $\angle PSQ = 100°$, then find $\angle SRQ$.

Sol. $\angle PSQ + \angle QSR = 180°$ [linear pair of angles]

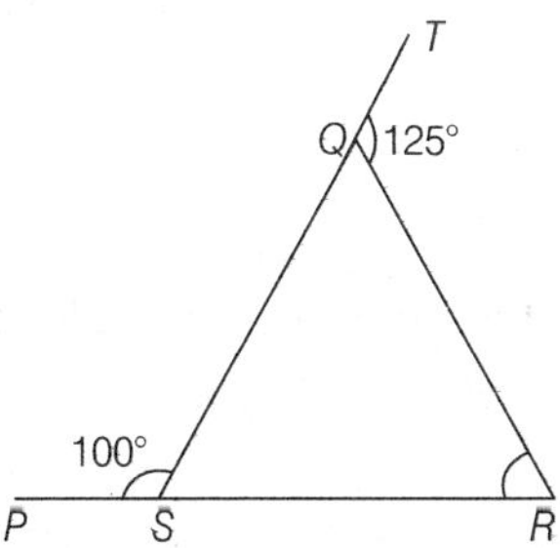

$\Rightarrow$ $100° + \angle QSR = 180°$

$\Rightarrow$ $\angle QSR = 80°$

Now, $\angle TQR + \angle SQR = 180°$ [linear pair of angles]

$\Rightarrow$ $125° + \angle SQR = 180°$

$\Rightarrow$ $\angle SQR = 55°$

Now, in ΔQSR,

$$\angle QSR + \angle SRQ + \angle SQR = 180° \quad \text{[Angle sum property of triangle]}$$

$$\Rightarrow \quad 80° + \angle SRQ + 55° = 180°$$

$$\Rightarrow \quad \angle SRQ = 180° - 80° - 55°$$

$$\Rightarrow \quad \angle SRQ = 45°$$

Q.11 Show that the sum of the three altitudes of a Δ is less than the sum of three sides of the triangle.

Sol. Given in ΔABC, AD, BE and CF are three altitudes of ΔABC.

To prove $AD + BE + CF < AB + BC + CA$

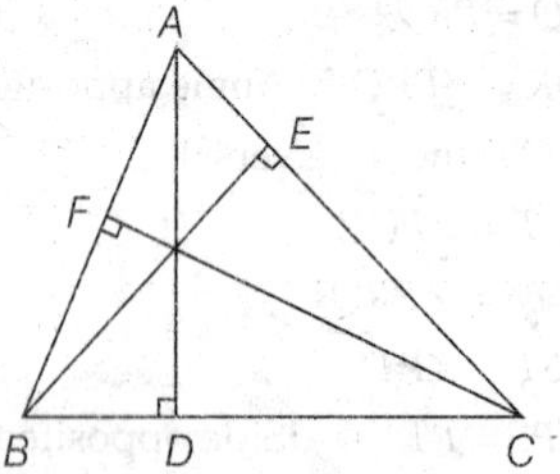

Proof In ΔABD, $\angle D = 90°$

Then, other two angles are acute angles

$\because \quad \angle B < \angle D$

$\therefore \quad AD < AB$ ...(i)

Similarly, in ΔBEC and ΔABE, we can prove that $BE < BC$ ...(ii)

and $CF < CA$ ...(iii)

On adding Eqs. (i), (ii) and (iii), we get

$$AD + BE + CF < AB + BC + CA$$ **Hence Proved.**

Q.12 If P is the point in the interior of triangle ABC. Prove that $PA + PB + PC > \frac{1}{2}(AB + BC + AC)$.

Sol. Given, P is an interior point.

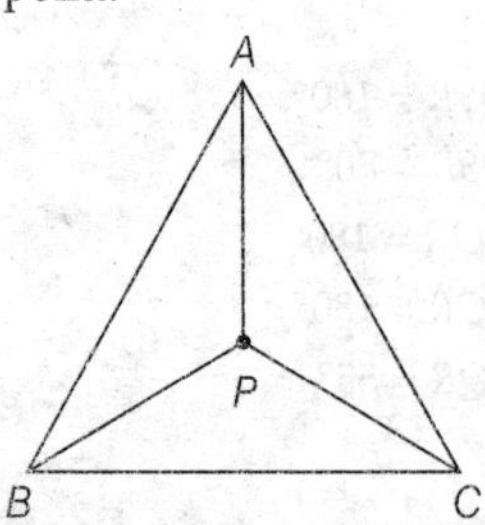

To prove

$$PA + PB + PC > \frac{1}{2}(AB + BC + AC)$$

Proof In ΔAPB,

$$AB < PA + PB \qquad \text{...(i)}$$

[Sum of two sides of a triangle is greater than the third side]

In ΔCPB,

$$BC < PC + PB \qquad \text{...(ii)}$$

[Sum of two sides of a triangle is greater than the third side]

In ΔAPC,

$$AC < PA + PC \qquad \text{...(iii)}$$

[Sum of two sides of a triangle is greater than the third side]

On adding eqs. (i), (ii) and (iii), we get

$$(AB + BC + CA) < PA + PB + PC + PB + PA + PC$$

$$\Rightarrow \quad (AB + BC + CA) < 2(PB + PB + PC)$$

$$\Rightarrow \quad PA + PB + PC > \frac{1}{2}(AB + BC + AC)$$ **Hence Proved.**

Q.13 Verify that the sum of three sides of a triangle is greater than the sum of its three medians.

Sol. Let ABC be the triangle and D, E and F the mid-points of BC, CA and AB respectively.

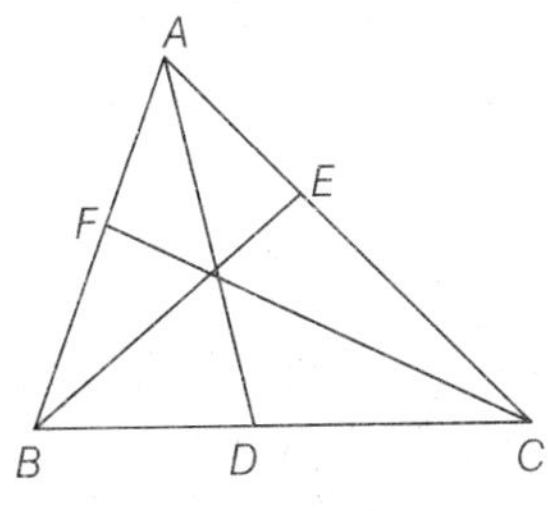

Recall that the sum of two sides of a triangle is greater than twice the median bisecting the third side.

So, in ΔABC, AD is median.

$$\Rightarrow \quad AB + AC > 2AD \qquad \text{...(i)}$$

Similarly, we get

$$BC + AC > 2CF \qquad \text{...(ii)}$$

and

$$BC + AB > 2BE \qquad \text{...(iii)}$$

On adding Eqs. (i), (ii) and (iii), we get

$$(AB + AC) + (BC + AC) + (BC + AB) > (2AD + 2CD + 2BE)$$

$$\Rightarrow \quad 2(AB + BC + AC) > 2(AD + BE + CF)$$

$$\therefore \quad AB + BC + AC > AD + BE + CF$$

Hence, we can say that the sum of three sides of a triangle is greater than the sum of its three medians. **Hence Proved.**

Q.14 In the bisector of the vertical angle of a triangle bisects the base, prove that the triangle is isosceles.

Sol.

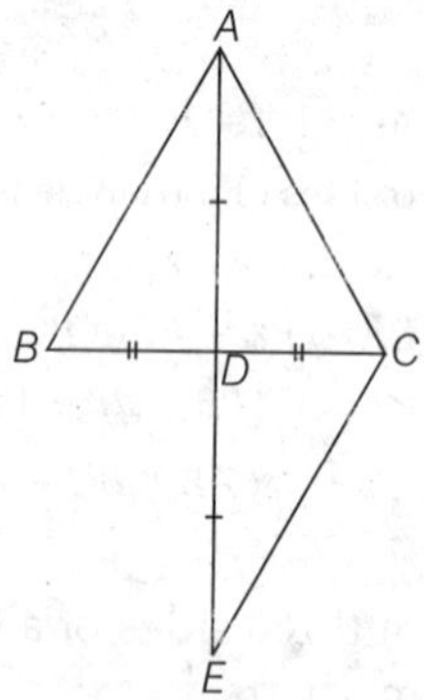

In ΔABC,

AD is the bisector of $\angle A$, then $BD = DC$

Now, extend AD to E such that $AD = DE$

In ΔABD and ΔECD,

$BD = DC$ [Proved above]

$AD = DE$ [Given]

$\angle ADB = \angle EDC$ [Vertically opposite angles]

$\Delta ABD \cong \Delta ECD$ [By SAS congruence axiom]

$AB = EC$ ...(i)(By CPCT)

$\angle BAD = \angle DEC$ (By CPCT)

$\angle DAC = \angle DEC$ [$\because \angle BAD = \angle DAC$]

$\angle AEC = \angle EAC$

$\therefore EC = AC$ (sides opposite to equal angle are equal).

So, from Eq. (i), we get

$$AB = AC$$

We know that in an isosceles triangle, at least two sides are equal that is

$$AB = AC,$$

Hence, ΔABC is an isosceles triangle.

Q.15 D, E and F are the mid-points of the sides BC, CA and AB of an equilateral triangle ABC. Prove that ΔDEF is also an equilateral triangle.

Sol. Since, D, E and F are the mid-points of side BC, CA and AB respectively.

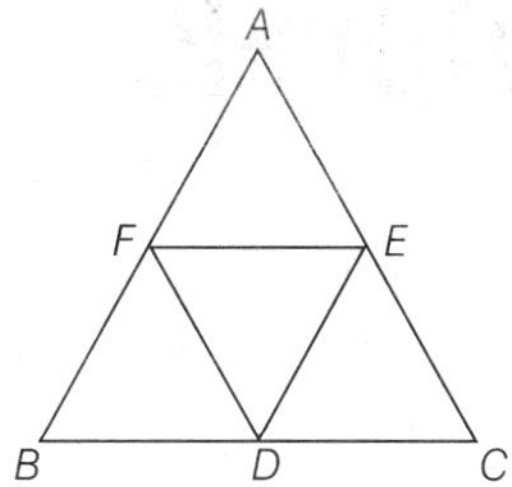

$\therefore$ $DE = \frac{1}{2} AB$ [by mid-point theorem]

Similarly, $FE = \frac{1}{2} BC$ and $DF = \frac{1}{2} CA$

Since, $AB = BC = CA$ [ΔABC is a equilateral]

So, $\frac{1}{2} AB = \frac{1}{2} BC = \frac{1}{2} CA$

$\Rightarrow$ $DE = FE = DF$

Hence, ΔDEF is an equilateral triangle.

Quadrilaterals

CHAPTER 08

Important Points

01 Quadrilateral A closed figure bounded by four lines segment is called a quadrilateral.

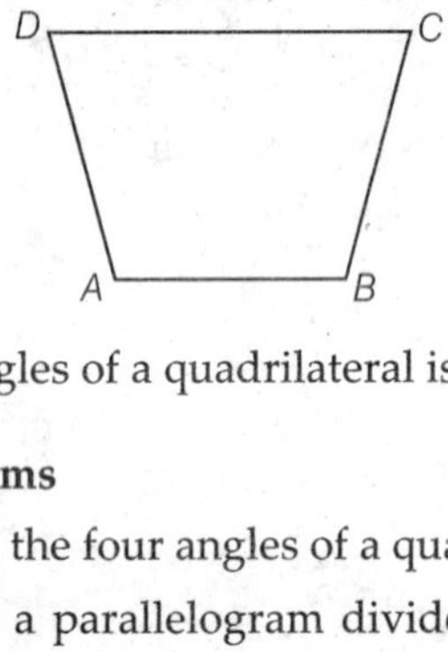

The sum of the angles of a quadrilateral is 360°.

02 Important Theorems

(i) The sum of all the four angles of a quadrilateral is 360°.

(ii) A diagonal of a parallelogram divides it into two congruent triangles.

(iii) A quadrilateral is a parallelogram, if

- opposite sides are equal.
- opposite angles are equal.
- diagonal bisect each other.

a pair of opposite sides is equal and parallel.

(iv) Diagonals of a rectangle bisect each other and they are equal and *vice-versa*.

(v) Consecutive angles of a parallelogram are supplementary.

(vi) Square, rectangle and rhombus are also a parallelogram.

(vii) All the interior angles of a rectangle are right angles.

(viii) Diagonals of a rhombus bisect each other at right angles and they are not equal and *vice-versa.*

(ix) Diagonals of a square bisect each other at right angles and they are equal and *vice-versa.*

(x) The line segment joining the mid-points of any two sides of a triangle is parallel to the third side and equal to half of it. (Mid-point theorem)

(xi) The line drawn through the mid-point of one side of a triangle, parallel to another side, intersects the third side at its mid-point. (By converse of mid-point theorem)

(xii) The quadrilateral formed by joining the mid-points of the sides of a quadrilateral, taken in order, is a parallelogram.

Exercise 8.1

Question 1 If the diagonals of a parallelogram are equal, then show that it is a rectangle.

◎ *Thinking Process* In a parallelogram, if one of the angle is right angle. Then the parallelogram is rectangle.

Sol. Let given parallelogram is $ABCD$ whose diagonals AC and BD are equal. *i.e.,* $AC = BD$.

Now, we have to prove that $ABCD$ is a rectangle.

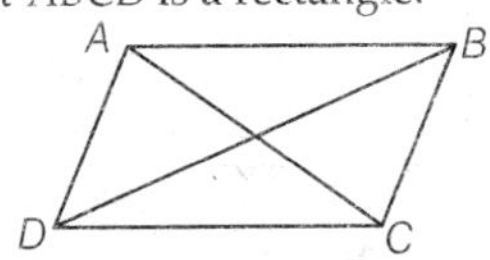

Proof In $\Delta\ ABC$ and $\Delta\ DCB$, we have

	$AB = CD$	(Opposite sides of parallelogram)
	$BC = BC$	(Common in both triangles)
and	$AC = BD$	(Given)
∴	$\Delta\ ABC \cong \Delta DCB$	(By SSS rule)
∴	$\angle ABC = \angle DCB$	...(i)

(Corresponding part of congruent triangle)

But $DC \parallel AB$ and transversal CB intersect them.

$\therefore$ $\angle ABC + \angle DCB = 180°$

($\because$ Both are interior angles on the same side of the transversal)

$\Rightarrow$ $\angle ABC + \angle ABC = 180°$ [From Eq. (i)]

$\Rightarrow$ $2\angle ABC = 180°$

$\Rightarrow$ $\angle ABC = 90° = \angle DCB$

Thus, $ABCD$ is a parallelogram and one of angles is 90°.

Hence, $ABCD$ is a rectangle. **Hence Proved.**

Question 2 Show that the diagonals of a square are equal and bisect each other at right angles.

Sol. Let a square $ABCD$ whose diagonals AC and BD intersect at O.

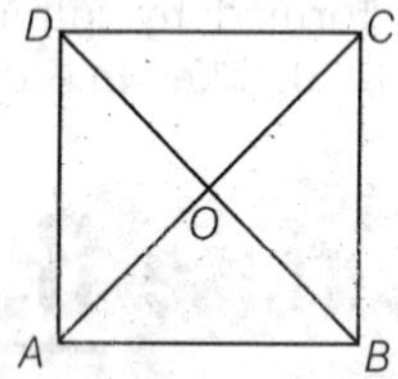

To prove Diagonals are equal and bisect each other at right angles.

i.e., $AC = BD, OD = OB, OA = OC$ and $AC \perp BD$

Proof In $\Delta\ ABC$ and $\Delta\ BAD$, we have

$AB = BA$ (Common)

$BC = AD$ (Sides of a square)

$\angle ABC = \angle BAD = 90°$

$\therefore$ $\Delta ABC \cong \Delta BAD$ (By SAS rule)

Hence, $AC = BD$

(Corresponding Parts of Congruent Triangle)

In ΔOAB and ΔOCD

$AB = DC$ (Side of square)

$\angle OAB = \angle DCO$

($\because AB \parallel CD$ and transversal AC intersect)

and $\angle OBA = \angle BDC$

($\because AB \parallel CD$ and transversal BD intersect)

$\therefore$ $\Delta OAB \cong \Delta OCD$ (By ASA rule)

$\therefore$ $OA = OC$ and $OB = OD$

(Corresponding Parts of Congruent Triangle)

Now, in ΔAOB and ΔAOD, we have

$OB = OD$ (Prove in above)

$AB = AD$ (Sides of a square)

$AO = OA$ (Common)

$\therefore$ $\Delta AOB \cong \Delta AOD$ (By SSS rule)

$\therefore$ $\angle AOB = \angle AOD$ (By CPCT)

But $\angle AOB + \angle AOD = 180^\circ$ (Linear pair)

$\angle AOB + \angle AOB = 180^\circ$ ($\because \angle AOB = \angle AOD$)

$2\angle AOB = 180^\circ$

$\angle AOB = 90^\circ$

$\therefore$ $\angle AOB = \angle AOD = 90^\circ$

Thus, $AO \perp BD$ *i.e.*, $AC \perp BD$.

Hence, $AC = BD, OA = OC, OB = OD$ and $AC \perp BD$ **Hence Proved.**

Question 3 Diagonal AC of a parallelogram $ABCD$ bisects $\angle A$ (see figure). Show that

(i) it bisects $\angle C$ also, (ii) $ABCD$ is a rhombus.

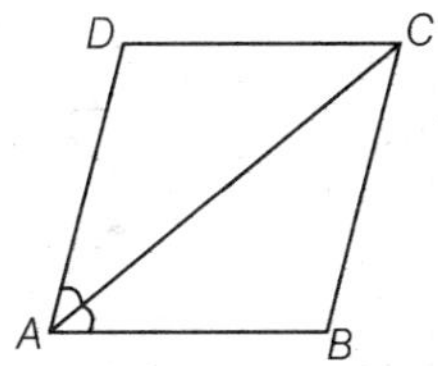

◎ ***Thinking Process*** If a transversal lines intersects the two parallel lines, then alternate angles are equal.

Sol. Given, diagonal AC of a parallelogram $ABCD$ bisects $\angle A$.

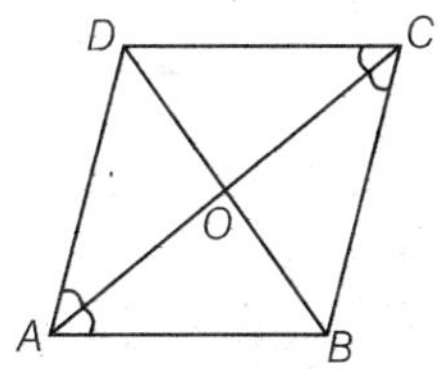

i.e., $\angle DAC = \angle BAC = \frac{1}{2}\angle BAD$ ...(i)

Here, $AB \parallel CD$ and AC is transversal.

$\therefore$ $\angle DCA = \angle CAB$ (Pair of alternate angle)...(ii)

and $\angle BCA = \angle DAC$ (Pair of alternate angle)...(iii)

From Eqs. (i), (ii) and (iii), we get

$\angle DAC = \angle BCA = \angle BAC = \angle DCA$

Hence, $\angle ACD = \angle BCA$

$= \angle DAC + \angle CAB$ [$\because$ From Eqs. (i) and (iii)]

$= \angle BAD$

$\therefore$ Diagonal AC also bisects $\angle C$.

Again, in ΔABC and ΔADC, we have

$AC = AC$ [Common line]

$\angle BAC = \angle DAC$ [from Eq. (i)]

$\angle BCA = \angle DAC$ [from Eq. (iii)]

$\Delta ABC \cong \Delta ADC$ [By ASA rule]

$\therefore$ $AB = AD$ and $BC = DC$

$\because$ $AB = CD$ and $BC = AD$

$\therefore$ $AB = BC = CD = AD$

Hence, $ABCD$ is a rhombus. **Hence Proved.**

Question 4 $ABCD$ is a rectangle in which diagonal AC bisects $\angle A$ as well as $\angle C$. Show that (i) $ABCD$ is a square (ii) Diagonal BD bisects $\angle B$ as well as $\angle D$.

Sol. Given $ABCD$ is a rectangle.

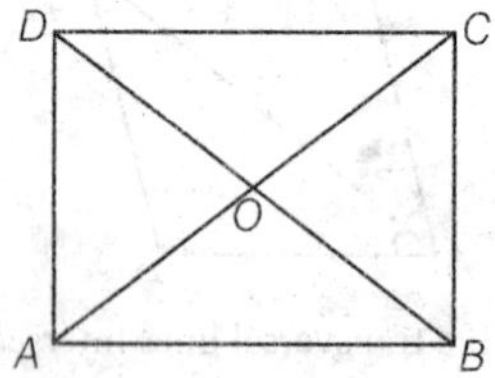

We know that in a rectangle opposite sides are equal

$\therefore$ $AB = CD$ and $BC = AD$ ...(i)

To Prove

(i) $ABCD$ is a square.

i.e., $AB = BC = CD = DA$

(ii) Diagonal BD bisects $\angle B$ as well as $\angle D$.

Proof (i) In ΔADC and ΔABC, we have

$\angle DAC = \angle BAC$ (Given)

$\angle DCA = \angle BCA$ (Given)

and $AC = CA$ (Common)

$\therefore$ $\Delta ADC \cong \Delta ABC$ (By ASA rule)

$\therefore$ $AD = AB$ (By CPCT)

and $CD = BC$ (By CPCT)...(ii)

Hence, from Eqs. (i) and (ii), we get

$AB = BC = AD = CD$

$\therefore \square ABCD$ is a square.

In ΔAOB and ΔCOB, we have

$AB = BC$ (Side of square)

$BO = OB$ (Common)

$$OA = OC \quad (\because \text{Diagonal of square bisect each other})$$

$\therefore \quad \Delta AOB \cong \Delta COB$ (By SSS rule)

$\therefore \quad \angle OBA = \angle OBC$ (By CPCT)

This shows that BO or BD bisect $\angle B$.

Similarly, in $\Delta\ AOD$ and $\Delta\ COD$, we have

$AD = CD$ (Side of square)

$OD = DO$ (Common)

and $OA = OC$

($\because$ Diagonal of square bisect each other)

$\therefore \quad \Delta\ AOD \cong \Delta\ COD$ (By SSS rule)

$\therefore \quad \angle ADO = \angle CDO$ (By CPCT)

This shows that DO or DB bisect $\angle D$.

Therefore, diagonal BD bisects $\angle B$ as well as $\angle D$. **Hence Proved.**

Mistake Alert Diagonals of a rectangle are equal in length and bisects each other. But those are not perpendicular bisector.

Question 5 In parallelogram $ABCD$, two points P and Q are taken on diagonal BD such that $DP = BQ$ (see figure). Show that

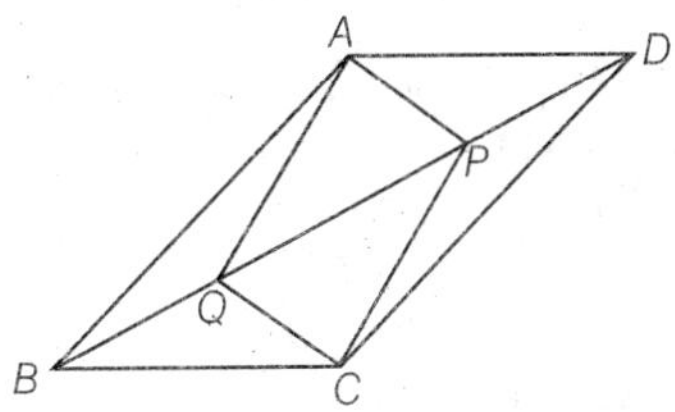

(i) $\Delta APD \cong \Delta CQB$ (ii) $AP = CQ$

(iii) $\Delta AQB \cong \Delta CPD$ (iv) $AQ = CP$

(v) $APCQ$ is a parallelogram.

Thinking Process Two triangles are congruent if their corresponding sides and angles are equal in length and measure are respectively.

Sol. Given, $ABCD$ is a parallelogram and P and Q are lie on BD such that

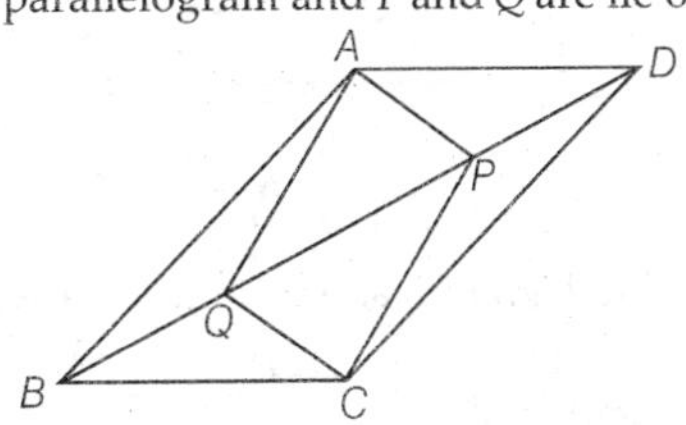

$$DP = BQ \quad ...(i)$$

(i) We have to show, $\Delta APD \cong \Delta CQB$

Now, in ΔAPD and ΔCQB, we have

$DP = BQ$ (Given)

$AD = BC$ (Opposite sides are equal in parallelogram)

$\because$ $AD \parallel BC$ and BD is a transversal.

$\therefore$ $\angle ADP = \angle QBC$ (Alternate interior angle)

$\therefore$ $\Delta APD \cong \Delta CQB$ (By SAS rule)

(ii) Since, $\Delta APD \cong \Delta CQB$

$\therefore$ $AP = CQ$ (By CPCT)

(iii) Here, we have to show, $\Delta AQB \cong \Delta CPD$

Now, in ΔAQB and ΔCPD, we have

$BQ = DP$ (Given)

$AB = CD$ (Opposite sides of parallelogram)

$\because$ $AB \parallel CD$ and BD is a transversal.

$\therefore$ $\angle ABQ = \angle CDP$ (Alternate interior angle)

$\therefore$ $\Delta AQB \cong \Delta CPD$ (By SAS rule)

(iv) Since, $\Delta AQB \cong \Delta CPD$

$\therefore$ $AQ = CP$ (By CPCT)

(v) We know that, if both pairs of opposite sides are equal in quadrilateral, then it is a Parallelogram.

Now, in ΔAPQ and ΔPCQ, we have

$AQ = CP$ [From part (iv)]

$AP = CQ$ [From part (ii)]

Hence, $APCQ$ is a parallelogram. **Hence Proved.**

Question 6 $ABCD$ is a parallelogram and AP and CQ are perpendiculars from vertices A and C on diagonal BD (see figure). Show that

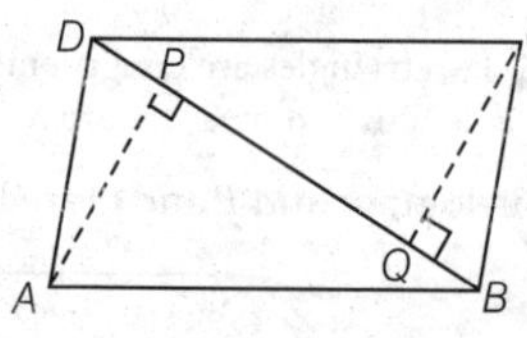

(i) $\Delta APB \cong \Delta CQD$ (ii) $AP = CQ$.

Sol. Given, $ABCD$ is a parallelogram and AP and CQ are perpendicular from vertices A and C on diagonal BD.

$\because$ $AB \parallel CD$ and BD is a transversal.

$\therefore$ $\angle CDB = \angle DBA$ ...(i)(Alternate interior angles)

(i) Now, in $\Delta\ APB$ and $\Delta\ CQD$, we have

$CD = AB$ (Sides of parallelogram)

$\angle CQD = \angle APB = 90°$ (Given)

$\angle CDQ = \angle ABP$ [From Eq. (i)]

$\therefore$ $\Delta APB \cong \Delta CQD$ (By ASA rule)

(ii) $\because$ $\Delta APB \cong \Delta CQD$

$\therefore$ $AP = CQ$ (By CPCT)

Hence Proved.

Mistake Alert Diagonals of parallelogram are not the angle bisector.

Question 7 $ABCD$ is a trapezium in which $AB \parallel CD$ and $AD = BC$ (see figure). Show that

(i) $\angle A = \angle B$ (ii) $\angle C = \angle D$

(iii) $\Delta ABC \cong \Delta BAD$ (iv) diagonal AC = diagonal BD

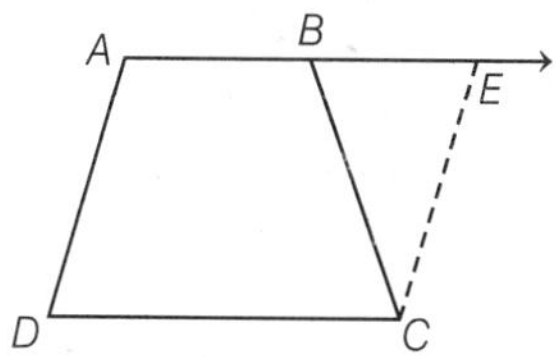

Hint Extend AB and draw a line through C parallel to DA intersecting AB produced at E.

Sol. Given, $ABCD$ is a trapezium.

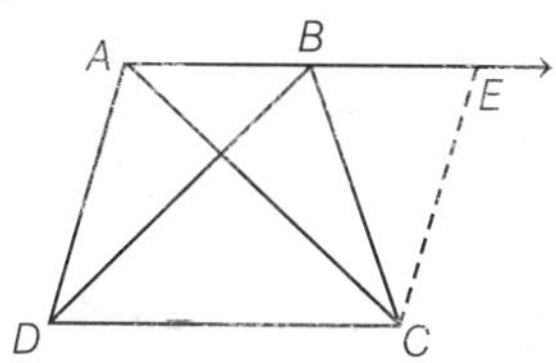

$AB \parallel CD$ and $AD = BC$

Now, extend AB and draw a line through C parallel to DA intersecting AB produced at E.

Now, $ADCE$ is a parallelogram.

$\therefore$ $AD \parallel CE$ and $AD = CE$

But $AD = BC$

$\therefore$ $AD = BC = CE$

(i) We know that, $\angle A + \angle E = 180°$

($\because$ Interior angles on the same side of the transversal AE)

$\Rightarrow$ $\angle E = 180° - \angle A$

Since, $BC = EC$

$\therefore$ $\angle CBE = \angle CEB$

(In a triangle angle opposite to equal sides are equal)

$\therefore$ $\angle E = \angle CBE = 180° - \angle A$

Also, $\angle ABC = 180° - \angle CBE$ ($\because$ ABE is straight line)

$= 180° - 180° + \angle A$

$\Rightarrow$ $\angle B = \angle A$ ...(i)

(ii) Now, $\angle A + \angle D = 180°$

($\because$ Interior angles on the same side of the transversal AD)

$\Rightarrow$ $\angle D = 180° - \angle A$

$\Rightarrow$ $\angle D = 180° - \angle B$ [From Eq. (i)]...(ii)

Also, $\angle C + \angle B = 180°$

($\because$ Interior angles on the same side of the transversal BC)

$\Rightarrow$ $\angle C = 180° - \angle B$ ...(iii)

From Eqs. (ii) and (iii), we get

$\angle C = \angle D$

(iii) Now, in Δ ABC and Δ BAD, we have

$AB = BA$ (Common)

$AD = BC$ (Given)

$\angle A = \angle B$ [From Eq. (i)]

$\therefore$ $\Delta ABC \cong \Delta BAD$ (By SAS)

(iv) Since, $\Delta ABC \cong \Delta BAD$

$\therefore$ $AC = BD$ (By CPCT) **Hence Proved.**

Exercise 8.2

Question 1 $ABCD$ is a quadrilateral in which P, Q, R and S are mid-points of the sides AB, BC, CD and DA (see figure). AC is a diagonal. Show that

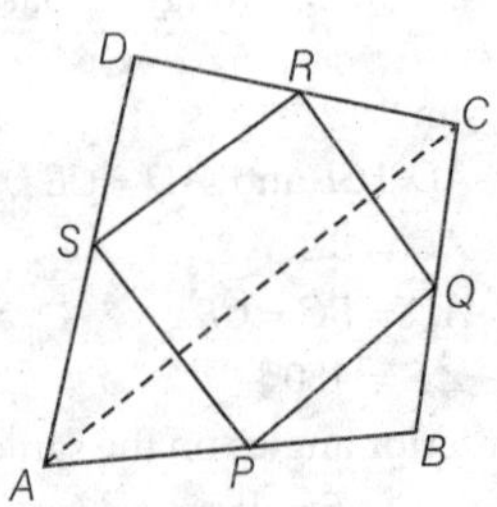

(i) $SR \parallel AC$ and $SR = \frac{1}{2} AC$

(ii) $PQ = SR$

(iii) $PQRS$ is a parallelogram.

◎ ***Thinking Process*** The line joining the two mid-points of sides of a triangle is parallel to third side and half its length.

Sol. Given, P, Q, R and S are mid-points of the sides.

$\therefore \quad AP = PB, BQ = CQ$

$CR = DR$

and $\quad AS = DS$

(i) In ΔADC, we have

S is mid-point of AD and R is mid-point of the DC.

We know that, the line segment joining the mid-points of two sides of a triangle is parallel to the third side.

$\therefore \quad SR \parallel AC \quad$ ...(i)

Also, $\quad SR = \frac{1}{2} AC \quad$ ...(ii)

Similarly, in ΔABC, we have

$PQ \parallel AC \quad$ ...(iii)

and $\quad PQ = \frac{1}{2} AC \quad$ ...(iv)

(ii) Now, from Eqs. (i) and (ii), we get

$PQ \parallel SR$

and $\quad PQ = SR \quad$ ...(v)

(iii) Now, from Eqs. (i) and (iii), we get

$PQ \parallel SR$

and from Eq. (v), $\quad PQ = SR$

Since, a pair of opposite sides of a quadrilateral $PQRS$ is equal and parallel.

So, $PQRS$ is a parallelogram. **Hence Proved.**

Question 2 $ABCD$ is a rhombus and P, Q, R and S are the mid-points of the sides AB, BC, CD and DA, respectively. Show that the quadrilateral $PQRS$ is a rectangle.

Sol. Given, $ABCD$ is a rhombus and P, Q, R and S are mid-points of AB, BC, CD and DA.

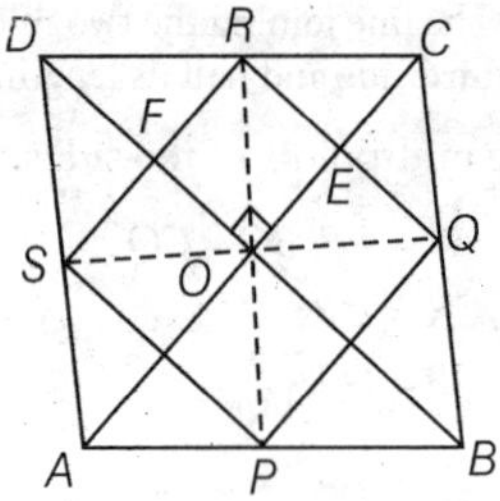

By mid-point theorem,

In ΔADC, $SR \parallel AC$ and $SR = \frac{1}{2} AC$ ...(i)

In ΔABC, $PQ \parallel AC$ and $PQ = \frac{1}{2} AC$ ...(ii)

From Eqs. (i) and (ii), we get

$$PQ \parallel SR \text{ and } PQ = SR = \frac{1}{2} AC$$

We know that in a quadrilateral $PQRS$ if it one pair of opposite sides PQ and SR is equal and parallel, then it is a parallelogram.

$\therefore PQRS$ is a parallelogram.

Now, we know that diagonals of a rhombus bisect each other at right angles.

$\therefore$ $\angle EOF = 90°$

Now, $RQ \parallel BD$ (By mid-point theorem)

$\Rightarrow$ $RE \parallel OF$

Also, $SR \parallel AC$ [From Eq. (i)]

$\Rightarrow$ $FR \parallel OE$

$\therefore OERF$ is a parallelogram.

So, $\angle ERF = \angle EOF = 90°$

(Opposite angle of a quadrilateral is equal)

Thus, $PQRS$ is a parallelogram with $\angle R = 90°$.

Hence, $PQRS$ is a rectangle.

Question 3 *ABCD* is a rectangle and *P*, *Q*, *R* and *S* are mid-points of the sides *AB*, *BC*, *CD* and *DA*, respectively. Show that the quadrilateral *PQRS* is a rhombus.

◎ ***Thinking Process*** The line joining the mid-point of two sides of a triangle is parallel to third side and half of its length.

Sol. Given, *ABCD* is a rectangle.

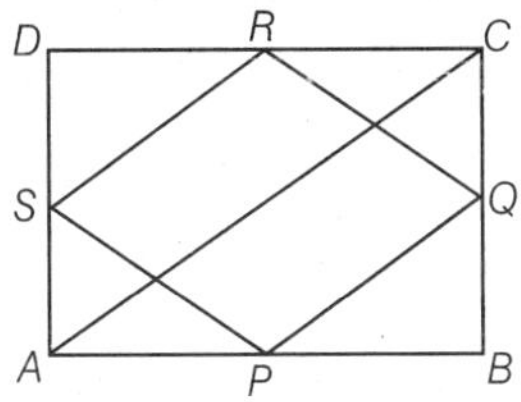

$\therefore \quad \angle A = \angle B = \angle C = \angle D = 90°$

and $\quad AD = BC,\ AB = CD$

Also, given *P*, *Q*, *R* and *S* are mid-points of *AB*, *BC*, *CD* and *DA*, respectively.

$\therefore \quad PQ \parallel AC$ and $PQ = \frac{1}{2} AC$ ...(i) (By mid-point theorem)

and $\quad SR \parallel AC$ and $SR = \frac{1}{2} AC$ ...(ii) (By mid-point theorem)

From Eqs. (i) and (ii), we get

$PQ \parallel SR$ and $PQ = SR$ ...(iii)

$\therefore$ *PQRS* is a parallelogram

Now, $\quad AD = BC$ ...(iv) (Opposite sides of rectangle *ABCD*)

$$\frac{1}{2} AD = \frac{1}{2} BC$$

$\Rightarrow \quad AS = BQ$ ...(v)

$\Rightarrow \quad DS = CQ$ ...(vi)

Now, in ΔASP and ΔBQP

$AP = BP$ (*P* is the mid-point of sides *AB*)

$AS = BQ$ [from Eq. (v)]

$\angle A = \angle B$ (Each 90°)

$\therefore \quad \Delta ASP \cong \Delta BQP$ (By SAS rule)

$\therefore \quad SP = PQ$ (By CPCT)...(vii)

Similarly, in ΔRDS and ΔRCQ,

$SD = CQ$ [from Eq. (vi)]

$DR = RC$ (*R* is the mid-point of sides *DC*)

$\angle C = \angle D$ (Each 90°)

$\therefore$ $\Delta RDS \cong \Delta RCQ$ (By SAS rule)

$\therefore$ $SR = RQ$ (By CPCT)...(viii)

From equation (iii), (vii) and (viii), we get

$$PS = PQ = QR = RS$$

It is clear that quadrilateral $PQRS$ is a rhombus.

Question 4 $ABCD$ is a trapezium in which $AB \parallel DC$, BD is a diagonal and E is the mid-point of AD. A line is drawn through E parallel to AB intersecting BC at F (see figure). Show that F is the mid-point of BC.

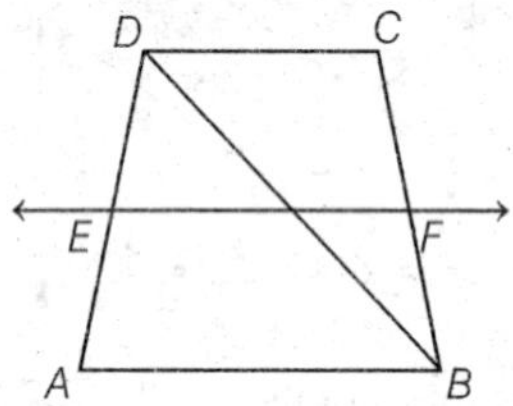

Sol. Given, $ABCD$ is a trapezium in which $AB \parallel CD$ and E is mid-point of AD and $EF \parallel AB$.

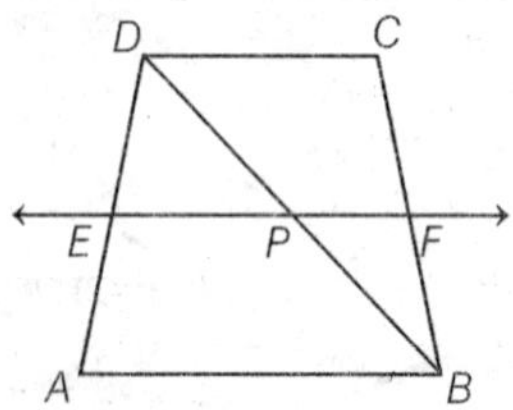

In ΔABD, we have

$$EP \parallel AB$$

and E is mid-point of AD.

So, by theorem, if a line drawn through the mid-point of one side of a triangle parallel to another side bisect the third side.

$\therefore$ P is mid-point of BD.

Similarly, in ΔBCD, we have,

$PF \parallel CD$ $[\because EF \parallel AB \parallel CD]$

and P is mid-point of BD.

So, by converse of mid-point theorem, F is mid-point of CB.

Mistake Alert In trapezium, only one pair of opposite sides are parallel but not equal.

Question 5 In a parallelogram $ABCD$, E and F are the mid-points of sides AB and CD respectively (see figure). Show that the line segments AF and EC trisect the diagonal BD.

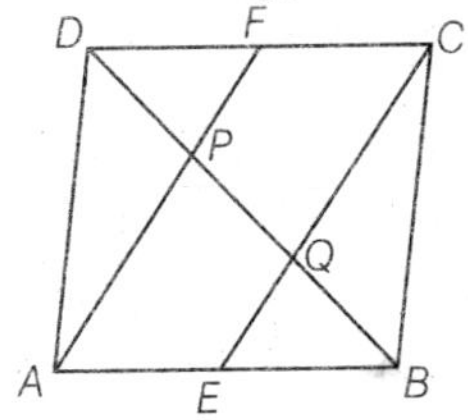

Sol. Given, $ABCD$ is a parallelogram and E, F are the mid-points of sides AB and CD respectively.

To prove Line segments AF and EC trisect the diagonal BD.

Proof Since, $ABCD$ is a parallelogram.

$AB \parallel DC$

and $AB = DC$ (Opposite sides of a parallelogram)

$\Rightarrow$ $AE \parallel FC$ and $\frac{1}{2} AB = \frac{1}{2} DC$

$\Rightarrow$ $AE \parallel FC$ and $AE = FC$

$\therefore$ $AECF$ is a parallelogram.

$\therefore$ $AF \parallel EC \Rightarrow EQ \parallel AP$ and $FP \parallel CQ$

In ΔBAP, E is the mid-point of AB and $EQ \parallel AP$, so Q is the mid-point of BP.

(By converse of mid-point theorem)

$\therefore$ $BQ = PQ$ ...(i)

Again, in ΔDQC, F is the mid-point of DC and $FP \parallel CQ$, so P is the mid-point of DQ. (By converse of mid-point theorem)

$\therefore$ $QP = DP$ ...(ii)

From Eqs. (i) and (ii), we get

$BQ = PQ = PD$

Hence, CE and AF trisect the diagonal BD.

Question 6 ABC is a triangle right angled at C. A line through the mid-point M of hypotenuse AB and parallel to BC intersects AC at D. Show that

(i) D is the mid-point of AC (ii) $MD \perp AC$

(iii) $CM = MA = \frac{1}{2} AB$

Sol. Given, ABC is a right angled triangle.

$$\angle C = 90^\circ$$

and M is the mid-point of AB.

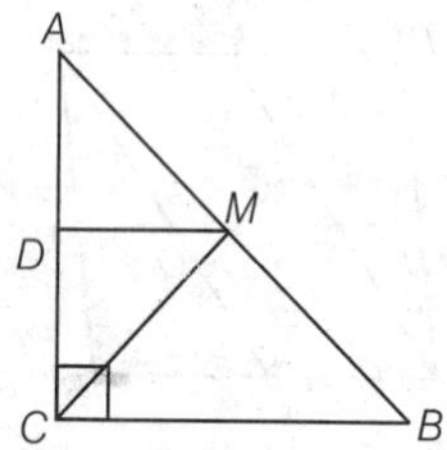

Also, $DM \parallel BC$

(i) In $\Delta\ ABC$, $BC \parallel MD$ and M is mid-point of AB.

$\therefore$ D is the mid-point of AC.

(By converse of mid-point theorem)

(ii) Since, $MD \parallel BC$ and CD is transversal.

$\therefore \quad \angle ADM = \angle ACB$ (Corresponding angles)

But $\quad \angle ACB = 90^\circ$

$\therefore \quad \angle ADM = 90^\circ \Rightarrow MD \perp AC$

(iii) Now, in $\Delta\ ADM$ and $\Delta\ CDM$, we have

$DM = MD$ (Common)

$AD = CD$ ($\because$ D is mid point of AC)

$\angle ADM = \angle MDC$ (Each equal to 90°)

$\therefore \quad \Delta\ ADM \cong \Delta\ CDM$ (By SAS)

$\therefore \quad CM = AM$ (By CPCT)...(i)

$\because$ M is mid-point of AB,

$\therefore \quad AM = BM = \frac{1}{2} AB$ ...(ii)

From Eqs. (i) and (ii), we get

$CM = AM = \frac{1}{2} AB$ **Hence Proved.**

DIKSHA APP Questions

☐ Multiple Choice Questions

Q.1 A parallelogram with one of its angles as a right angle is a

(a) rectangle (b) square

(c) rhombus (d) kite

Sol. (a) Let $\square PQRS$ is a parallelogram.

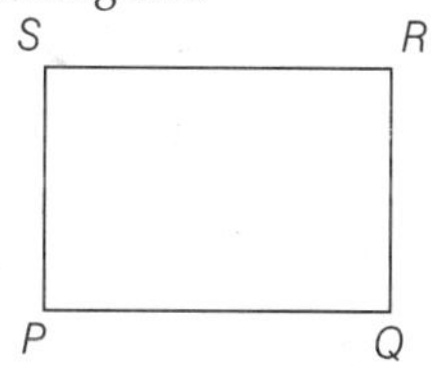

$$\angle SPQ = \angle SRQ$$

[$\because$ opposite angles are equal in parallelogram]...(i)

and $\qquad \angle SPQ + \angle PQR = 180°$

[$\because$ interior angles on the same side of the transversal PQ]...(ii)

Let $\angle SPQ$ is right angle.

$\therefore \qquad \angle SRQ = 90° \qquad$ [From Eq. (i)]

and $\qquad \angle PQR = 90° \qquad$ [From Eq. (ii)]

$\therefore \qquad \angle PSR = 90°$

$\because$ All the angle of parallelogram is 90°.

$\therefore \square PQRS$ is a rectangle.

Q.2 $ABCD$ is a parallelogram. X is the mid-point of BC and Y is the mid-point of CD. XY meet diagonal AC at P. Then, $CP = \ldots\ldots$

(a) $\dfrac{1}{2}AC$ (b) $\dfrac{1}{4}AC$

(c) $\dfrac{3}{4}AC$ (d) None of these

Sol. (b)

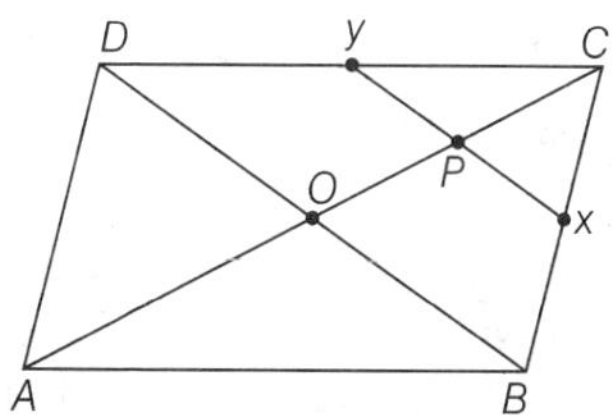

In parallelogram $ABCD$, X and Y are the mid-points of side BC and CD.

$\therefore AC$ and BD are diagonals of $ABCD$.

In ΔCBD by mid-point theorem

$$XY = \frac{BD}{2} \text{ and } XY \parallel BD \qquad \ldots(i)$$

From Eq. (i)

$$XY \parallel BD$$

$\therefore \qquad PY \parallel OD$

Now in ΔOCD,

Y is mid-point of CD and $PY \parallel OD$.

So, by converse of mid-point theorem,

P is mid-point of OC.

$\therefore \qquad CP = \frac{1}{2} OC$

$\Rightarrow \qquad CP = \frac{1}{2} \times \frac{1}{2} AC$

[Diagonal of parallelogram bisects each other.]

$\Rightarrow \qquad CP = \frac{1}{4} AC$

Q.3 The diagonals AC and BD of a parallelogram $ABCD$ intersect each other at the point O. If $\angle DAC = 32°$ and $\angle AOB = 72°$, then $\angle DBC$ is

(a) 32° (b) 40° (c) 24° (d) 60°

◎ ***Thinking Process*** The sum of all the angles of a triangle is 180°.

Sol. (b)

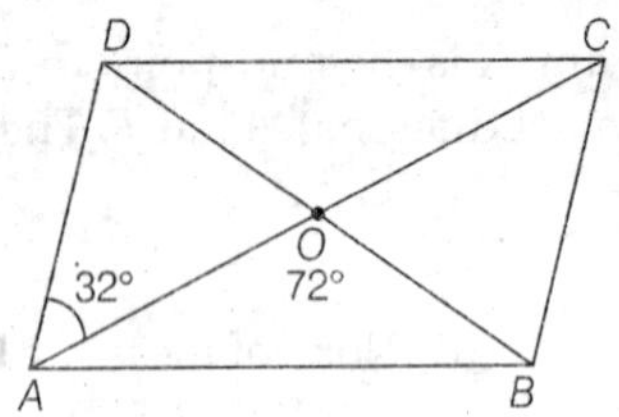

Given, $ABCD$ is a parallelogram and diagonals BD and AC intersect at O.

$$\angle DAC = 32° \text{ and } \angle AOB = 72°$$

To find $\angle DBC$

Now, $ABCD$ is a parallelogram

Then, $AD \parallel BC$, and AC is transversal

$\angle DAC = \angle BCO = 32°$ [Alternate interior angles]

$\angle AOB + \angle BOC = 180°$ (Linear pair axiom)

$72° + \angle BOC = 180°$

$\angle BOC = 108°$

Now, in ΔOBC

$\angle BOC + \angle OCB + \angle OBC = 180°$ [Angle sum property of triangle]

$108° + 32° + \angle OBC = 180°$

$\angle OBC = 180° - 140°$

$\angle OBC = 40° \Rightarrow \angle DBC = 40°$

Q.4 Which of the following statement is true?

(a) A trapezium is a parallelogram.

(b) Every rectangle is a parallelogram.

(c) Every parallelogram is a rectangle.

(d) Every rhombus is a square.

Sol. (b) Option (b) is correct because opposite sides of rectangle is equal and parallel to each other.

Q.5 The figure obtained by joining the mid-points of the sides of a rhombus,

(a) a square

(b) a rhombus

(c) a parallelogram

(d) a rectangle

Sol. (d) Consider $ABCD$ as a rhombus with P, Q, R and S as the mid-points of AB, BC, CD, AD respectively.

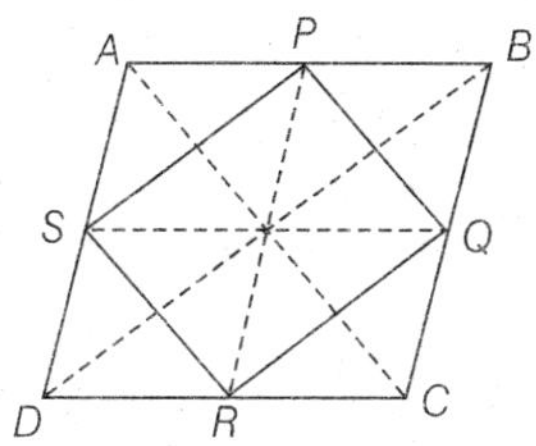

In ΔABC, P is the mid-point of AB and Q is the mid-point of BC.

$\therefore$ $$PQ \parallel AC \text{ and } PQ = \frac{1}{2} AC$$

[by using midpoint theorem] ...(i)

Similarly, in ΔDAC,

$$SR \parallel AC \text{ and } SR = \frac{1}{2} AC \quad \text{...(ii)}$$

From Eqs. (i) and (ii), we get

$$PQ \parallel SR \text{ and } PQ = SR$$

So, $PQRS$ is a parallelogram.

Also, $ABQS$ is a parallelogram.

$\therefore$ $$AB = SQ \quad \text{...(iii)}$$

[Opposite sides of a parallelogram are equal]

Similarly, *PBCR* is a parallelograms

$\therefore$ $BC = PR$ [opposite sides of parallelogram are equal]

$\therefore$ $AB = PR$ [$\because$ $BC = AB$ sides of a rhombus]

$\therefore$ $SQ = PR$

So, the diagonal of a parallelogram are equal.

Hence, *PQRS* is a rectangle.

Note If the diagonals of a parallelogram are equal then the parallelogram is a rectangle.

☐ Subjective Type Questions

Q.1 A diagonals of a parallelogram divides it into how many congruent triangles.

Sol. Two

Q.2 In a square *ABCD*, the diagonals *AC* and *BD* bisect at *O*, then ΔAOB is which type of triangle?

Sol.

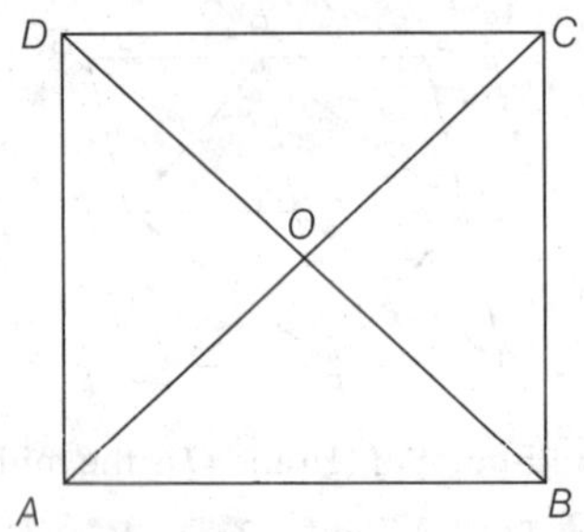

As we know, the diagonals of a square are equal in length and also perpendicular bisector of each other.

$\therefore$ $AC = BD \Rightarrow \frac{1}{2}AC = \frac{1}{2}BD$

$\Rightarrow$ $AO = OB$ and $\angle AOB = 90°$

$\therefore$ ΔAOB is a right angled isosceles triangle.

Q.3 *ABCD* is a rhombus such that $\angle ACB = 40°$, then what is $\angle ADB$?

◎ ***Thinking Process*** Diagonals of rhombus are perpendicular bisector.

Sol. Let $\angle ADB$ be x.

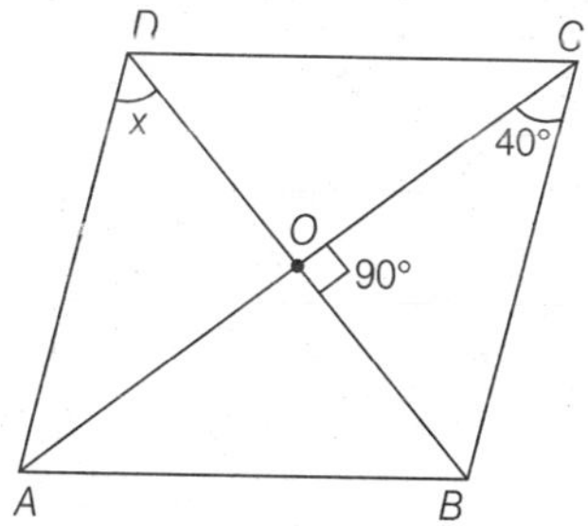

As we know, diagonals of rhombus are perpendicular bisector of each other.

$\therefore$ $\angle BOC = 90°$

In ΔBOC

$$\angle OBC + \angle BCO + \angle COB = 180°$$

$\Rightarrow$ $\angle OBC + 40° + 90° = 180°$

$\Rightarrow$ $\angle OBC + 130° = 180°$

$\Rightarrow$ $\angle OBC = 50°$

Since, $AD \parallel BC$

Thus $\angle ADB = \angle DBC$ [Alternate interior angles]

$\Rightarrow$ $x = 50°$

Hence, $\angle ADB = 50°$

Q.4 Three angles of a quadrilateral are 60°, 70° and 80° calculate the fourth angle.

Sol. Let the fourth angle be x.

So, $60° + 70° + 80° + x = 360°$

[By angle sum property of quadrilaterals]

$\Rightarrow$ $210° + x = 360°$

$\Rightarrow$ $x = 360° - 210°$

$\Rightarrow$ $x = 150°$

Hence, the fourth angle is 150°.

Q.5 In a parallelogram $ABCD$, if $\angle A = (4x + 20)$, $\angle C = 110 - 5x$, then find x.

Sol.

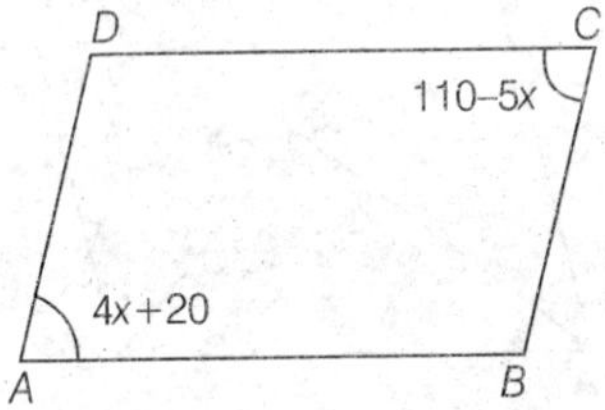

$\angle A = \angle C$ [Opposite angle of parallelogram are equal]

$\therefore$ $4x + 20 = 110 - 5x$

$\Rightarrow$ $4x + 5x = 110 - 20$

$\Rightarrow$ $9x = 90$

$\Rightarrow$ $x = 10$

Q.6 In figure, bisectors of $\angle B$ and $\angle D$ of quadrilateral $ABCD$ meets CD and AB, produced at P and Q respectively.
Prove that $\angle P + \angle Q = \frac{1}{2}(\angle ABC + \angle ADC)$

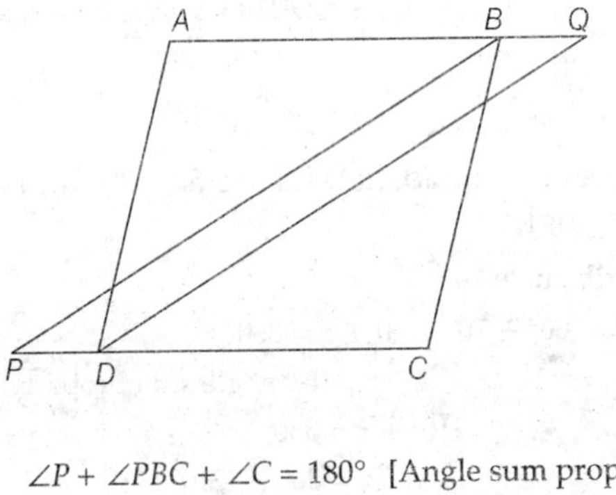

Sol. In ΔPBC

$\angle P + \angle PBC + \angle C = 180°$ [Angle sum property of triangle]

$\Rightarrow$ $\angle P + \frac{1}{2}\angle B + \angle C = 180°$ ... (i)

In ΔQAD

$\angle Q + \angle A + \angle ADQ = 180°$ [Angle sum property of triangle]

$\Rightarrow$ $\angle Q + \angle A + \frac{1}{2}\angle D = 180°$ ... (ii)

Adding Eqs. (i) and (ii), we get

$$\angle P + \frac{1}{2}\angle B + \angle C + \angle Q + \angle A + \frac{1}{2}\angle D = 360°$$

$$\Rightarrow \quad \angle P + \frac{1}{2}\angle B + \angle C + \angle Q + \angle A + \frac{1}{2}\angle D$$

$$= \angle A + \angle B + \angle C + \angle D \quad \text{[Angle of quadrilateral]}$$

$$\Rightarrow \quad \angle P + \angle Q = \angle B - \frac{1}{2}\angle B + \angle D - \frac{1}{2}\angle D$$

$$\Rightarrow \quad \angle P + \angle Q = \frac{\angle B}{2} + \frac{\angle D}{2}$$

$$\Rightarrow \quad \angle P + \angle Q = \frac{1}{2}(\angle B + \angle D)$$

$$\Rightarrow \quad \angle P + \angle Q = \frac{1}{2}(\angle ABC + \angle ADC)$$

Hence Proved.

Q.7 *ABCD* is a parallelogram. *AB* produced to *E* so that $BE = AB$. Prove that the *ED* bisects *BC*.

Sol.

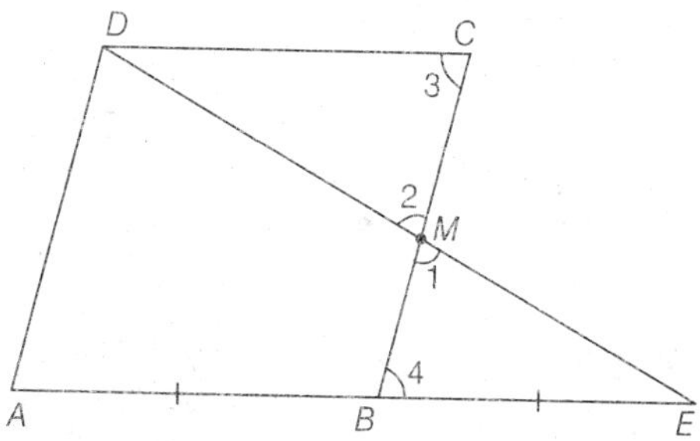

Given, *ABCD* is a parallelogram.

and $AB = BE$

To Prove *M* is the mid-point of side *BC*.

$\Rightarrow \quad BM = MC$

Proof As $AB = BE$

Then, *B* is the mid-point of side *AE*

ABCD is a parallelogram.

$\Rightarrow \quad AB \parallel CD \Rightarrow AE \parallel CD$, *CB* is the transversal

$\Rightarrow \quad \angle 3 = \angle 4$ [Alternate angles are equal]

Now, in ΔMCD and ΔMBE

$CD = AB = BE$ [Given]

$\angle 2 = \angle 1$ [Vertically opposite angles]

$\angle 3 = \angle 4$ [Alternate angles]

$\Delta MCD \cong \Delta MBE$ [By ASA rule]

$\Rightarrow \quad BM = MC$ [By CPCT]

M is the mid-point of side *BC*.

$\Rightarrow$ *ED* bisects side *BC*.

Q.8 In a parallelogram $ABCD$, bisectors of angles A and B intersect each other at E which lies on DC. Find $\angle AEB$.

Sol.

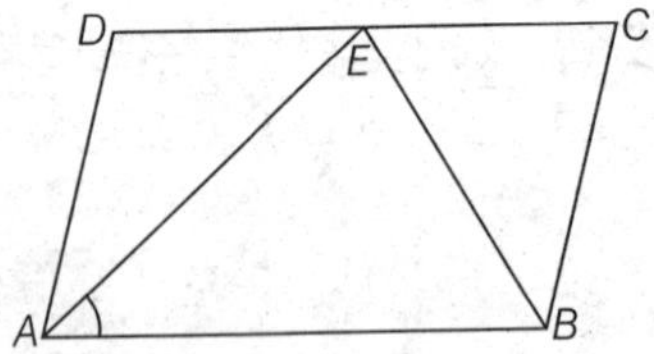

$ABCD$ is a parallelogram,

$\Rightarrow \quad \angle A + \angle B = 180°$

(Sum of adjacent angles of parallelogram are supplementary)

$\Rightarrow \quad \frac{1}{2}\angle A + \frac{1}{2}\angle B = \frac{180°}{2}$

$\Rightarrow \quad \angle EAB + \angle EBA = 90° \quad$ ... (i)

In ΔAEB,

$\Rightarrow \quad \angle AEB + \angle EAB + \angle EBA = 180° \quad$ [Angle sum property of triangle.]

$\Rightarrow \quad \angle AEB + 90° = 180° \quad$ [from Eq. (i)]

$\angle AEB = 90°$

Q.9 Complete the grid given below (write yes/no).

SN	Property	Square	Rhombus	Rectangle	Trapezium	Parallelog-ram
(i)	Opposite sides are equal and parallel					
(ii)	Adjacent sides are equal					
(iii)	Diagonals bisect each other					
(iv)	Diagonals bisect at 90°					
(v)	Diagonals are equal in length					

Sol.

SN.	Property	Square	Rhombus	Rectangle	Trapezium	Parallelog-ram
(i)	Opposite sides are equal and parallel	Yes	Yes	Yes	No	Yes
(ii)	Adjacent sides are equal	Yes	Yes	No	No	No
(iii)	Diagonals bisect each other	Yes	Yes	Yes	No	Yes
(iv)	Diagonals bisect at 90°	Yes	Yes	No	No	No
(v)	Diagonals are equal in length	Yes	No	Yes	No	Yes

Q.10 In ΔABC, find the measures of the angles of the triangle formed by joining the mid-points of the sides of this triangle.

Sol.

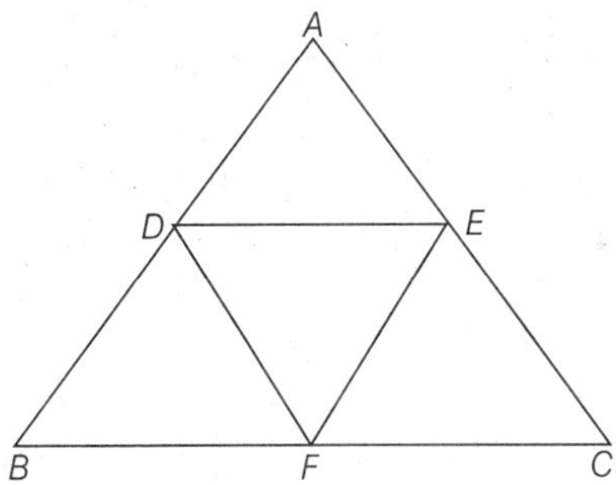

Let D, E, F are the mid-points of sides AB, AC, BC, respectively.

Now, $DE \parallel BC, DE = \frac{1}{2}BC$ ...(i) [By mid-point theorem]

Similarly, $EF \parallel AB, EF = \frac{1}{2}AB$ ... (ii)

$DF \parallel AC, DF = \frac{1}{2}AC$ ... (iii)

From Eqs. (i), (ii) and (iii), we get

$ADFE, DEFB, DFCE$ are a parallelogram

In parallelogram, opposite sides are equal or parallel and also opposite angles are equal.

$\therefore$ $\angle A = \angle F, \angle D = \angle C, \angle E = \angle B$ **Hence Proved.**

Q.11 Prove that the straight line joining the mid-points of the diagonals of the trapezium is parallel to parallel sides of it. And is equal to half of their difference.

Sol. Let $PQRS$ is a trapezium.

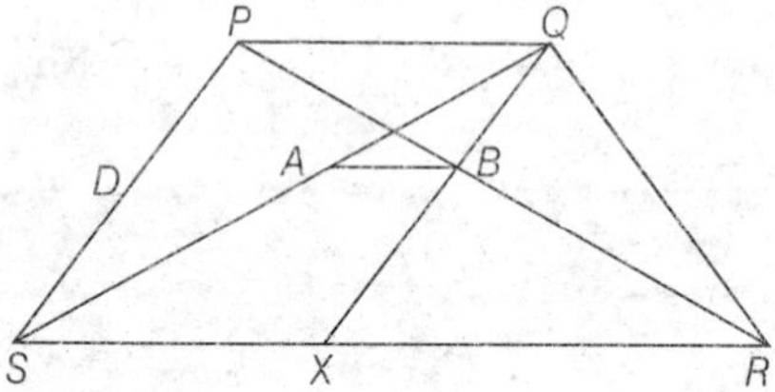

Given, $PQRS$ is a trapezium and B, A are the mid-points of diagonals PR and SQ of trapezium $PQRS$.

To Prove $PQ \parallel AB$ or $SR \parallel AB$ and

$$AB = \frac{SR - PQ}{2}$$

Proof Now, $PQ \parallel SR$ and SQ and PR are diagonals.

$$\angle QSR = \angle PQS \quad \text{... (i) [Alternate interior angles]}$$

$$\angle QPR = \angle PRS \quad \text{... (ii)[Alternate interior angles]}$$

In ΔQBP and ΔXBR

$$RB = BP \quad (B \text{ is the mid-point of side } PR)$$

$$\angle QPB = \angle BRX \quad \text{[From Eq. (ii)]}$$

$$\angle PQB = \angle BXR \quad [\because PQ \parallel XR \text{ and transversal} \times Q \text{ intersect}]$$

$$\Delta QBP \cong \Delta XBR \quad \text{[By AAS Rule]}$$

$$\Rightarrow \quad BQ = XB$$

$$PQ = XR \quad \text{[By CPCT]}$$

Again in ΔQSX

A, B are the mid-points of side SQ and XQ

So, by mid point theorem $AB \parallel SX$

$$\therefore \quad AB \parallel PQ$$

Also,
$$AB = \frac{SX}{2} = \frac{SR - XR}{2} = \frac{SR - PQ}{2} \quad [\because XR = PQ]$$

Q.12 In the following figure, $BE \perp AC$. AD is any line from A to BC intersecting BE in H. P, Q, R are respectively the mid-points of AH, AB and BC. Prove that $\angle PQR = 90°$.

Sol.

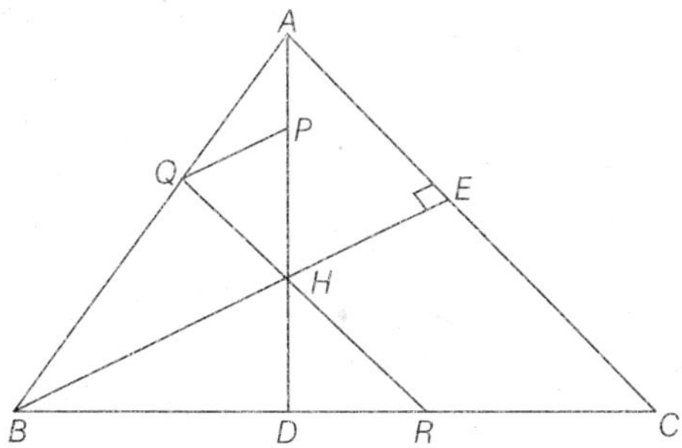

In ΔABC, Q, R are the mid-point of AB and BC respectively.

$\therefore$ $$QR \parallel AC \quad \text{... (i)[By mid-point theorem]}$$

In ΔABH, Q and P are the mid-points of AB and AH respectively.

$\therefore$ $$QP \parallel BH \Rightarrow QP \parallel BE \quad \text{... (ii)}$$

But $AC \perp BE$ therefore from Eqs. (i) and (ii)

$$QP \perp QR \Rightarrow \angle PQR = 90°$$ **Hence Proved.**

Q.13 P, Q, R are respectively, the mid-points of sides BC, CA and AB of a ΔABC. PR and BQ meet at X. CR and PQ meet at Y.

Prove that $XY = \frac{1}{4} BC$

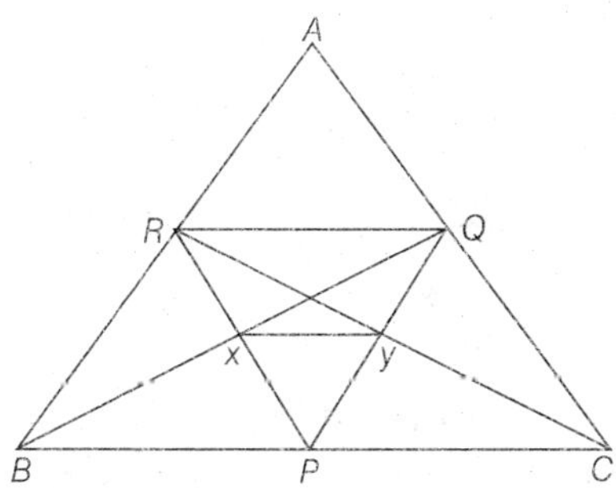

Sol. In a triangle, line joining mid-points of two sides are parallel and half of third side.

$\therefore$ $$PQ \parallel AB$$

and $$PQ = \frac{1}{2} AB \quad \text{... (i)}$$

$$QR \parallel BC \Rightarrow QR = \frac{1}{2} BC \quad \text{...(ii)}$$

$$PR \parallel AC \Rightarrow PR = \frac{1}{2} AC \quad \text{...(iii)}$$

From Eqs. (i) and (ii), we get

Two pairs are parallel, so $BPQR$ is parallelogram

$$BP = QR = \frac{BC}{2} \quad \text{...(iv)}$$

In parallelogram diagonals bisect each other.

So, X is mid-point to PR,

Similarly, Y is the mid-point on QP.

In ΔRPQ

$$XY = \frac{1}{2} QR \quad \text{[By mid-point theorem]}$$

$$\Rightarrow \quad XY = \frac{1}{2}\left(\frac{1}{2} BC\right) \quad \text{[From Eq. (iv)]}$$

$$\Rightarrow \quad XY = \frac{1}{4} BC$$

Hence Proved.

Circles

CHAPTER 09

Important Points

01 Circle The collection of all points in a plane which are at a fixed distance from a fixed point is called a circle.

e.g.,

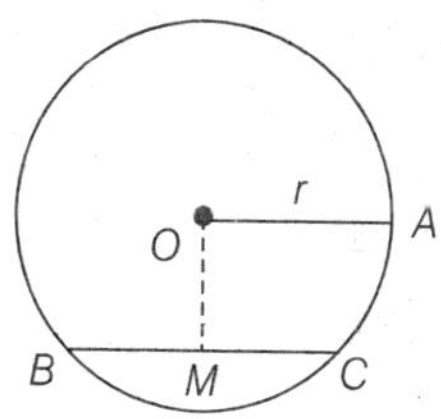

Here, O is the centre of the circle.

OA is radius of the circle.

BC is a chord and OM is the perpendicular distance from centre to the chord BC.

02 Important Theorems

(i) The perpendicular from the centre of a circle to a chord bisects the chord and it is *vice-versa*.

(ii) Equal chords of a circle (or of congruent circles) are equidistant from the centre.

(iii) If two chords of a circle are equal, then their corresponding arcs (major, minor or semi-circle) are congruent and conversely, if two arcs are congruent, then their corresponding chords are equal.

(iv) Congruent arcs of a circle subtend equal angles at the centre.

(v) The angle subtended by an arc at the centre is double the angle subtended by it at any point on the remaining part of the circle.

(vi) Angles in the same segment of a circle are equal.

(vii) The sum of either pair of opposite angles of a cyclic quadrilateral is 180° and *vice-versa.*

(viii) The angle in a semi-circle is a right angle.

(ix) Equal chords of a circle subtend equal angles at the centre.

(x) If the angles subtended by the chords of a circle at the centre are equal. Then, the chords are equal.

(xi) Chords equidistant from the centre of a circle are equal in length.

(xii) If a line segment joining two points subtends equal angles at two other points lying on the same side of the line containing the line segment, the points lie on a circle.

(xiii) The sum of either pair of opposite angles of a cyclie quadrilateral is 180°.

(xiv) If the sum of a pair of opposite angles of a quadrilateral is 180°, the quadrilateral is cyclic.

03 Cyclic Quadrilaterals A quadrilaterals *ABCD* is called cyclic if all the four vertices of its lie on a circle.

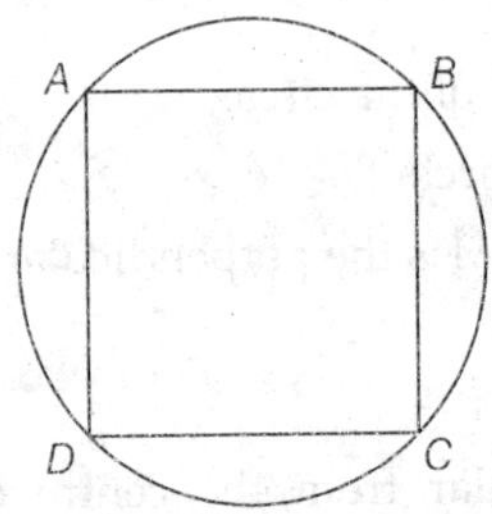

Exercise 9.1

Question 1 Recall that two circles are congruent, if they have the same radii. Prove that equal chords of congruent circles subtend equal angles at their centres.

◎ *Thinking Process* If all three sides of one triangle are equal to the corresponding sides of another triangle, then the two triangles are congruent.

Sol. Given, MN and PQ are two equal chords of two congruent circles with centre at O and O'.

To prove $\angle MON = \angle PO'Q$

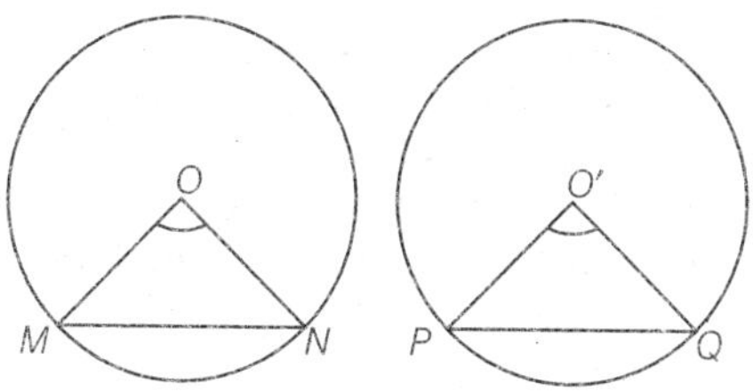

Proof In $\Delta\, MON$ and $\Delta\, PO'Q$, we have

$MO = PO'$ (Radii of congruent circles)

$NO = QO'$ (Radii of congruent circles)

and $MN = PQ$ (Given)

$\therefore$ By SSS criterion, we get

$$\Delta\, MON \cong \Delta\, PO'Q$$

Hence, $\angle MON = \angle PO'Q$ (By CPCT)

Question 2 Prove that, if chords of congruent circles subtend equal angles at their centres, then the chords are equal.

Sol. Given, MN and PQ are two chords of congruent circles such that angles subtended by these chords at the centres O and O' of the circles are equal.

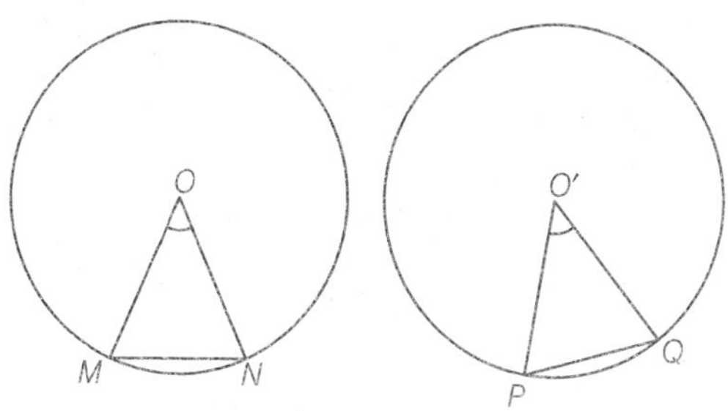

i.e., $\angle MON = \angle PO'Q$

To prove $MN = PQ$

Proof In ΔMON and $\Delta PO'Q$, we get

$MO = PO'$ (Radii of congruent circles)

$NO = QO'$ (Radii of congruent circles)

and $\angle MON = \angle PO'Q$ (Given)

$\therefore$ By SAS criterion, we get

$\Delta MON \cong \Delta PO'Q$

Hence, $MN = PQ$ (By CPCT)

Exercise 9.2

Question 1 Two circles of radii 5 cm and 3 cm intersect at two points and the distance between their centres is 4 cm. Find the length of the common chord.

Sol. Let O and O' be the centres of the circles of radii 5 cm and 3 cm, respectively. Let AB be their common chord.

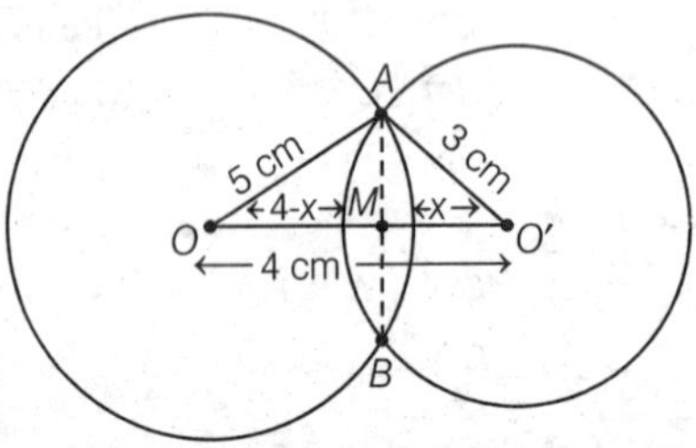

Given, $OA = 5\text{ cm}, O'A = 3\text{ cm}$ and $OO' = 4\text{ cm}$

Let $O'M = x$, then $OM = 4 - x$

$\because$ In two intersecting circles, the line joining their centres is perpendicular bisector of the common chord.

$\therefore$ $\angle OMA = \angle OMB = 90°$ and $AM = MB$

Now, in right ΔOMA, we have

$$AM^2 + OM^2 = OA^2 \quad [\because \text{Pythagoras theorem}]$$

$$\Rightarrow AM^2 + (4-x)^2 = 5^2$$

$$\Rightarrow AM^2 = 5^2 - (4-x)^2$$

$$\Rightarrow AM^2 = 25 - 16 - x^2 + 8x \quad [\because (a-b)^2 = a^2 + b^2 - 2ab]$$

$$\Rightarrow AM^2 = 9 - x^2 + 8x \quad \text{...(i)}$$

Again, in right $\Delta O'MA$,

$$AM^2 = AO'^2 - MO'^2 \quad [\because \text{Pythagoras theorem}]$$
$$= 3^2 - x^2 = 9 - x^2 \quad \ldots(ii)$$

From Eqs. (i) and (ii), we have

$$9 - x^2 + 8x = 9 - x^2 \Rightarrow 8x = 0 \Rightarrow x = 0$$

$\Rightarrow M$ and O' coincide

$\therefore$ AB is diameter of smaller circle

So, $AM = 3$ cm

But $AM = MB$

$\therefore$ $MB = 3$ cm

$\therefore$ $AB = AM + MB = 3 + 3 = 6$ cm

Thus, the required length of the common chord = 6 cm

Mistake Alert Students may assume that chord AB bisects OO' which will give an incorrect result.

Question 2 If two equal chords of a circle intersect within the circle, prove that the segments of one chord are equal to corresponding segments of the other chord.

Sol. Given, MN and AB are two chords of a circle with centre O, AB and MN intersect at P and $MN = AB$

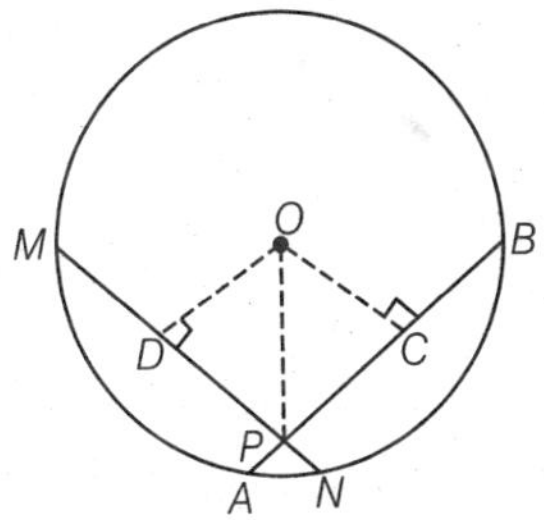

To prove $MP = PB$ and $PN = AP$

Construction Draw $OD \perp MN$ and $OC \perp AB$.

Join OP.

Proof $\because$ $DM = DN = \frac{1}{2} MN$

(Perpendicular from centre bisects the chord)

and $AC = CB = \frac{1}{2} AB$

(Perpendicular from centre bisects the chord)

$\therefore$ $MD = BC$ ...(i)

and $DN = AC$ ($\because MN = AB$) ...(ii)

In ΔODP and ΔOPC,

$$OD = OC$$

(Equal chords of a circle are equidistant from the centre)

$$\angle ODP = \angle OCP \quad \text{(each equal to } 90^\circ\text{)}$$

$$OP = OP \quad \text{(Common)}$$

$\therefore$ RHS criterion of congruence,

$$\Delta ODP \cong \Delta OCP$$

$\therefore$ $DP = PC$ (By CPCT)...(iii)

On adding Eqs. (i) and (iii), we get

$$MD + DP = BC + PC$$

$$MP = PB$$

On subtracting Eq. (iii) from Eq. (ii), we get

$$DN - DP = AC - PC$$

$\Rightarrow$ $PN = AP$

So, $MP = PB$ and $PN = AP$ **Hence Proved.**

Question 3 If two equal chords of a circle intersect within the circle, prove that the line joining the point of intersection to the centre makes equal angles with the chords.

Sol. Given, RQ and MN are chords of a circle with centre O. MN and RQ intersect at P and $MN = RQ$

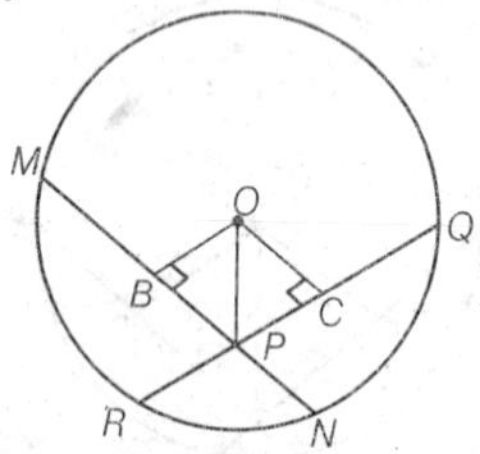

To prove $\angle OPC = \angle OPB$

Construction Draw $OC \perp RQ$ and $OB \perp MN$.
Join OP.

Proof In ΔOCP and ΔOBP, we get

$$\angle OCP = \angle OBP \quad \text{(Each} = 90^\circ\text{)}$$

$$OP = OP \quad \text{(Common)}$$

$$OC = OB$$

(Equal chords of a circle are equidistant from the centre)

$\therefore$ By RHS criterion of congruence, we get

$$\Delta OCP \cong \Delta OBP$$

$\therefore$ $\angle OPC = \angle OPB$ (By CPCT)

Question 4 If a line intersects two concentric circles (circles with the same centre) with centre O at A, B, C and D, prove that $AB = CD$ (see figure).

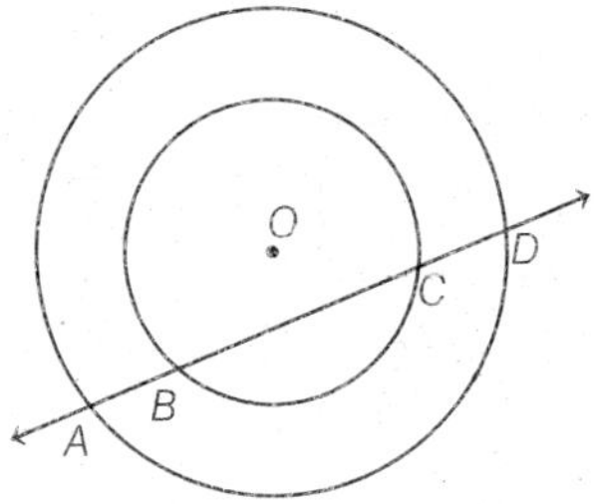

Sol. Let OP be the perpendicular from O on line l. Since, the perpendicular from the centre of a circle to a chord bisects the chords.

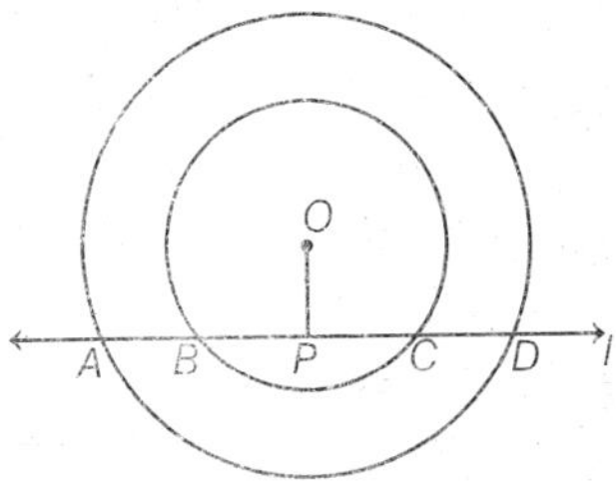

Since, BC is the chord of the smaller circle and $OP \perp BC$.

$\therefore \quad BP = PC \quad \ldots(i)$

Since, AD is a chord of the larger circle and $OP \perp AD$.

$\therefore \quad AP = PD \quad \ldots(ii)$

On subtracting Eq. (i) from Eq. (ii), we get

$$AP - BP = PD - PC$$

$\Rightarrow \quad AB = CD$ **Hence Proved.**

Question 5 Three girls Reshma, Salma and Mandip are playing a game by standing on a circle of radius 5m drawn in a park. Reshma throws a ball to Salma, Salma to Mandip, Mandip to Reshma. If the distance between Reshma and Salma and between Salma and Mandip is 6 m each, what is the distance between Reshma and Mandip?

Sol. Let O be the centre of the circle and the points R, S and M denote Reshma, Salma and Mandip respectively.

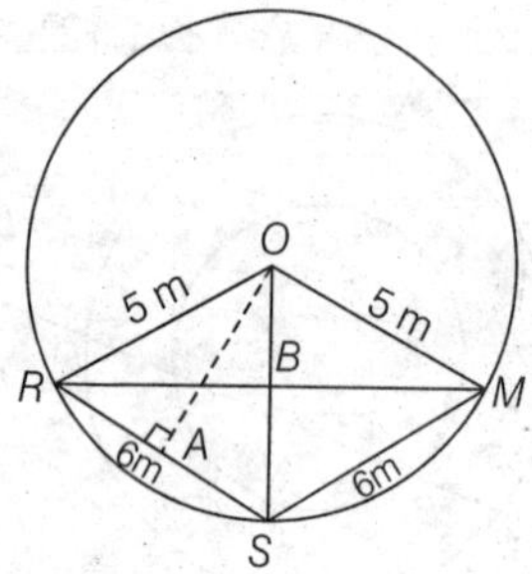

Now, draw a perpendicular OA to RS from O.

$\therefore$ $$RA = AS = 3\text{ m}$$

[$\because$ A perpendicular drawn from the centre of a circle to a chord, bisects the chord]

Now, in ΔORA,

$$(OR)^2 = (OA)^2 + (AR)^2 \quad \text{[By Pythagoras theorem]}$$

$\Rightarrow$ $$(5)^2 = (OA)^2 + (3)^2$$

$\Rightarrow$ $$(OA)^2 = 25 - 9 = 16$$

$\Rightarrow$ $$OA = 4\text{ m}$$

$\therefore$ Area of $$\Delta ORS = \frac{1}{2} \times RS \times OA$$

$$= \frac{1}{2} \times 6 \times 4 = 12\text{ m}^2 \quad \ldots\text{(i)}$$

As, $OR = OM = 5$ cm and $RS = SM = 6$ m

$\therefore$ Quadrilateral $ORSM$ is a kite.

We know that, the diagonals of a kite are perpendicular and the diagonal common to both the isosceles triangle is bisected by the another diagonal.

$\therefore$ $$\angle RBS = 90° \text{ and } RB = BM$$

Also, area of $$\Delta ORS = \frac{1}{2} \times OS \times RB$$

$$= \frac{1}{2} \times 5 \times RB \quad \ldots\text{(ii)} [\because OS \text{ is the radius of the circle}]$$

From Eqs. (i) and (ii), we get

$$12 = \frac{1}{2} \times 5 \times RB$$

$\Rightarrow$ $$RB = \frac{24}{5} = 4.8\text{ m}$$

$\therefore$ $$RM = 2 \times RB = 2 \times 4.8 = 9.6\text{ m}$$

So, the distance between Reshma and Salma is 9.6 m.

Question 6 A circular park of radius 20 m is situated in a colony. Three boys Ankur, Syed and David are sitting at equal distance on its boundary each having a toy telephone in his hands to talk each other. Find the length of the string of each phone.

◎ ***Thinking Process*** Three sides are equal in length form an equilateral triangle and in an equilateral triangle altitudes bisect their sides.

Sol. Let Ankur, Syed and David standing on the point P, Q and R.

Let $PQ = QR = PR = x$

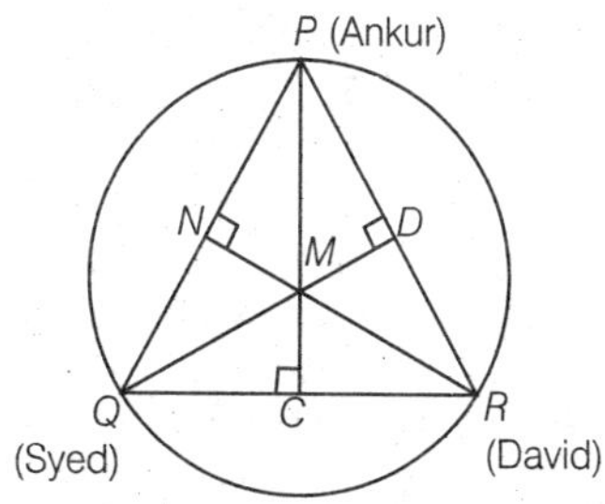

Therefore, ΔPQR is an equilateral triangle. Drawn altitudes PC, QD and RN from vertices to the sides of a triangle and intersect these altitudes at the centre of a circle M. As PQR is an equilateral triangle, therefore these altitudes bisects their sides.

In right ΔPCQ,

$$PQ^2 = PC^2 + QC^2 \qquad \text{(By Pythagoras theorem)}$$

$$\Rightarrow \quad x^2 = PC^2 + \left(\frac{x}{2}\right)^2 \qquad \left(\because QC = \frac{1}{2}QR = \frac{x}{2}\right)$$

$$\Rightarrow \quad PC^2 = x^2 - \frac{x^2}{4} = \frac{3x^2}{4}$$

$$\therefore \quad PC = \frac{\sqrt{3}x}{2}$$

Now,
$$MC = PC - PM = \frac{\sqrt{3}x}{2} - 20 \qquad (\because PM = \text{radius} = 20\,\text{m})$$

In right ΔQCM,
$$QM^2 = QC^2 + MC^2 \qquad \text{[By Pythagoras theorem]}$$

$$\therefore \quad (20)^2 = \left(\frac{x}{2}\right)^2 + \left(\frac{\sqrt{3}x}{2} - 20\right)^2 \qquad (\because QM = \text{radius} = 20\,\text{m})$$

$$\Rightarrow \quad 400 = \frac{x^2}{4} + \frac{3x^2}{4} - 20\sqrt{3}x + 400 \Rightarrow 0 = x^2 - 20\sqrt{3}x$$

$$\Rightarrow \quad x^2 = 20\sqrt{3}x \Rightarrow x = 20\sqrt{3} \qquad \text{(Divide by } x\text{)}$$

Hence,
$$PQ = QR = PR = 20\sqrt{3}\text{ m}$$

Mistake Alert Students may incorrectly apply the identity as $(x-y)^2 = x^2 - y^2 + 2xy$ instead of $(x-y)^2 = x^2 + y^2 - 2xy$.

Exercise 9.3

Question 1 In figure A, B and C are three points on a circle with centre O such that $\angle BOC = 30°$ and $\angle AOB = 60°$. If D is a point on the circle other than the arc ABC, find $\angle ADC$.

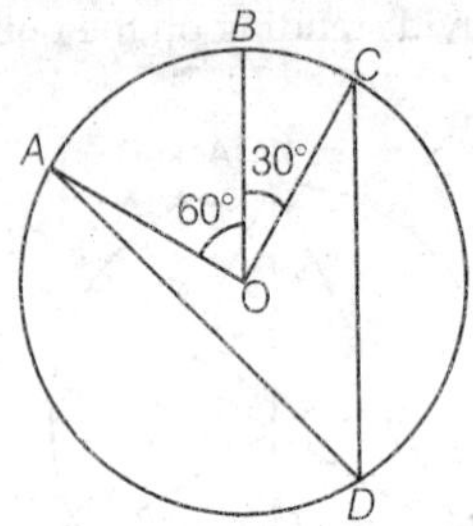

Sol. $\because \angle AOC = \angle AOB + \angle BOC = 60° + 30° = 90°$

$\therefore$ Arc ABC makes 90° at the centre of the circle.

($\because$ The angle subtended by an arc at the centre is double the angle subtended by it at any point on the remaining part of the circle.)

$\therefore \quad \angle ADC = \frac{1}{2}\angle AOC = \frac{1}{2} \times 90° = 45° \quad (\because \angle AOC = 90°)$

Mistake Alert Students may mistakenly take $\angle ADC = 2\angle AOC$ instead of $\angle ADC = \frac{1}{2}\angle AOC$.

Question 2 A chord of a circle is equal to the radius of the circle. Find the angle subtended by the chord at a point on the minor arc and also at a point on the major arc.

Sol. Let BC be chord, which is equal to the radius. Join OB and OC.

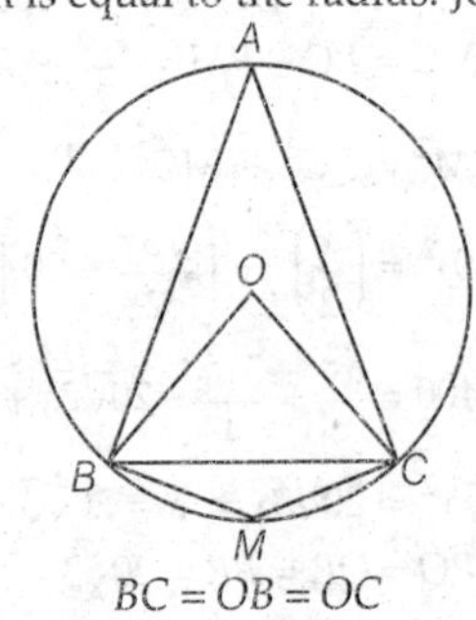

Given, $\quad BC = OB = OC$

$\therefore \Delta OBC$ is an equilateral triangle.

$$\therefore \quad \angle BOC = 60^\circ$$

$$\therefore \quad BAC = \frac{1}{2} \angle BOC = \frac{1}{2} \times 60^\circ = 30^\circ$$

($\because$ The angle subtended by an arc at the centre is double the angle subtended by it at any point on the remaining part of the circle.)

Since, $ABMC$ is a cyclic quadrilateral.

$$\therefore \quad \angle BAC + \angle BMC = 180^\circ$$

($\because$ In a cyclic quadrilateral the sum of opposite angles is 180°)

$$\Rightarrow \quad \angle BMC = 180^\circ - 30^\circ = 150^\circ \quad (\because \angle BAC = 30^\circ)$$

So, the angles subtended by chord at a point on the minor arc and also at a point on the major arc are 150° and 30°.

Question 3 In figure, $\angle PQR = 100^\circ$, where P, Q and R are points on a circle with centre O. Find $\angle OPR$.

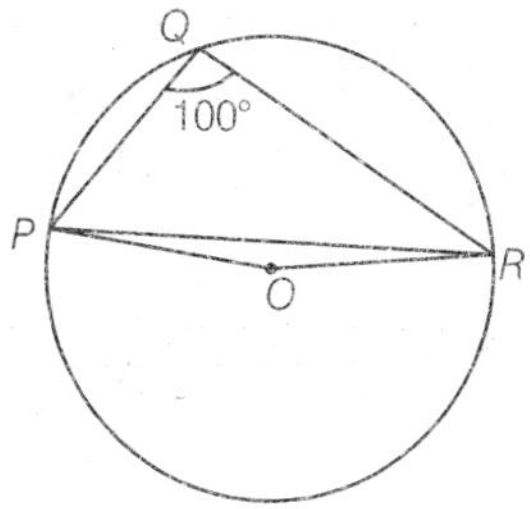

◎ ***Thinking Process*** End points of a chord joined with centre of a circle form an isosceles triangle and in an isosceles triangle angles opposite to equal sides are equal.

Sol. Given. $\angle PQR = 100^\circ$

$$\because \quad \angle POR = 2\angle PQR = 2 \times 100^\circ = 200^\circ$$

[Since, the angle subtended by an arc at the centre is double the angle subtended by it at any point on the remaining part of the circle.]

Since, in ΔOPR, $\angle POR = 360^\circ - 200^\circ = 160^\circ$ ...(i)

Again, ΔOPR, $OP = OR$ (Radii of the circle)

$\therefore \quad \angle OPR = \angle ORP$ (Opposite angles of an isosceles triangle)

In ΔPOR, $\angle OPR + \angle ORP + \angle POR = 180^\circ$

(Angle sum property of triangle)...(ii)

From Eqs. (i) and (ii), we get

$$\angle OPR + \angle OPR + 160^\circ = 180^\circ \quad [\because \angle POR = 160^\circ]$$

$$\therefore \quad 2\angle OPR = 180^\circ - 160^\circ = 20^\circ$$

$$\therefore \quad \angle OPR = \frac{20^\circ}{2} = 10^\circ$$

Question 4 In figure, $\angle ABC = 69°, \angle ACB = 31°$, find $\angle BDC$.

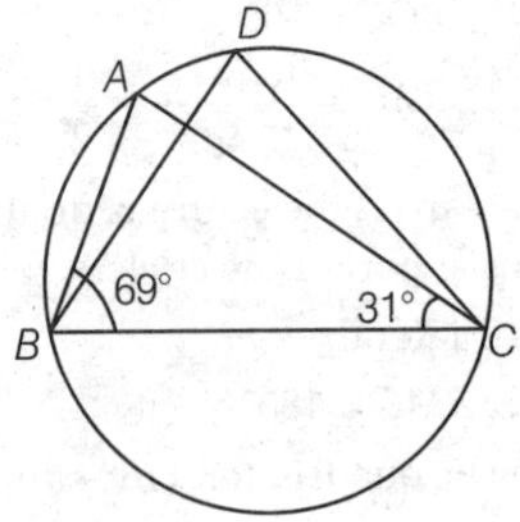

Sol. $\because$ $\angle BDC = \angle BAC$ ...(i)

(Since, the angles in the same segment are equal)

Now, in ΔABC, we have

$\angle ABC + \angle ACB + \angle BAC = 180°$ (Angle sum property of triangle)

$\Rightarrow$ $\angle BAC + 69° + 31° = 180°$ [Given, $\angle ABC = 69°$, $\angle ACB = 31°$]

$\Rightarrow$ $\angle BAC + 100° = 180°$

$\therefore$ $\angle BAC = 180° - 100° = 80°$

$\Rightarrow$ $\angle BAC = 80°$

$\therefore$ From Eq. (i), we get $\angle BDC = 80°$ ($\because \angle BOC = \angle BAC$)

Question 5 In figure, A, B and C are four points on a circle. AC and BD intersect at a point E such that $\angle BEC = 130°$ and $\angle ECD = 20°$. Find $\angle BAC$.

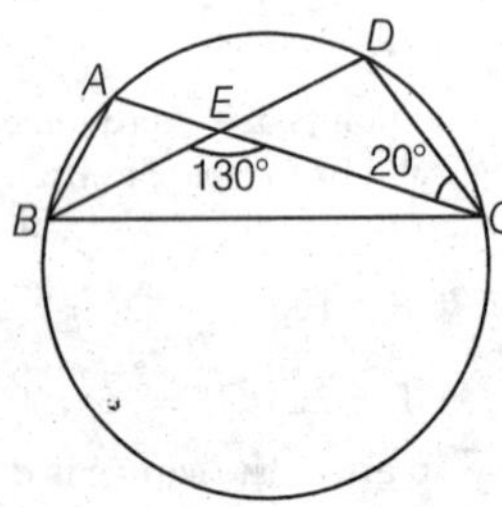

Sol. $\angle AEB = 180° - 130° = 50°$ (Linear pair)...(i)

$\therefore$ $\angle CED = \angle AEB = 50°$ (Vertically opposite)

In ΔCDE, we get

$\angle DEC + \angle DCE + \angle EDC = 180°$ (Angle sum property of triangle)

$50° + 20° + \angle EDC = 180°$

$\Rightarrow$ $\angle EDC = 180° - 70°$

$\Rightarrow$ $\angle EDC = 110°$

$\therefore$ $\angle BDC = \angle BAC$ (Angles in same segement)

Hence, $\angle BAC = 110°$

Question 6 $ABCD$ is a cyclic quadrilateral whose diagonals intersect at a point E. If $\angle DBC = 70°$, $\angle BAC$ is $30°$, find $\angle BCD$. Further, if $AB = BC$, find $\angle ECD$.

Sol. $\because$ Angles in the same segment are equal.

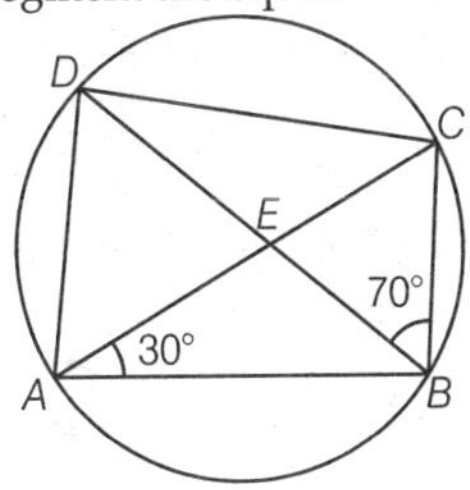

$\therefore$ $\angle BDC = \angle BAC$ (Angles in same segment)

$\therefore$ $\angle BDC = 30°$ ($\because \angle BAC = 30°$)

In ΔBCD, we have

$\therefore$ $\angle BDC + \angle DBC + \angle BCD = 180°$ (Angle sum property of triangle)

$\therefore$ $30° + 70° + \angle BCD = 180°$ (Given, $\angle DBC = 70°$ and $\angle BDC = 30°$)

$\Rightarrow$ $\angle BCD = 180° - 30° - 70° = 80°$

If $AB = BC$, then $\angle BCA = \angle BAC = 30°$

(Angles opposite to equal sides in a triangle are equal)

Now, $\angle ECD = \angle BCD - \angle BCA = 80° - 30° = 50°$

($\because \angle BCD = 80°$ and $\angle BCA = 30°$)

Hence, $\angle BCD = 80°$ and $\angle ECD = 50°$

Question 7 If diagonals of a cyclic quadrilateral are diameters of the circle through the vertices of the quadrilateral, prove that it is a rectangle.

Sol. Given, Diagonals NP and QM of a cyclic quadrilateral are diameters of the circle through the vertices M, P, Q and N of the quadrilateral $NQPM$.

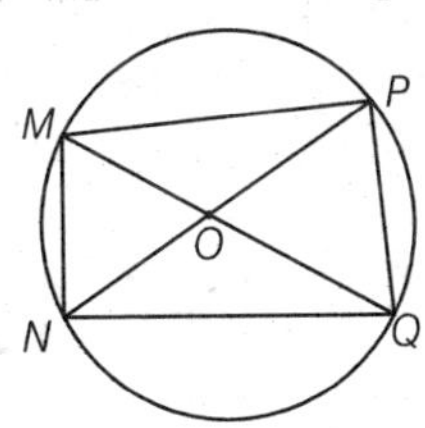

To prove Quadrilateral $NQPM$ is a rectangle.

Proof $\because$ $ON = OP = OQ = OM$ (Radii of a circle)

Now, $ON = OP = \frac{1}{2} NP$ ...(i)(O is the mid-point of side NP)

and $OM = OQ = \frac{1}{2} MQ$...(ii)(O is the midpoint of side MD)

From Eqs. (i) and (ii), we get

$\therefore$ $NP = MQ$

Hence, the diagonals of the quadrilateral $MPQN$ are equal and bisect each other. So, quadrilateral $NQPM$ is a rectangle. **Hence Proved.**

Question 8 If the non-parallel sides of a trapezium are equal, prove that it is cyclic.

Sol. Given, Non-parallel sides PS and QR of a trapezium $PQRS$ are equal.

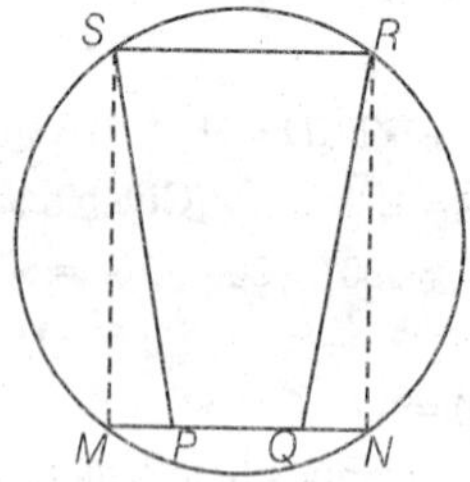

To prove $PQRS$ is a cyclic trapezium.

Construction Draw $SM \perp PQ$ and $RN \perp PQ$.

Proof In ΔSMP and ΔRNQ, we get

$SP = RQ$ (Given)

$\angle SMP = \angle RNQ$ (Each = 90°)

and $SM = RN$

($\because$ Distance between two parallel lines is always equal)

$\therefore$ By RHS criterion, we get

$\Delta SMP \cong \Delta RNQ$

So, $\angle SPM = \angle NQR$ (By CPCT)

and $\angle PSM = \angle QRN$ (By CPCT)

Now, $\angle PSM = \angle QRN$

Then, we can write $-\angle PSM = -\angle QRN$

$\therefore$ $90° - \angle PSM = 90° - \angle QRN$ (Adding both sides 90°)

$\therefore$ $\angle MSR - \angle PSM = \angle NRS - \angle QRN$ ($\because \angle MSR = \angle NRS = 90°$)

So, $\angle PSR = \angle QRS$

i.e., $\angle S = \angle R$

Thus, $\angle P = \angle Q$ and $\angle R = \angle S$ ...(i)

$\therefore$ $\angle P + \angle Q + \angle R + \angle S = 360°$

(∵ Sum of the angles of a quadrilateral is 360°)

$\therefore$ $2\angle S + 2\angle Q = 360°$ [From Eq. (i)]

$\angle S + \angle Q = 180°$

and $\angle P + \angle R = 180°$

Since, the sum of opposite angles of a quadrilateral is 180°.

Hence, $PQRS$ is a cyclic trapezium.

Question 9 Two circles intersect at two points B and C. Through B, two line segments ABD and PBQ are drawn to intersect the circles at A, D and P, Q respectively (see figure). Prove that $\angle ACP = \angle QCD$.

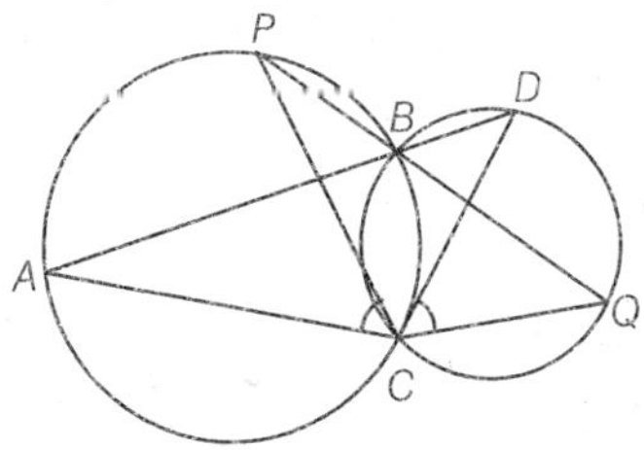

◎ *Thinking Process* Angles in the same segment of a circle are equal.

Sol. Given, Two circles intersect at two points B and C. Through B two line segments ABD and PBQ are drawn to intersect the circles at A, D and P, Q, respectively.

To prove $\angle ACP = \angle QCD$

Proof In circle I, we have $\angle ACP = \angle ABP$ ...(i)(Angles in the same segment)

In circle II, we have $\angle QCD = \angle QBD$ ...(ii)(Angles in the same segment)

$\angle ABP = \angle QBD$ ...(iii)(Vertically opposite angles)

From Eqs. (i) and (ii), (iii), we get $\angle ACP = \angle QCD$ **Hence Proved.**

Question 10 If circles are drawn taking two sides of a triangle as diameters, prove that the point of intersection of these circles lie on the third side.

Sol. Given, Two circles are drawn with sides AC and AB of ΔABC as diameters. Both circles intersect each other at D.

To prove D lies on BC.

Construction Join AD.

Proof Since, AC and AB are the diameters of the two circles.

$\angle ADB = 90°$ (∵ Angles in a semi-circle) ...(i)

and $\angle ADC = 90°$ (Angles in a semi-circle) ...(ii)

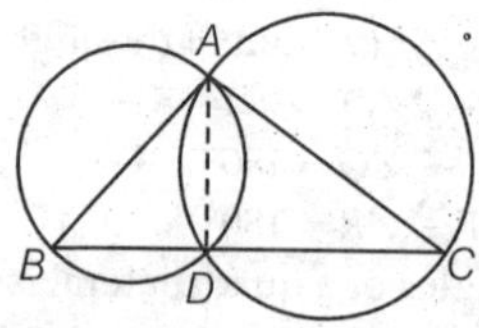

On adding Eqs (i) and (ii), we get

$$\angle ADB + \angle ADC = 90° + 90° = 180°$$

Hence, BCD is a straight line.

So, D lies on BC.

Hence, point of intersection of circles lies on the third side BC.

Question 11 ABC and ADC are two right angled triangles with common hypotenuse AC. Prove that $\angle CAD = \angle CBD$.

◎ ***Thinking Process*** Two right triangles with common hypotenuse drawn, then the hypotenuse will be the diameter of a circle. Also remember the angles in a semi-circle is right angle.

Sol. Since, ΔADC and ΔABC are right angled triangles with common hypotenuse.

Case I If both the triangles are not in the same semi-circle.

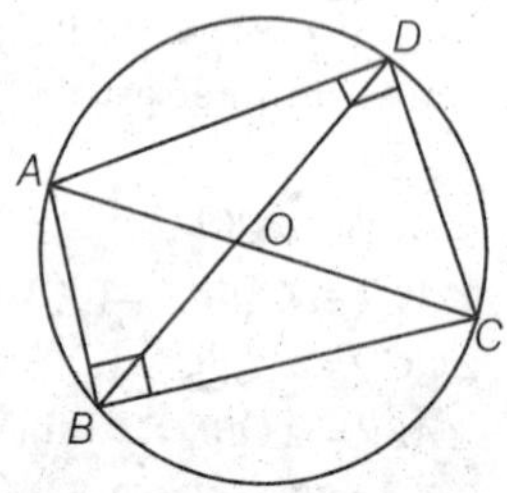

Draw a circle with AC as diameter passing through B and D. Join BD, DC is a chord.

$\because$ Angles in the same segment are equal.

$\therefore$ $\angle CBD = \angle CAD$

Case II If both the triangles are in the same semi-circle

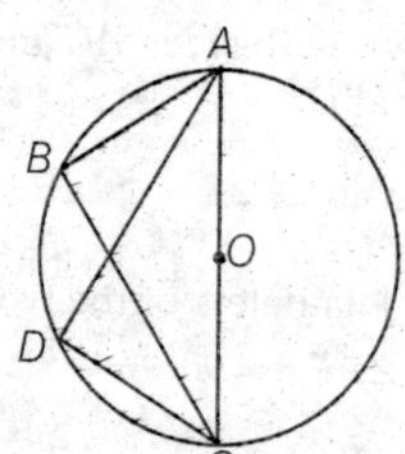

$\Rightarrow$ A, B, C and D are concylic. Join BD.

DC is a chord.

$\therefore$ $\angle CAD$ and $\angle CBD$ are formed in the same segment.

$\Rightarrow$ $$\angle CAD = \angle CBD$$

Question 12 Prove that a cyclic parallelogram is a rectangle.

Sol. Given, $PQRS$ is a parallelogram inscribed in a circle.

To prove $PQRS$ is a rectangle.

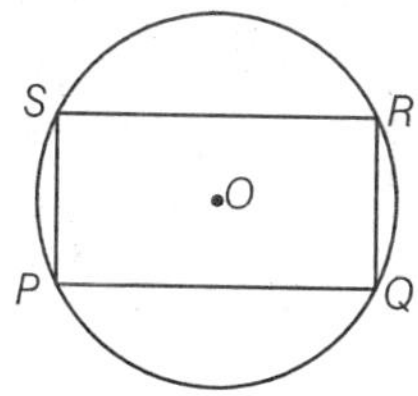

Proof Since, $PQRS$ is a cyclic quadrilateral.

$\therefore$ $$\angle P + \angle R = 180° \quad ...(i)$$

($\because$ Sum of opposite angles in a cyclic quadrilateral is 180°)

But $\angle P = \angle R$ ($\because$ In parallelogram opposite angles are equal) ...(ii)

From Eqs. (i) and (ii), we get

$$\angle P = \angle R = 90°$$

Similarly, $$\angle Q = \angle S = 90°$$

$\therefore$ Each angle of $PQRS$ is 90°.

Hence, cyclic parallelgram $PQRS$ is a rectangle. **Hence Proved.**

DIKSHA APP Questions

☐ Multiple Choice Questions

Q.1 The sum of either pair of opposite angles of a cyclic quadrilateral.

(a) 160° (b) 120° (c) 140° (d) 180°

Sol. (d) Opposite angles of a cyclic quadrilateral are supplementry.

Q.2 If an arc of a circle subtend an angle of 120° at the centre, what will be the measure of the angle subtended by it at any point in the remaining part?

(a) 120° (b) 20° (c) 60° (d) 160°

Sol. (c) The angle subtended by an arc at the centre is double the angle subtended by it any point on the remaining part of circle.

Q.3 In a circle with centre O, AB and CD are two diameters perpendicular to each other. The length of the chord AC is

(a) $2\,AB$ (b) $\frac{AB}{\sqrt{2}}$ (c) AB (d) $3\,AB$

Sol. (b)

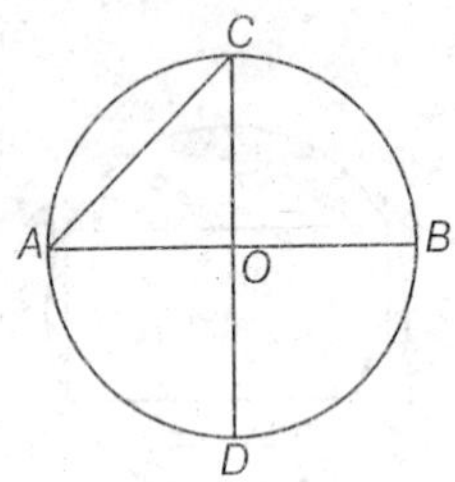

In ΔAOC, we have

$$AC^2 = OA^2 + OC^2 \quad \text{[By Pythagoras theorem]}$$

$\Rightarrow$ $$AC^2 = OA^2 + OA^2 \quad [\because OA = OC \text{ Radii of circle}]$$

$\Rightarrow$ $$AC^2 = 2OA^2 \quad \text{... (i)}$$

Now, $$OC = OA = OB = \frac{AB}{2}$$

On squaring and multiplying by 2 on both sides, we get

$$2OA^2 = 2\left(\frac{AB}{2}\right)^2 = 2 \times \frac{AB^2}{4}$$

$\Rightarrow$ $$2OA^2 = \frac{AB^2}{2}$$

On putting the value of $2OA^2$ in Eq. (i), we get

$$AC^2 = \frac{AB^2}{2}$$

$\Rightarrow$ $$AC = \frac{1}{\sqrt{2}}AB$$

Q.4 The region between a chord and either of the arc is called

(a) chord (b) segment

(c) sector (d) diameter

Sol. (b) The region between a chord and either of the arc is called segment.

Q.5 How many circles can pass through three non collinear points?

(a) 1 (b) 0

(c) 2 (d) 4

Sol. (a) Only one circle can pass through three non-collinear points.

☐ Subjective Type Questions

Q.1 Justify your statement. "Two chords of a circle of lengths 10 cm and 8 cm are at the distance 8 cm and 3.5 cm, respectively from the centre".

Sol. The statements is not correct because the longer chord will be at smaller distance from the centre.

Q.2 Justify your statement. "The angles subtended by a chord at any two points of a circle are equal".

Sol. The angles subtended by a chord at any two points of circle are equal if both the points lie in the same segment, otherwise they are not equal.

Q.3 If $ABCD$ is a cyclic quadrilateral and ABC is an equilateral triangle, find $\angle BDC$.

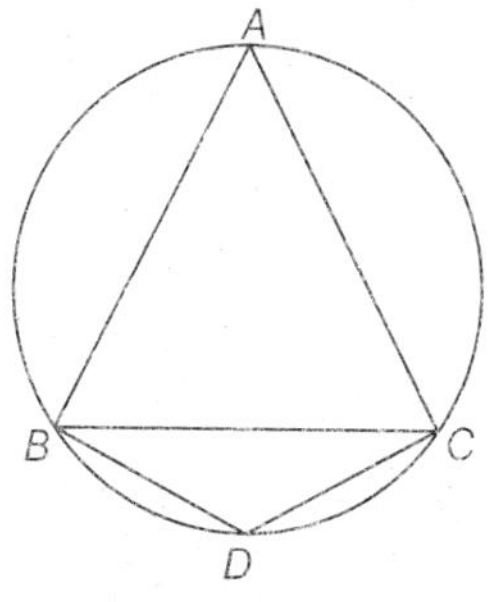

Sol. Since, ΔABC is an equilateral triangle and each angle of an equilateral triangle is 60°.

$\therefore \quad \angle BAC = 60°$

Since, $ABCD$ is a cyclic quadrilateral.

$\therefore \quad \angle A + \angle D = 180°$ (opposite angles of cyclic quadrilateral are supplementary)

$\Rightarrow \quad 60° + \angle D = 180°$

$\Rightarrow \quad \angle D = 180° - 60°$

$\Rightarrow \quad \angle D = 120°$

$\Rightarrow \quad \angle BDC = 120°$

Q.4 Find $\angle PRQ$ in the following figure.

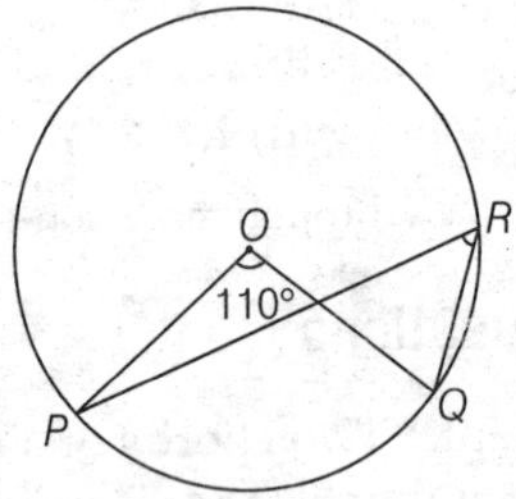

Sol. We know that angle subtended by an arc at the centre is double the angle subtended by it at the remaining part of the circle.

$$\therefore \quad \angle PRQ = \frac{1}{2} \angle POQ$$

$$= \frac{1}{2} \times 110° = 55°$$

Q.5 Find x in the following figure.

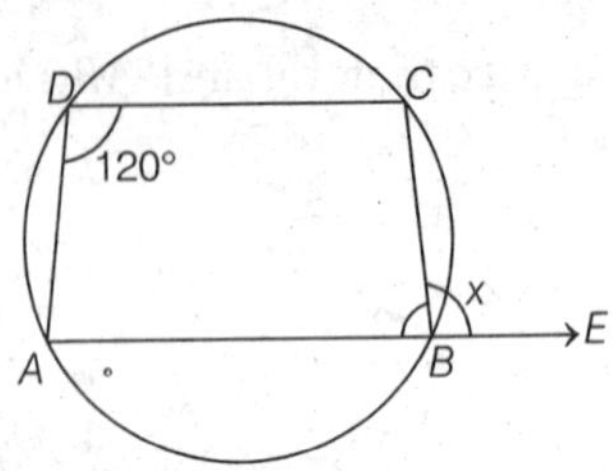

Sol. In the given figure, we have $\angle ADC = 120°$ and $ABCD$ is a cyclic quadrilateral.

$$\therefore \quad \angle ADC + \angle ABC = 180°$$

[Opposite angles of cyclic quadrilateral are supplementary]

$$\Rightarrow \quad 120° + \angle ABC = 180°$$

$$\Rightarrow \quad \angle ABC = 60°$$

Now, $\angle ABC + \angle CBE = 180°$ (Linear pair axiom)

$$\Rightarrow \quad 60° + \angle CBE = 180°$$

$$\Rightarrow \quad \angle CBE = 180° - 60°$$

$$\Rightarrow \quad \angle CBE = 120°$$

$$\therefore \quad x = 120°$$

Q.6 In the following figure, find $\angle AOB$.

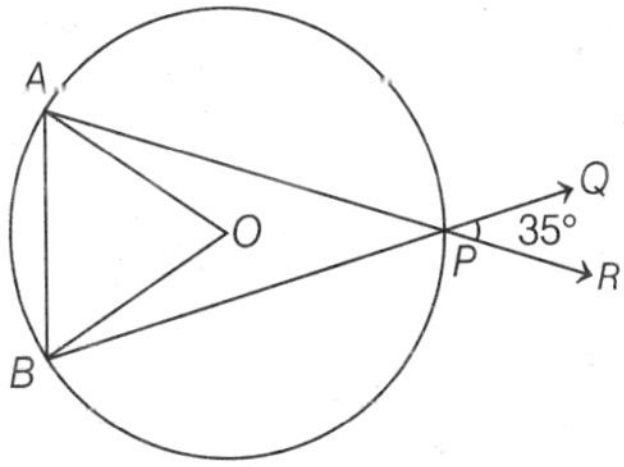

◎ *Thinking Process* Angle subtended by an arc at the centre is double the angle subtended by it at the remaining part of the circle.

Sol. $\angle APB = \angle RPQ = 35°$ (Vertically opposite angles)

Now, $\angle AOB$ and $\angle APB$ are angles subtended by an arc AB at centre and at the remaining part of the circle respectively.

$\therefore$ $$\angle AOB = 2\angle APB = 2 \times 35° = 70°$$

Q.7 What is a cyclic quadrilateral?

Sol. It is a quadrilateral whose all the four vertices lie on the circumference of the circle and the sum of opposite angle of cyclic quadrilateral is 180°.

Q.8 If two circles intersect at two points, prove that the line through the centre is perpendicular bisector of the common chord.

Sol.

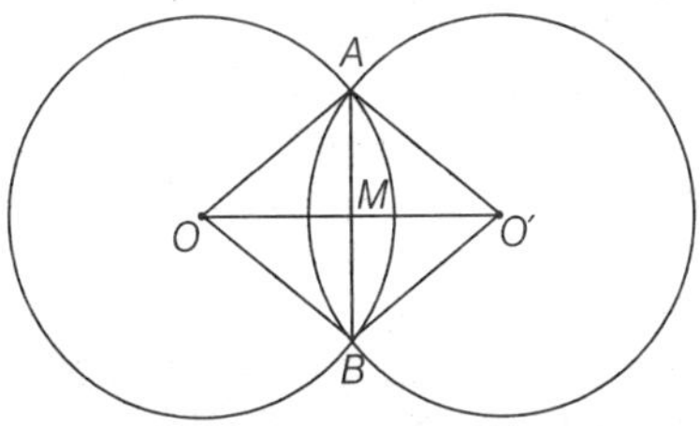

Let two circles with centres O and O' intersect at two points A and B, so that AB is the common chord of two circles and OO' is the line segment joining the centres.

Let OO' intersect AB at M.

Now, draw line segments OA, OB, $O'A$ and $O'B$.

In $\Delta OAO'$ and OBO',

We have, $OA = OB$ (radii of same circle)

$O'A = O'B$ (radii of same circle)

$OO' = OO'$ (common)

$\therefore$ $\Delta OAO' \cong \Delta OBO'$ (by SSS congruency)

$\Rightarrow \quad \angle AOO' = \angle BOO'$ (By CPCT)

$\therefore \quad \angle AOM = \angle BOM$ ...(i)

Now, in ΔAOM and ΔBOM,

$OA = OB$ [radii of same circle]

$\angle AOM = \angle BOM$ (from Eq. (i))

$OM = OM$ [common side]

$\Rightarrow \quad \Delta AOM \cong \Delta BOM$ [by SAS congruency]

$\Rightarrow \quad AM = BM$ and $\angle AMO = \angle BMO$ [by CPCT]

But $\quad \angle AMO + \angle BMO = 180°$ ... (ii)

$\Rightarrow \quad \angle AMO + \angle AMO = 180°$ [by Eq. (i)]

$\Rightarrow \quad 2\angle AMO = 180°$

$\Rightarrow \quad \angle AMO = 90°$

Thus, $AM = BM$ and $\angle AMO = \angle BMO = 90°$

Hence we can say that the line through the centre is perpendicular bisector of the common chord. **Hence Proved.**

Q.9 Distance of chord AB from the centre is 12 cm and length of the chord is 10 cm, then find the diameter

Sol.

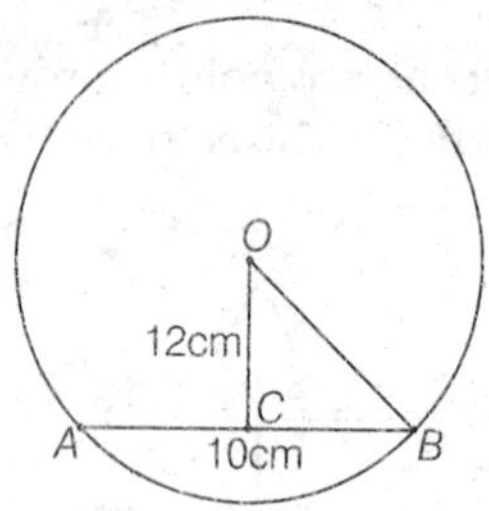

We have, the distance of chord AB from the centre, $OC = 12$ cm

Length of chord $AB = 10$ cm

In ΔOCB, we have

$\angle C = 90°$ and $CB = 5$ cm

(Perpendicular drawn from the centre bisects the chord)

In right ΔOCB, by Pythagoras theorem

$$OB^2 = OC^2 + CB^2 \Rightarrow OB^2 = 12^2 + 5^2$$

$$\Rightarrow \quad OB^2 = 144 + 25 \quad \Rightarrow OB^2 = 169$$

$$OB = 13 \text{ cm}$$

Radii $= OB = 13$ cm, $OA = 13$ cm

Then, Diameter $= 2 \times$ radius

$= 2 \times 13 = 26$ cm

Q.10 In the given figure, O is the centre of the circle. The angle subtended by the arc BCD at the centre is 140°. Find $\angle BAD$ and $\angle DCP$.

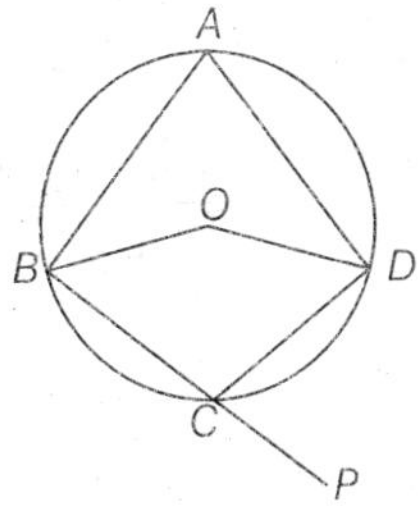

◎ **Thinking Process** If four points A, B, C and D lie on the circumference of the circle, then quadrilateral made by joining these all four points is cyclic and sum of opposite angles of cyclic quadrilateral is 180°.

Sol.

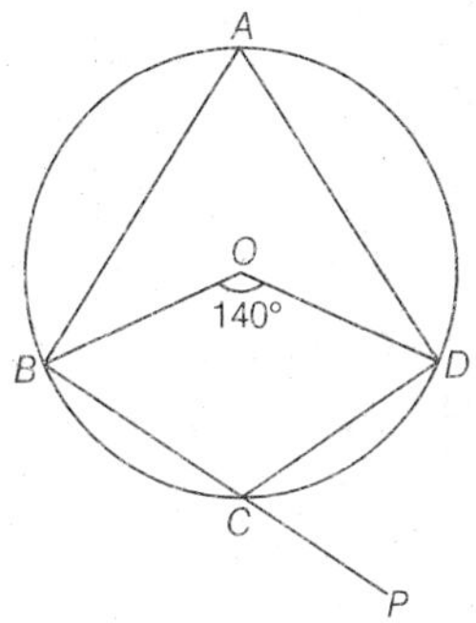

We know that, angle subtended by an arc at the centre is double the angle subtended by it at the remaining part of the circle.

$\therefore \quad \angle BAD = \frac{1}{2} BOD = \frac{1}{2} \times 140° \quad$ [Given $\angle BOD = 140°$]

$\Rightarrow \quad \angle BAD = 70°$

Since, $ABCD$ is a cyclic quadrilateral

$\therefore \quad \angle BAD + \angle BCD = 180°$

[Sum of opposite angles of cyclic quadrilateral is 180°]

$\Rightarrow \quad 70° + \angle BCD = 180°$

$\Rightarrow \quad \angle BCD = 110°$

Now, $\quad \angle BCD + \angle DCP = 180° \quad$ (Linear pair axiom)

$\Rightarrow \quad 110° + \angle DCP = 180°$

$\Rightarrow \quad \angle DCP = 180° - 110°$

$\Rightarrow \quad \angle DCP = 70°$

Q.11 AB and CD are parallel chords of a circle whose centre is O and radius 20 cm. If $AB = 24$ cm and $CD = 32$ cm, find the distance between AB and CD when it is given that they lie on the opposite sides of the centre O.

Sol.

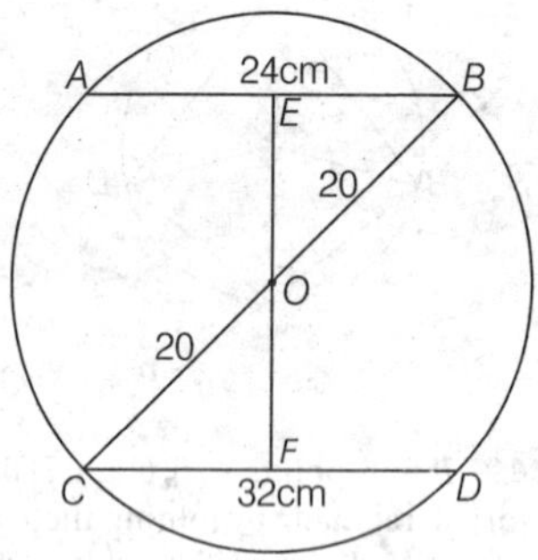

Construction Draw $OE \perp AB, OF \perp CD$.

Proof $AE = BE = 12$ cm (⊥ from centre bisects the chord)

In ΔEBO,

$$OB^2 = OE^2 + EB^2 \quad \text{(By Pythagoras theorem)}$$

$\Rightarrow$ $(20)^2 = OE^2 + 12^2$

$\Rightarrow$ $400 = OE^2 + 144$

$\Rightarrow$ $400 - 144 = OE^2$

$\Rightarrow$ $OE^2 = 256$

$\Rightarrow$ $OE = 16$ cm

Now, $CF = FD = 16$ cm

(Perpendicular (⊥) from centre bisects the chord)

In ΔCOF,

$$OC^2 = OF^2 + CF^2 \quad \text{(By Pythagoras theorem)}$$

$\Rightarrow$ $(20)^2 = OF^2 + (16)^2$

$\Rightarrow$ $400 = OF^2 + 256$

$\Rightarrow$ $400 - 256 = OF^2$

$\Rightarrow$ $OF^2 = 144$

$\Rightarrow$ $OF = 12$ cm

Given $AB \parallel CD$

$\therefore$ Distance between AB and CD is EF.

$$EF = OE + OF$$

$$= 16 + 12 = 28 \text{ cm}$$

Q.12 AC and BD are chords of a circle which bisect each other. Prove that AC and BD are diameters of the circle and $ABCD$ is a rectangle.

Sol.

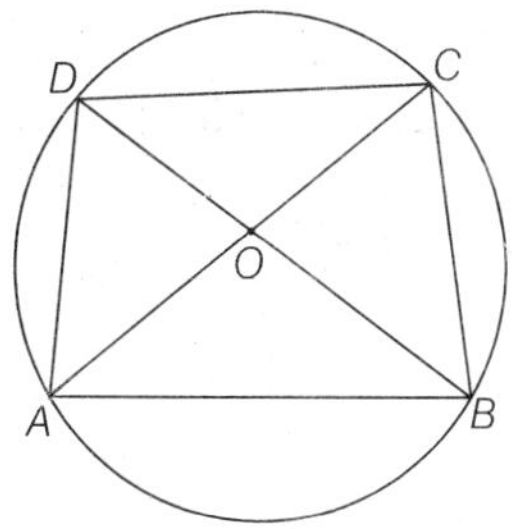

Let two chords AC and BD are intersecting each other at point O.

In ΔAOB and ΔCOD, we have

$$OA = OC \quad \text{(Given)}$$
$$OB = OD \quad \text{(Given)}$$
$$\angle AOB = \angle COD \quad \text{(Vertically opposite angle)}$$
$$\Delta AOB \cong \Delta COD \quad \text{(By SAS congruence rule)}$$
$$AB = CD \quad \text{[By CPCT]}$$

Similarly, it can be proved that

$$\Delta AOD \cong \Delta COB$$
$$\therefore \quad AD = CB \quad \text{(By CPCT)}$$

Since, in quadrilateral $ABCD$, opposite sides are equal in length.

So, $ABCD$ is a parallelogram.

We know that opposite angles of a parallelogram are equal.

$$\therefore \quad \angle A = \angle C,$$
$$\text{And} \quad \angle A + \angle C = 180° \quad \text{(Cyclic quadrilateral)}$$
$$\Rightarrow \quad \angle A + \angle A = 180° \quad (\because \angle A = \angle C)$$
$$\Rightarrow \quad 2\angle A = 180°$$
$$\Rightarrow \quad \angle A = 90°$$

One of its interior angles is 90°.

Therefore, it is a rectangle.

$\because \angle A$ is the angle subtended by chord BD at circumference.

Therefore, BD should be the diameter of the circle.

Similarly, AC is the diameter of the circle.

Q.13 If O is the circumcentre of a ΔABC and $OD \perp BC$, prove that $\angle BOD = \angle A$.

Sol. In ΔBOD and ΔCOD, we have

$$BO = CO \quad \text{(Both are radii)}$$
$$\angle BDO = \angle CDO = 90^\circ$$
$$OD = OD \quad \text{(common)}$$
$$\Delta BOD \cong \Delta COD \quad \text{(By RHS property)}$$

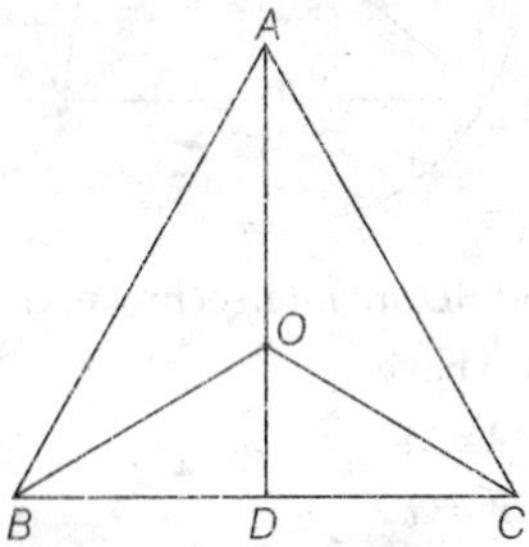

So, $\angle BOD = \angle COD$ (By CPCT)

We know that, the angle subtended by an arc at the centre is double the angle subtended by it at any point on the remaining part of the circle.

$$\angle BOC = 2\angle BAC$$
$$\Rightarrow \angle BOD + \angle DOC = 2\angle BAC$$
$$\Rightarrow \angle BOD + \angle BOD = 2\angle BAC$$
$$\Rightarrow 2\angle BOD = 2\angle BAC$$
$$\Rightarrow \angle BOD = \angle A$$

Hence Proved.

Q.14 Two circles of radii 13 cm and 5 cm intersect at two points in such a way that the distance between their centres is 12 cm. Find the length of the common chord of the two circles.

Sol.

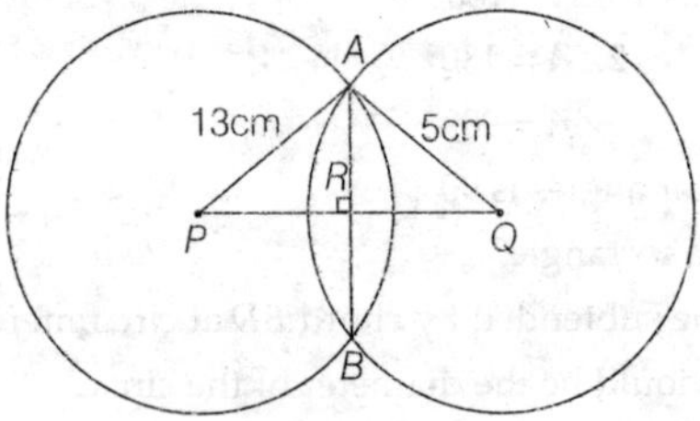

Let the common chord be AB and P and Q be the centres of the two circles.

$\therefore$ $AP = 13$ cm and $AQ = 5$ cm

$PQ = 12$ cm (Given)

Now $PQ \perp$ chord AB.

$\therefore \quad AR = RB = \frac{1}{2} AB$

(Perpendicular from centre to the chord, bisects the chord)

Let $\quad PR = x$ cm

So, $\quad RQ = 12 - x$ cm

In ΔARP, we have

$$AP^2 = AR^2 + PR^2 \quad \text{(By pythagoras theorem)}$$

$$\Rightarrow \quad (13)^2 = AR^2 + x^2$$

$$\Rightarrow \quad 169 = AR^2 + x^2 \Rightarrow AR^2 = 169 - x^2 \quad \text{... (i)}$$

In ΔARQ, we have $\quad AQ^2 = AR^2 + QR^2$

$$\Rightarrow \quad 5^2 = AR^2 + (12 - x)^2 \quad \text{(By pythagoras theorem)}$$

$$\Rightarrow \quad 25 = AR^2 + 144 + x^2 - 24x$$

$$\Rightarrow \quad 25 - 144 - x^2 + 24x = AR^2$$

$$\Rightarrow \quad AR^2 = -x^2 + 24x - 119 \quad \text{... (ii)}$$

From Eqs (i) and (ii), we get

$$169 - x^2 = -x^2 + 24x - 119$$

$$\Rightarrow \quad -24x = -119 - 169 \Rightarrow -24x = -288$$

$$\Rightarrow \quad x = 12$$

$\Rightarrow R$ and Q coincide.

$\therefore AB$ is diameter of smaller circle.

On substitute the value of x in Eq. (i), we get

$$AR^2 = 169 - (12)^2 \Rightarrow AR^2 = 169 - 144$$

$$\Rightarrow \quad AR^2 = 25 \Rightarrow AR = 5 \text{ cm}$$

$$\Rightarrow \quad AB = 2 \times AR = 2 \times 5 = 10 \text{ cm}$$

So, length of common chord AB is 10 cm.

Mistake Alert Students may assume AR bisects PQ instead of PR bisects the AB.

Q.15 BC is a chord of a circle with centre O. A is a point on major arc BC as shown in the figure. Prove that $\angle BAC + \angle OBC = 90°$.

Sol.

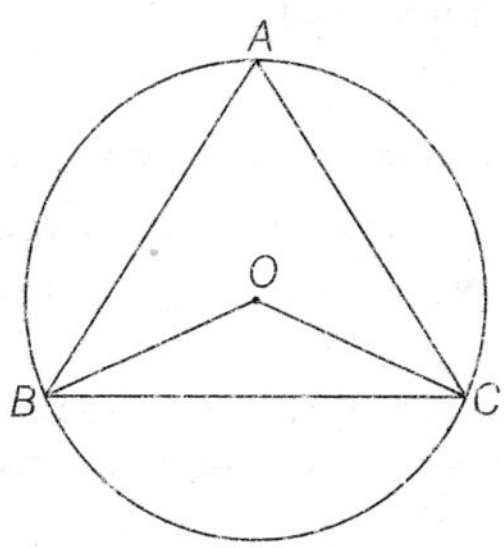

In ΔOBC, we have $OB = OC$ (Both are radiii)

Then $\angle OBC = \angle OCB$ (Angle opposite to equal sides are equal)

Now, in ΔOBC,

$\angle OBC + \angle OCB + \angle BOC = 180°$ (Angle sum property of triangle)

$\Rightarrow \angle OBC + \angle OBC + \angle BOC = 180°$ $(\because \angle OBC = \angle OCB)$

$\Rightarrow$ $2\angle OBC = 180° - \angle BOC$

$\Rightarrow$ $\angle OBC = 90° - \dfrac{\angle BOC}{2}$ ... (i)

We know that $\angle BAC = \dfrac{1}{2}\angle BOC$ ... (ii)

The angle subtended by an arc at the centre is double the angle subtended by it at any point on the remaining part of circle.

From Eqs. (i) and (ii), we get

$\angle OBC = 90° - \angle BAC$

$\Rightarrow$ $\angle OBC + \angle BAC = 90°$ **Hence Proved.**

Q.16 $ABCD$ is a cyclic quadrilateral in which $AB \parallel CD$.
If $\angle DAB = 115°$, determine the measure of $\angle DCB$ and $\angle ABC$.

Sol.

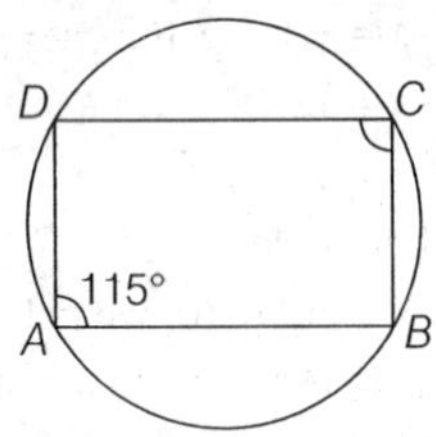

Since, $ABCD$ is a cyclic quadrilateral,

$\therefore$ $\angle A + \angle C = 180°$ (Opposite angles of cyclic quadrilateral are supplementary)

$\Rightarrow$ $115° + \angle C = 180°$

$\Rightarrow$ $\angle C = 180° - 115°$

$\Rightarrow$ $\angle C = 65°$ or $\angle DCB = 65°$

As $AB \parallel CD$, BC is the transversal

Then,

$\angle C + \angle B = 180°$ (Angle on the same side of the transversal.)

$\Rightarrow$ $65° + \angle B = 180° \Rightarrow \angle B = 180° - 65°$

$\Rightarrow$ $\angle B = 115° \Rightarrow \angle ABC = 115°$

Mistake Alert If a transversal intersects two parallel lines, then each pair of interior angles on the same side of the transversal is supplementary not in equal.

Heron's Formula

CHAPTER 10

Important Points

01 Triangle A plane figure bounded by three line segments is called a triangle.

In ΔABC has

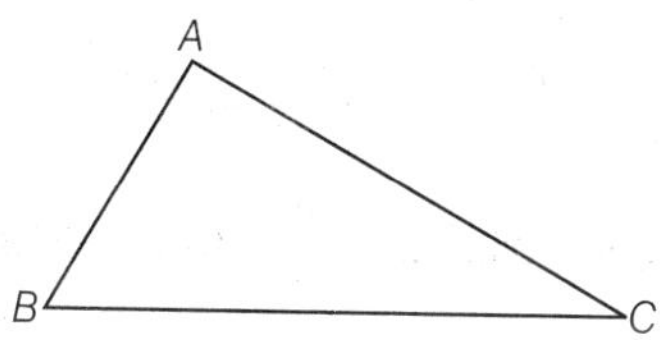

(i) three vertices, namely A, B and C.

(ii) three sides, namely AB, BC and CA.

(iii) three angles, namely $\angle A$, $\angle B$ and $\angle C$.

02 Types of Triangle on the Basis of Sides

(i) **Equilateral Triangle** A triangle having all sides equal is called an equilateral triangle.

i.e., in an equilateral ΔABC, $AB = BC = CA$

For an equilateral triangle of side 'a'.

Area $= \dfrac{\sqrt{3}}{4}a^2$, perimeter $= 3a$

(ii) **Isosceles Triangle** A triangle having two sides equal is called an isosceles triangle.

i.e. in an isosceles ΔABC, $AB = AC$

(iii) **Scalene Triangle** A triangle in which all the sides are of different lengths is called scalene triangle.

i.e., in scalene ΔABC, $AB \neq BC \neq CA$

03 Perimeter of a Triangle The sum of the lengths of three sides of a triangle is called its perimeter.

Let, $AB = c$, $BC = a$, $CA = b$

$\therefore$ Perimeter of ΔABC, $s = a + b + c$

04 Area of a Triangle The measure of the surface enclosed by the boundary of triangle is called its area.

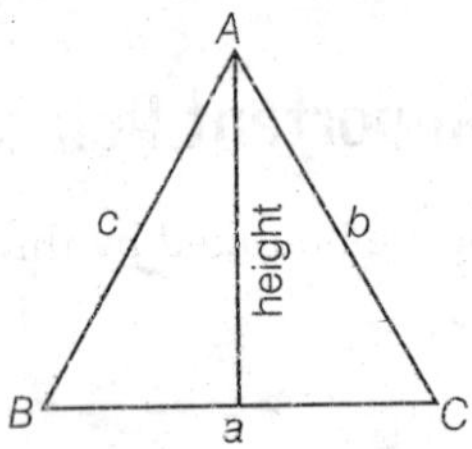

$$\text{Area of a triangle} = \frac{1}{2} \times \text{Base} \times \text{Height}$$

$$\text{Area of right angled triangle} = \frac{1}{2} \times \text{Base} \times \text{Perpendicular}$$

05 Area of a Triangle by Heron's Formula If a triangle has a, b and c as sides, then the area of a triangle by Heron's formula

$$= \sqrt{s(s-a)(s-b)(s-c)}$$

where, s (semi-perimeter) $= \dfrac{a+b+c}{2}$

Note This formula is highly applicable in the case when we don't have the exact idea about height and applicable to all types of triangles. Whether it is a right triangle or an isosceles triangle or an equilateral triangle.

Exercise 10.1

Question 1 A traffic signal board, indicating 'SCHOOL AHEAD', is an equilateral triangle with side a. Find the area of the signal board, using Heron's formula.If its perimeter is 180 cm, what will be the area of the signal board?

Sol. We know that, an equilateral triangle has equal sides. Let a be the length of each side of an equilateral triangle.

Perimeter of triangle = 180 cm (Given)

$\Rightarrow \quad a + a + a = 180$

$\Rightarrow \quad 3a = 180$

$\Rightarrow \quad a = 60$ cm

$\therefore$ Semi-perimeter, $s = \dfrac{a + a + a}{2}$

$= \dfrac{180}{2}$ $\quad (\because 2s = a + b + c)$

$s = 90$ cm

Area of an equilateral triangle $= \sqrt{s(s-a)(s-a)(s-a)}$

[by Heron's formula]

$= \sqrt{90(90-60)(90-60)(90-60)}$

$(\because a = b = c = 60)$

$= \sqrt{30 \times 3 \times 30 \times 30 \times 30}$

$= 30 \times 30\sqrt{3}$

$= 900\sqrt{3}$ cm^2

Quick Solution

We have, perimeter of equilateral triangle = 180 cm

$\Rightarrow \quad 3 \times \text{Side} = 180$

$\Rightarrow \quad \text{Side} = 60$ cm

$\therefore$ Area of equilateral triangle

$= \dfrac{\sqrt{3}}{4}(\text{Side})^2$

$= \dfrac{\sqrt{3}}{4} \times 60 \times 60$

$= 900\sqrt{3}$ cm^2

Question 2 The triangular side walls of a flyover have been used for advertisements. The sides of the walls are 122 m, 22 m and 120 m (see figure). The advertisements yield an earning of ₹ 5000 per m^2 per year. A company hired one of its walls for 3 months. How much rent did it pay?

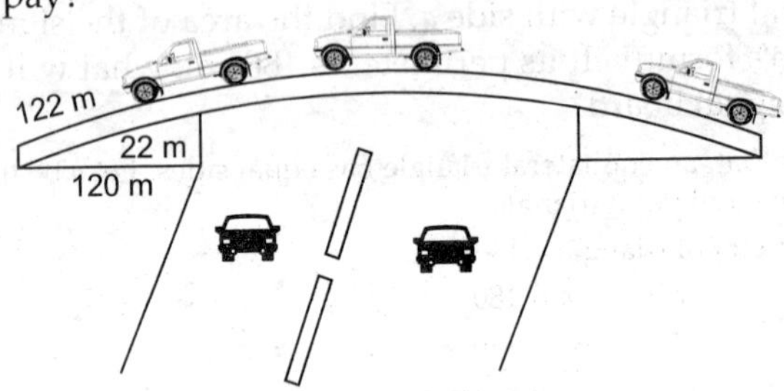

Sol. Let the sides of the triangular wall are $a = 122$ m, $b = 22$ m and $c = 120$ m

$\therefore$ Semi-perimeter, $s = \dfrac{a+b+c}{2} = \dfrac{122+22+120}{2} = \dfrac{264}{2} = 132$ m

Area of triangle $= \sqrt{s(s-a)(s-b)(s-c)}$

$= \sqrt{132(132-122)(132-22)(132-120)}$

$= \sqrt{132 \times 10 \times 110 \times 12} = \sqrt{11 \times 12 \times 10 \times 11 \times 10 \times 12}$

$= 1320 \text{ m}^2$

Rent for 1 year per m^2 = ₹ 5000

Company hired one of its walls for 3 months.

$\therefore$ Rent for 3 months per m^2 = ₹ $5000 \times \dfrac{3}{12}$

Thus, rent paid by the company for 3 months per 1320 m^2 $= 5000 \times \dfrac{3}{12} \times 1320$

= ₹ 1650000

$\therefore$ The company had to pay ₹ 1650000.

Question 3 There is a slide in a park. One of its side walls has been painted in some colour with a message "KEEP THE PARK GREEN AND CLEAN" (see figure). If the sides of the wall are 15 m, 11 m and 6m, find the area painted in colour.

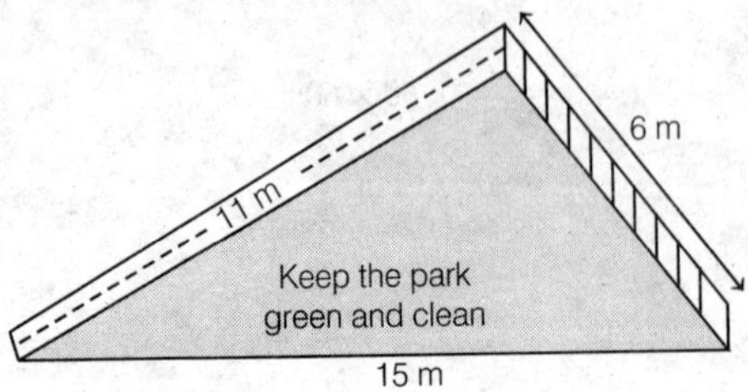

Sol. The given figure formed a triangle whose sides are $a = 15$ m, $b = 11$ m and $c = 6$ m

Now, semi-perimeter $s = \frac{15 + 11 + 6}{2}$ m

$= \frac{32}{2} = 16$ m

Therefore, area painted in colour $= \sqrt{16(16-15)(16-11)(16-6)}$

[∵ Heron's formula, area $= \sqrt{s(s-a)(s-b)(s-c)}$]

$= \sqrt{16 \times 1 \times 5 \times 10}$

$= \sqrt{2 \times 2 \times 2 \times 2 \times 5 \times 5 \times 2} = 2 \times 2 \times 5\sqrt{2}$

$= 20\sqrt{2}$ m^2

Hence, the area painted in colour is $20\sqrt{2}\,\text{m}^2$.

Mistake Alert Students may forget to divide the sum of the sides of triangle by 2, leading to an incorrect value of s, which affects the entire calculations.

Question 4 Find the area of a triangle two sides of which are 18 cm and 10 cm and the perimeter is 42 cm.

Sol. Let $a = 18$ cm, $b = 10$ cm and third side of the triangle be c.

We have, perimeter = 42 cm

$\Rightarrow \quad a + b + c = 42$

$\Rightarrow \quad 18 + 10 + c = 42$

$\Rightarrow \quad c = (42 - 28)$ cm

$\Rightarrow \quad c = 14$ cm

Now, semi-perimeter $s = \frac{a + b + c}{2}$

$\Rightarrow \quad s = \frac{42}{2} = 21$ cm

$\therefore$ Area of a triangle $= \sqrt{s(s-a)(s-b)(s-c)}$ [by Heron's formula]

$= \sqrt{21(21-18)(21-10)(21-14)}$

$= \sqrt{21 \times 3 \times 11 \times 7}$

$= \sqrt{7 \times 3 \times 3 \times 11 \times 7}$

$= 21\sqrt{11}$ cm^2

Question 5 Sides of a triangle are in the ratio of 12 : 17 : 25 and its perimeter is 540 cm. Find its area.

Sol. Suppose that the sides in cm, are $12x$, $17x$ and $25x$.

We have, perimeter of triangle = 540

$\Rightarrow \quad 12x + 17x + 25x = 540$

$\Rightarrow \quad 54x = 540 \Rightarrow x = 10$

So, the sides of the triangle are 12×10 cm, 17×10 cm, 25×10 cm *i.e.*, 120 cm, 170 cm, 250 cm.

Now, semi-perimeter, $s = \frac{540}{2}$ cm [∵ Perimeter = 540]

$= 270$ cm

∴ Area of triangle $= \sqrt{270\,(270-120)\,(270-170)\,(270-250)}$

[by Heron's formula]

$= \sqrt{27 \times 10 \times 150 \times 100 \times 20}$

$= 100\sqrt{27 \times 15 \times 10 \times 2}$

$= 100\sqrt{9 \times 3 \times 3 \times 5 \times 10 \times 2}$

$= 100\sqrt{3 \times 3 \times 3 \times 3 \times 10 \times 10}$

$= 100 \times 3 \times 3 \times 10$

$= 9000 \text{ cm}^2$

Question 6 An isosceles triangle has perimeter 30 cm and each of the equal sides is 12 cm. Find the area of the triangle.

Sol. Let ABC be an isosceles triangle in which $AB = AC$.

∴ $AB = AC = 12$ cm

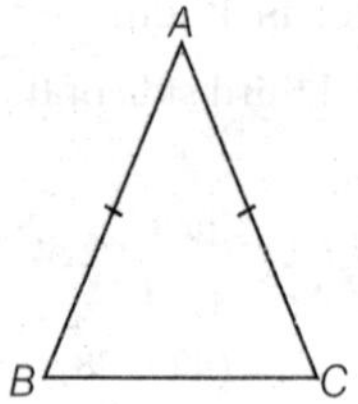

Perimeter of $\Delta ABC = 30$ cm

⇒ $AB + AC + BC = 30$

⇒ $12 + 12 + BC = 30$ [Given]

⇒ $BC = 30 - 24$

⇒ $BC = 6$ cm

Now, semi-perimeter, $s = \frac{30}{2}$ cm $= 15$ cm (∵ Perimeter = 30)

Area of isosceles triangle $= \sqrt{s\,(s-a)\,(s-b)\,(s-c)}$ [∵ by Heron's formula]

$= \sqrt{15\,(15-12)\,(15-12)\,(15-6)}$

$= \sqrt{15 \times 3 \times 3 \times 9}$

$= \sqrt{5 \times 3 \times 3 \times 3 \times 3 \times 3} = 9\sqrt{15} \text{ cm}^2$

DIKSHA APP Questions

☐ Multiple Choice Questions

Q.1 The perimeter of a right angled triangle is 24 cm and its hypotenuse is 10 cm, the area of triangle is

(a) 28 cm^2 (b) 29 cm^2

(c) 24 cm^2 (d) 21 cm^2

Sol. (c)

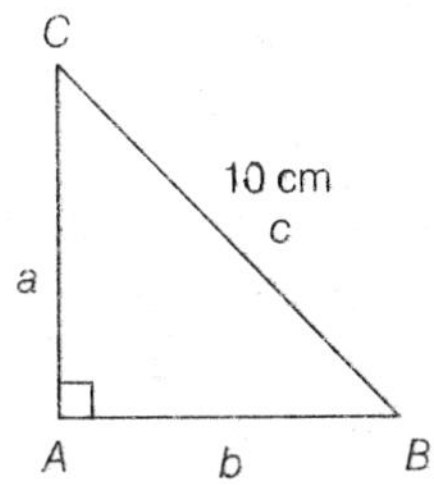

Let base and perpendicular of right angled triangle are a and b respectively and its hypotenuse be c.

Then, according to question, the perimeter of triangle is 24 cm.

$\Rightarrow \quad a + b + c = 24$

$\Rightarrow \quad a + b + 10 = 24$

$\Rightarrow \quad a + b = 14$

$\Rightarrow \quad a = 14 - b$

Now, by Pythagoras theorem

$c^2 = a^2 + b^2$

$\Rightarrow \quad (10)^2 = (14 - b)^2 + b^2$

$\Rightarrow \quad 100 = 196 + b^2 - 28b + b^2 \quad [\because (a - b)^2 = a^2 + b^2 - 2ab]$

$\Rightarrow \quad 100 = 2b^2 - 28b + 196$

$\Rightarrow \quad 100 - 196 - 2b^2 - 28b$

$\Rightarrow \quad -96 = 2b^2 - 28b$

$\Rightarrow \quad -48 = b^2 - 14b$

$\Rightarrow \quad b^2 - 14b + 48 = 0$

$\Rightarrow \quad b^2 - 8b - 6b + 48 = 0$

$\Rightarrow \quad b(b - 8) - 6(b - 8) = 0$

$\Rightarrow \quad (b - 8)(b - 6) = 0$

$\Rightarrow \quad b = 8, 6, \text{ then } a = 6, 8$

Now, semi-perimeter, $s = \frac{24}{2} = 12$ cm $\quad [\because$ Perimeter = 24 cm$]$

$\therefore$ Area of triangle $= \sqrt{12(12-6)(12-8)(12-10)}$ [by Heron's formula]

$= \sqrt{12 \times 6 \times 4 \times 2}$

$= \sqrt{12 \times 12 \times 4}$

$= 12 \times 2 = 24 \text{ cm}^2$

Mistake Alert Students may incorrectly apply the identity as $(a-b)^2 = a^2 - b^2 + 2ab$ instead of $(a-b)^2 = a^2 + b^2 - 2ab$

Q.2 The area of an isosceles triangle whose perimeter is 11 cm and base 5 cm is

(a) $\frac{5}{4}\sqrt{11} \text{ cm}^2$ (b) $\sqrt{11} \text{ cm}^2$

(c) $20\sqrt{11} \text{ cm}^2$ (d) $5\sqrt{11} \text{ cm}^2$

Sol. (a) Let x be the length of each of the equal sides of the triangle.

Given, the base of an isosceles triangle is 5 cm and perimeter 11 cm.

According to question, $5 + x + x = 11$

$\Rightarrow \quad 5 + 2x = 11$

$\Rightarrow \quad 2x = 11 - 5$

$\Rightarrow \quad 2x = 6$

$\Rightarrow \quad x = 3$

So, the sides of the isosceles triangle are 3 cm, 3 cm and 5 cm.

Now, semi-perimeter

$= \frac{3+3+5}{2} = \frac{11}{2}$

$\therefore$ Area of triangle $= \sqrt{\frac{11}{2}\left(\frac{11}{2}-3\right)\left(\frac{11}{2}-3\right)\left(\frac{11}{2}-5\right)}$ [by Heron's formula]

$= \sqrt{\frac{11}{2} \times \frac{5}{2} \times \frac{5}{2} \times \frac{1}{2}}$

$= \frac{5}{2} \times \frac{1}{2}\sqrt{11} = \frac{5}{4}\sqrt{11} \text{ cm}^2$

Q.3 The perimeter of an equilateral triangle is 12 cm. The area is

(a) $8\sqrt{3} \text{ cm}^2$ (b) $4\sqrt{3} \text{ cm}^2$

(c) $5\sqrt{3} \text{ cm}^2$ (d) $18\sqrt{3} \text{ cm}^2$

Sol. (b) Given, the perimeter of an equilateral triangle is 12 cm.

Let the length of each side of an equilateral triangle be x.

Then, $\quad x + x + x = 12$ (all sides equal)

$\Rightarrow \quad 3x = 12$

$\Rightarrow \quad x = 4 \text{ cm}$

Now, semi-perimeter $= \dfrac{x + x + x}{2}$

$= \dfrac{4 + 4 + 4}{2} = \dfrac{12}{2} = 6$ cm

$\therefore$ Area of triangle $= \sqrt{6(6-4)(6-4)(6-4)}$

$= \sqrt{6 \times 2 \times 2 \times 2}$

$= \sqrt{2 \times 3 \times 2 \times 2 \times 2}$

$= 2 \times 2\sqrt{3} = 4\sqrt{3}$ cm^2

Quick Solution

We have, perimeter of equilateral triangle = 12

$\Rightarrow \quad 3 \times \text{Side} = 12$

$\Rightarrow \quad \text{Side} = 4$ cm

$\therefore$ Area of equilateral triangle

$= \dfrac{\sqrt{3}}{4}(\text{Side})^2$

$= \dfrac{\sqrt{3}}{4} \times 4 \times 4$

$= 4\sqrt{3}$ cm^2

Mistake Alert Students may incorrectly apply the formula for area of an equilateral as $\dfrac{4}{\sqrt{3}}(\text{Side})^2$ instead of $\dfrac{\sqrt{3}}{4}(\text{Side})^2$.

Q.4 Two sides of a triangle are 8 cm and 11 cm and perimeter of triangle is 32 cm. The value of 's' is

(a) 20 cm (b) 19 cm (c) 12 cm (d) 16 cm

Sol. (a) Given, two sides of triangle are 8 cm and 11 cm and perimeter of triangle is 32 cm.

Let third side of the triangle be x.

$\therefore \quad 8 + 11 + x = 32$

$\Rightarrow \quad 19 + x = 32$

$\Rightarrow \quad x = 13$

Now, $\quad s = \dfrac{a + b + c}{2}$

$= \dfrac{8 + 11 + 13}{2} = \dfrac{32}{2} = 16$ cm

Mistake Alert Students may incorrectly find the values of s as $\dfrac{a+b+c}{3}$ instead of $\dfrac{a+b+c}{2}$.

Q.5 The sides of a triangle are 3 cm, 4 cm, 5 cm the length of the shortest altitude is

(a) 2.4 cm (b) 2.7 cm

(c) 3 cm (d) 2.1 cm

Thinking Process

- First find the area of the triangle with the given sides, then draw an altitude on the hypotenuse which is the smallest altitude.
- Put, area of triangle $= \frac{1}{2} \times$ Base $\times$ Height which we found earlier to find the required value.

Sol. (a) Let $a = 3$ cm, $b = 4$ cm and $c = 5$ cm

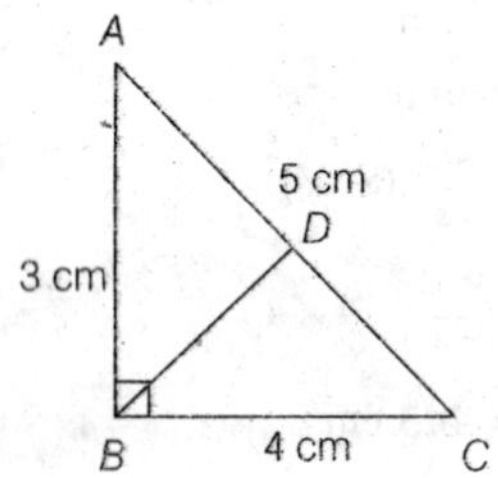

$$\therefore \quad s = \frac{a+b+c}{2}$$

$$= \frac{3+4+5}{2} = \frac{12}{2} = 6$$

$\therefore$ Area of triangle ΔABC

$$= \sqrt{s(s-a)(s-b)(s-c)}$$

$$= \sqrt{6(6-3)(6-4)(6-5)}$$

$$= \sqrt{6 \times 3 \times 2 \times 1}$$

$$= \sqrt{2 \times 3 \times 3 \times 2} = 6 \text{ cm}^2$$

As, we know, 3, 4 and 5 are triplet and form a right angle triangle.

So, the shortest altitude will be an hypotenuse which is 5 cm.

$\therefore$ Area of ΔABC

$$= \frac{1}{2} \times \text{Base} \times \text{Height}$$

$$= \frac{1}{2} \times AC \times BD$$

$$\Rightarrow \quad 6 = \frac{1}{2} \times 5 \times BD$$

$$\Rightarrow \quad BD = \frac{12}{5} = 2.4 \text{ cm}$$

☐ Subjective Type Questions

Q.1 Find the area of triangle, two sideds of which are 8 cm and 11 cm and the perimeter is 32 cm.

◎ ***Thinking Process*** First find the third side of triangle to evaluate the area.

Sol. Let, third side of the triangle be c and $a = 8$ cm, $b = 11$ cm

$\therefore \quad 8 + 11 + c = 32$

$\Rightarrow \quad 19 + c = 32$

$\Rightarrow \quad c = 13$

Then, $\quad s = \dfrac{32}{2} = 16 \quad$ [$\because$ Perimeter = 32 cm]

$$\therefore \text{Area of triangle} = \sqrt{s(s-a)(s-b)(s-c)}$$
$$= \sqrt{16(16-8)(16-11)(16-13)}$$
$$= \sqrt{16 \times 8 \times 5 \times 3}$$
$$= \sqrt{2 \times 2 \times 2 \times 2 \times 2 \times 2 \times 2 \times 5 \times 3}$$
$$= 8\sqrt{30} \text{ cm}^2$$

Q.2 Perimeter of a triangular ground is 900 m and its sides are in the ratio 3 : 5 : 4. Using Heron's formula, find the area of ground.

Sol. Let the sides of triangular ground be $3x$, $5x$ and $4x$.

Given, perimeter = 900 m

$\Rightarrow \quad 3x + 5x + 4x = 900$

$\Rightarrow \quad 12x = 900$

$\Rightarrow \quad x = \dfrac{900}{12} = 75$ m

Then, sides of the triangle are $3 \times 75, 5 \times 75$ and 4×75

i.e., 225 cm, 375 cm and 300 cm.

Now, find area of triangle by using Heron's formula

$s = \dfrac{900}{2} = 450 \quad$ [$\because$ Perimeter = 900 m]

$$\therefore \text{Area of triangle is } \Delta = \sqrt{s(s-a)(s-b)(s-c)}$$
$$= \sqrt{450(450-225)(450-375)(450-300)}$$
$$= \sqrt{450 \times 225 \times 75 \times 150}$$
$$= \sqrt{(2 \times 3 \times 3 \times 5 \times 5) \times (3 \times 3 \times 5 \times 5) \times (3 \times 5 \times 5) \times (2 \times 3 \times 5 \times 5)}$$
$$= 2 \times 3 \times 3 \times 3 \times 5 \times 5 \times 5 \times 5 = 33750 \text{ m}^2$$

Q.3 A NGO want to use a vacant triangular plot in the village whose sides are 9 cm, 12 cm and 15 cm for imparting free education to villagers. What is the area of the plot?

Sol. The three sides of the triangular plot are 9 cm, 12 cm and 15 cm.

Then, $s = \frac{9 + 12 + 15}{2} = \frac{36}{2} = 18$ cm

$$\begin{aligned}\text{Area of triangle} &= \sqrt{s(s-a)(s-b)(s-c)}\\ &= \sqrt{18(18-9)(18-12)(18-15)}\\ &= \sqrt{18 \times 9 \times 6 \times 3}\\ &= \sqrt{2 \times 3 \times 3 \times 3 \times 3 \times 2 \times 3 \times 3}\\ &= 2 \times 3 \times 3 \times 3\\ &= 54 \text{ cm}^2\end{aligned}$$

Quick Solution

As we know, 9, 12 and 15 are triplet and form a right triangle.

∴ Area of triangular plot

$$\begin{aligned}&= \frac{1}{2} \times \text{Base} \times \text{Height}\\ &= \frac{1}{2} \times 12 \times 9\\ &= 54 \text{ cm}^2\end{aligned}$$

Q.4 What is the altitude of an equilateral triangle?

Sol. The altitude of an equilateral tringle is $\frac{\sqrt{3}}{2} \times$ side.

Q.5 What is the area of an equilateral triangle?

Sol. Area of an equilateral triangle $\frac{\sqrt{3}}{4} \times (\text{side})^2$.

Q.6 The perimeter of an isosceles triangle is 42 cm and its base is 1.5 times each of the equal sides. Find the length of each side of triangle, the area of the triangle and height of triangle.

Sol. Let the length of equal sides of an isosceles triangle be x. Then, its base $= 1.5x$

We have perimeter = 42 cm

Now, $1.5x + x + x = 42$ cm

$$\begin{aligned}\Rightarrow \quad 3.5x &= 42\\ \Rightarrow \quad x &= \frac{42}{3.5}\\ \Rightarrow \quad x &= 12 \text{ cm}\end{aligned}$$

So, length of each side of the triangle

$$= 12 \text{ cm}$$

$\therefore$ Base $= 12 \times 1.5 = 18$ cm

Now, semi-perimeter $(s) = \frac{42}{2} = 21$ cm [$\because$ Perimeter = 42 cm]

$\because$ Area of triangle $= \sqrt{21(21-12)(21-12)(21-18)}$ [by Heron's formula]

$$= \sqrt{21 \times 9 \times 9 \times 3}$$
$$= \sqrt{3 \times 7 \times 3 \times 3 \times 3 \times 3 \times 3}$$
$$= 3 \times 3 \times 3\sqrt{7}$$
$$= 27\sqrt{7} \text{ cm}^2$$

Now, height of triangle

$$= \frac{1}{2} \times \text{Base} \times \text{Height}$$

$\Rightarrow$ $27\sqrt{7} = \frac{1}{2} \times 18 \times \text{Height}$

$\Rightarrow$ $\text{Height} = \frac{27\sqrt{7}}{9} = 3\sqrt{7}$ cm

Q.7 The perimeter of an isosceles triangle is 100 cm. If each of its equal sides is 26 cm. Find the area of the triangle.

Sol. Let third side of the triangle be c.

The equal sides of an isoscels triangle is 26 cm.

Then, $a = 26$ cm and $b = 26$ cm

$\therefore$ $a + b + c = 100$ [$\because$ Perimeter = 100 cm]

$\Rightarrow$ $26 + 26 + c = 100$

$\Rightarrow$ $c = 100 - 52$

$\Rightarrow$ $c = 48$

Now, $s = \frac{100}{2} = 50$ cm [$\because$ Perimeter = 100 cm]

$\therefore$ Area of triangle $= \sqrt{s(s-a)(s-b)(s-c)}$

$$= \sqrt{50(50-26)(50-26)(50-48)}$$
$$= \sqrt{50 \times 24 \times 24 \times 2}$$
$$= \sqrt{2 \times 5 \times 5 \times 2 \times 2 \times 2 \times 3 \times 2 \times 2 \times 2 \times 3 \times 2}$$
$$= 2 \times 2 \times 2 \times 2 \times 3 \times 5$$
$$= 240 \text{ cm}^2$$

Q.8 Find the cost of levelling the ground in the form of a triangle with sides 40 m, 70 m and 90 m at ₹ 4 per sq. m.
An organisation wants to conduct an environment awareness programme in which they will plant plants around the boundary of the ground. What values are reflected from the organisation doing the plantations?

Sol. By using Heron's formula, we will find the area

$$s = \frac{40 + 70 + 90}{2} = \frac{200}{2} = 100 \text{ m}$$

$$\text{Area of triangle} = \sqrt{s(s-a)(s-b)(s-c)}$$
$$= \sqrt{100(100-40)(100-70)(100-90)}$$
$$= \sqrt{100 \times 60 \times 30 \times 10}$$
$$= 10\sqrt{10 \times 6 \times 6 \times 5 \times 10}$$
$$= 10 \times 10 \times 6\sqrt{5}$$
$$= 600\sqrt{5}$$
$$= 600 \times 2.24 = 1344 \text{ m}^2$$

$\because$ Cost of levelling for 1 m^2 = ₹4

$\therefore$ Cost of levelling the ground

= 4 × ₹1344

= ₹5376

Tree plantation initiatives can help organisations align their sustainability goals with environmental conservation.

Q.9 If each side of the triangle is doubled, then its area increased by which percent?

Sol. Let a, b and c be the sides of the original triangle and s be its semi-perimeter.

$$\therefore \quad s = \frac{a+b+c}{2} = 2s = a + b + c \quad \text{...(i)}$$

The sides of a new triangle are $2a$, $2b$, $2c$.

$$\therefore \quad s' = \frac{(2a + 2b + 2c)}{2} \quad \text{(given : side is doubled)}$$
$$= \frac{2(a+b+c)}{2} = a + b + c$$

Let s' be the new semi-perimeter.

$$\Rightarrow \quad s' = 2s \quad \text{...(ii)[from Eq. (i)]}$$

Let Δ be area of original triangle and Δ' be area of new triangle.

$$\therefore \quad \Delta = \sqrt{s(s-a)(s-b)(s-c)} \quad \text{...(iii)}$$
$$\Delta' = \sqrt{s'(s'-2a)(s'-2b)(s'-2c)}$$

$$= \sqrt{2s(2s-2a)(2s-2b)(2s-2c)} \quad \text{[from Eq. (ii)]}$$
$$= \sqrt{2s \times 2(s-a) \times 2(s-b) \times 2(s-c)}$$
$$= \sqrt{16s(s-a)(s-b)(s-c)}$$
$$= 4\sqrt{s(s-a)(s-b)(s-c)}$$

$$\Rightarrow \quad \Delta' = 4\Delta \quad \text{[from Eq. (iii)]}$$

Increase in the area of triangle

$$= \Delta' - \Delta$$
$$= 4\Delta - \Delta$$
$$= 3\Delta$$

Percentage increase in area $= \frac{3\Delta}{\Delta} \times 100 = 300\%$

Hence, the percentage increase in the area of triangle is 300%.

Q.10 Prove that the area of an equilateral triangle with each of its side as 'a' is $\frac{\sqrt{3}}{4}a^2$.

Sol. Given, each side of the an equilateral triangle $= a$

$\therefore$ Semi-perimeter, $s = \frac{a+a+a}{2} = \frac{3a}{2}$

Area of an equilateral triangle

$$= \sqrt{s(s-a)(s-b)(s-c)}$$
$$= \sqrt{\frac{3a}{2}\left(\frac{3a}{2}-a\right)\left(\frac{3a}{2}-a\right)\left(\frac{3a}{2}-a\right)}$$
$$= \sqrt{\frac{3a}{2} \times \frac{a}{2} \times \frac{a}{2} \times \frac{a}{2}}$$
$$= \frac{a}{2} \times \frac{a}{2}\sqrt{3}$$
$$= \frac{\sqrt{3}}{4}a^2$$

Hence Proved.

Surface Areas and Volumes

CHAPTER 11

Important Points

01 Cone A right circular cone is a solid generated by revolving of a triangle about one of its sides (other than hypotenuse).

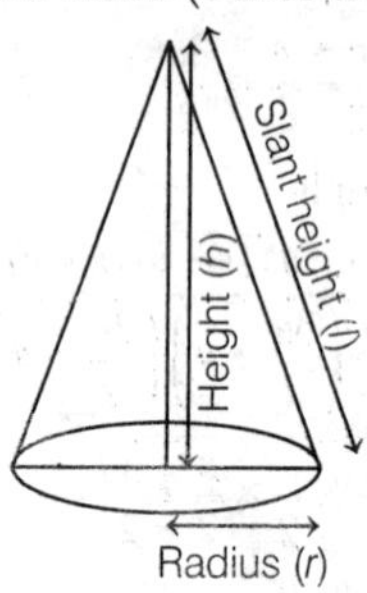

Volume of cone $= \frac{1}{3}\pi r^2 h$

Curved surface area or lateral surface area $= \pi rl$

Total surface area = Curved surface area + Base area

$$= \pi rl + \pi r^2$$

$$= \pi r(l + r)$$

where $\quad l = \sqrt{h^2 + r^2}$

$$h = \sqrt{l^2 - r^2}$$

and $\quad r = \sqrt{l^2 - h^2}$

02 Sphere A solid which is surrounded by curved surface and each point of surface are same distance from a fixed point. The fixed point is called the centre of sphere. The line segment joining from the centre of sphere to the any point of surface is called the radius of sphere.

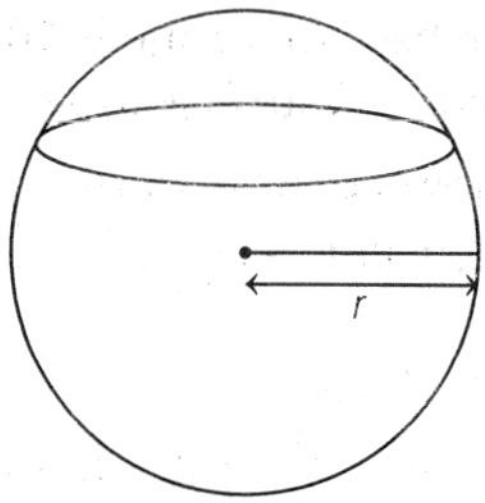

Volume of sphere $= \frac{4}{3}\pi r^3$

Surface area of sphere $= 4\pi r^2$

Note A sphere is like the surface of a ball. The word solid sphere is used for the solid whose surface is sphere.

03 Hemisphere A plane passing through the centre of a sphere divides the sphere into two equal parts. Each part is called a hemisphere.

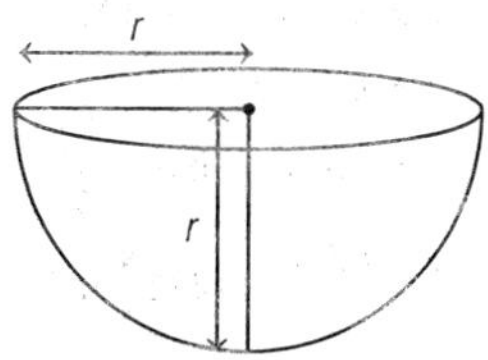

Volume of hemisphere $= \frac{2}{3}\pi r^3$

Curved surface area of hemisphere $= 2\pi r^2$

Total surface area of hemisphere $= 2\pi r^2 + \pi r^2 = 3\pi r^2$

Note
- The solids having the same curved surface area do not necessarily occupy the same volume.
- When an object is dropped into a liquid the volume of the displaced liquid is equal to the volume of object that is dipped.

Exercise 11.1

- Assume $\pi = \frac{22}{7}$, unless stated otherwise.

Question 1 Diameter of the base of a cone is 10.5 cm and its slant height is 10 cm. Find its curved surface area.

Sol. Given, diameter of the base of cone = 10.5 cm

$\therefore$Radius of the base of cone $(r) = \frac{10.5}{2} = 5.25$ cm $\qquad \left(\because r = \frac{\text{Diameter}}{2}\right)$

and slant height of the cone, $l = 10$ cm

Curved surface area of cone $= \pi r l = \frac{22}{7} \times 5.25 \times 10 = 165 \text{cm}^2$

Question 2 Find the total surface area of a cone, if its slant height is 21 m and diameter of its base is 24 m.

Sol. We have, slant height of the cone $l = 21$ m

and diameter of the base of cone = 24 cm

$\therefore$ Radius of the base of cone, $(r) = \frac{24}{2} = 12$m $\qquad \left(\because r = \frac{\text{Diameter}}{2}\right)$

$$\begin{aligned} \text{Total surface area of cone} &= \pi r(l + r) \\ &= \pi \times 12(21 + 12) \\ &= \pi \times 12 \times 33 \\ &= 396\pi = 396 \times \frac{22}{7} \\ &= \frac{8712}{7} = 1244\frac{4}{7} \text{ m}^2 \end{aligned}$$

Question 3 Curved surface area of a cone is 308 cm^2 and its slant height is 14 cm. Find

(i) radius of the base and (ii) total surface area of the cone.

Sol. We have, slant height of a cone, $l = 14$cm

Let the radius of the cone be r.

(i) Given, Curved surface area of a cone = 308 cm^2

$$\therefore \qquad \pi r l = 308$$

$$\Rightarrow \qquad \frac{22}{7} \times r \times 14 = 308$$

$$\Rightarrow \qquad r = \frac{308}{22 \times 2} \Rightarrow r = 7\text{cm}$$

Hence, radius of the base is 7 cm.

(ii) Total surface area of a cone $= \pi r(r + l) = \frac{22}{7} \times 7(7 + 14)$

$$= 22 \times 21$$
$$= 462 \text{ cm}^2$$

Question 4 A conical tent is 10 m high and the radius of its base is 24 m. Find

(i) slant height of the tent.

(ii) cost of the canvas required to make the tent, if the cost of 1 m^2 canvas is ₹ 70.

Sol. We have height of the conical tent, $(h) = 10$ m

and radius of base of conical tent, $(r) = 24$ m

(i) We know that $l^2 = h^2 + r^2$ where l = slant height of the cone

$$\Rightarrow \quad l = \sqrt{r^2 + h^2}$$
$$\Rightarrow \quad l = \sqrt{(24)^2 + 10^2}$$
$$= \sqrt{576 + 100}$$
$$= \sqrt{676} = 26 \text{ m}$$

Hence, the slant height of the conical tent is 26 m.

(ii) Canvas required to make the tent = Curved surface area of tent

$$= \pi r l$$
$$= \pi \times 24 \times 26 = 624\pi \text{ m}^2$$

$\because$ Cost of 1 m^2 canvas = ₹ 70

$\therefore$ Cost of $624\pi \text{ m}^2$ canvas = ₹ $70 \times 624\pi$

$$= ₹\ 70 \times 624 \times \frac{22}{7}$$
$$= ₹\ 10 \times 624 \times 22 = ₹\ 137280$$

Hence, the cost of the canvas is ₹ 137280.

Question 5 What length of tarpaulin 3 m wide will be required to make conical tent of height 8 m and base radius 6m? Assume that the extra length of material that will be required for stitching margins and wastage in cutting is approximately 20 cm. (use $\pi = 3.14$)

Thinking Process Firstly find the slant height and surface area of conical tent. Then, curved surface area of conical tent = Area of tarpaulin required

= Length of tarpaulin × Width of tarpaulin

$$\Rightarrow \text{Length of tarpaulin} = \frac{\text{Curved surface area of conical tent}}{\text{Width of tarpaulin}}$$

Sol. Let r, h and l be the radius, height and slant height of the tent, respectively.

Given, $r = 6$ m, $h = 8$ m

$\because$ $l = \sqrt{r^2 + h^2}$

$\therefore$ $l = \sqrt{6^2 + 8^2} = \sqrt{36 + 64}$

$= \sqrt{100} = 10$ m

Area of the canvas used for the tent

= Curve surface area of the cone

$= \pi r l$

$= 3.14 \times 6 \times 10$

$= 188.4 \text{ m}^2$

$$\therefore \text{Length of tarpaulin required} = \frac{\text{Area of tarpaulin required}}{\text{Width of tarpaulin}}$$

$$= \frac{188.4}{3} \quad (\because \text{Width of tarpaulin} = 3, \text{given})$$

$= 62.8$ m

The extra material required for stitching margins and cutting = 20 cm = 0.2 m $\left[\because 1\text{ cm} = \frac{1}{100}\text{ m}\right]$

Hence, the total length of tarpaulin required = 62.8 + 0.2 = 63 m

Question 6 The slant height and base diameter of a conical tomb are 25 m and 14 m respectively. Find the cost of white-washing its curved surface at the rate of ₹210 per 100 m^2.

Sol. We have, slant height of the conical tomb, (l) = 25 m

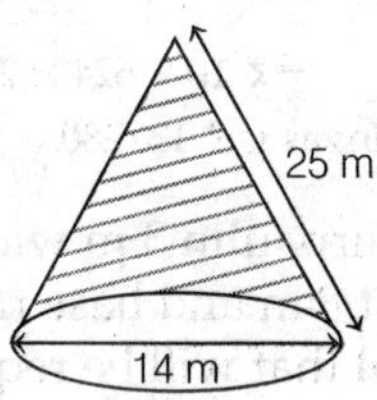

and diameter of the base of the conical tomb = 14 m

$\therefore$ Radius of the base of the conical tomb, $r = 7$ m

Curved surface area of the conical tomb $= \pi r l = \frac{22}{7} \times 7 \times 25$

$= 22 \times 25 = 550 \text{ m}^2$

Cost of white washing per 100 m^2 = ₹ 210

Cost of white washing per 1 m^2 = ₹ $\frac{210}{100}$

Cost of white washing 550 m^2 = ₹ $\frac{210 \times 550}{100}$ = ₹1155

Question 7 A joker's cap is in the form of a right circular cone of base radius 7 cm and height 24 cm. Find the area of the sheet required to make 10 such caps.

Sol. We have, radius of the base of the circular cone, $r = 7$ cm and height of the circular cone, $h = 24$ cm.

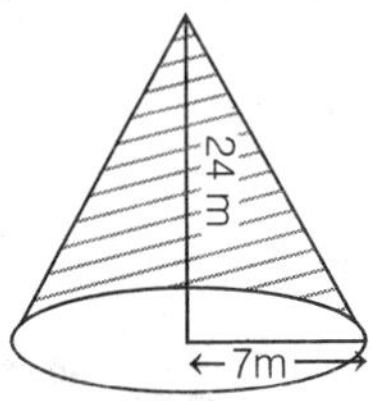

We know that, $l = \sqrt{h^2 + r^2}$

$\therefore$ $l = \sqrt{(24)^2 + 7^2} = \sqrt{576 + 49} = \sqrt{625}$

$\Rightarrow$ $l = 25\text{cm}$

Curved surface area of joker's cap $= \pi r l = \frac{22}{7} \times 7 \times 25$

$= 22 \times 25 = 550 \text{ cm}^2$

$\because$ The sheet required to make 1 cap $= 550 \text{ cm}^2$

$\therefore$ The sheet required to make 10 caps $= 550 \times 10 = 5500 \text{ cm}^2$

Mistake Alert Students makes the mistake by using the wrong formula for surface area or volume. So, ensure that you are using the correct formula for surface area or volume.

Question 8 A bus stop is barricaded from the remaining part of the road, by using 50 hollow cones made of recycled cardboard. Each cone has a base diameter of 40 cm and height 1 m. If the outer side of each of the cones is to be painted and the cost of painting is ₹12 per m^2, what will be the cost of painting all these cones? (Use $\pi = 3.14$ and take $\sqrt{1.04} = 1.02$)

Thinking Process Firstly find the slant height and curved surface area of the cone. After that find the cost of painting of one cone and using this find the cost of 50 cones.

Sol. We have, diameter of the base of the cone = 40 cm

$\therefore$ Radius of the base of the cone, $r = \frac{40}{2} = 20$ cm

$= \frac{20}{100} \text{ m} = 0.2 \text{ m}$ $\left(\because 1 \text{ cm} = \frac{1}{100} \text{ m}\right)$

and height of the cone $h = 1\text{m}$

$\because$ $l = \sqrt{r^2 + h^2}$

$\therefore$ $l = \sqrt{(0.2)^2 + 1^2} = \sqrt{0.04 + 1}$

$= \sqrt{1.04} = 1.02 \text{ m}$

Curved surface area of a cone $= \pi rl = 3.14 \times 0.2 \times 1.02 = 0.64056 \text{ m}^2$

Cost of painting per m^2 = ₹12

Cost of painting 0.64056 m^2 = ₹12 × 0.64056 = ₹ 7.68672

Cost of painting for 1 cone = ₹ 7.68672

Cost of painting 50 cones = ₹ 7.68672 × 50 = ₹ 384.336 = ₹ 384.34 (approximately)

Exercise 11.2

Question 1 Find the surface area of a sphere of radius

(i) 10.5 cm (ii) 5.6 cm (iii) 14 cm

Sol. (i) We have radius of a shpere, $r = 10.5\text{cm}$

Surface area of a sphere $= 4\pi r^2 = 4 \times \frac{22}{7} \times 10.5 \times 10.5$

$= 88 \times 1.5 \times 10.5 = 1386 \text{ cm}^2$

(ii) We have, r = radius of the sphere = 5.6 cm

$\therefore$ Surface area of the sphere $= 4\pi r^2$

$= 4 \times \frac{22}{7} \times 5.6 \times 5.6 = 88 \times 0.8 \times 5.6$

$= 394.24 \text{ cm}^2$

(iii) We have, r = radius of the sphere = 14 cm

$\therefore$ Surface area of the sphere $= 4\pi r^2$

$= 4 \times \frac{22}{7} \times 14 \times 14$

$= 88 \times 2 \times 14 = 2464 \text{ cm}^2$

Question 2 Find the surface area of a sphere of diameter

(i) 14 cm (ii) 21 cm (iii) 3.5 m

Sol. (i) We have, diameter of a sphere = 14 cm

$\therefore$ Radius of a sphere, $r = 7\text{cm}$

Surface area of a sphere $= 4\pi r^2 = 4 \times \frac{22}{7} \times 7^2 = 4 \times 22 \times 7 = 616 \text{ cm}^2$

(ii) We have, diameter of a sphere = 21 cm

$\therefore$ Radius of a sphere, $r = \frac{21}{2} = 10.5 \text{ cm}$

$\therefore$ Surface area of a sphere $= 4\pi r^2 = 4 \times \frac{22}{7} \times 10.5 \times 10.5$

$= 88 \times 1.5 \times 10.5$

$= 1386 \text{ cm}^2$

(iii) We have, diameter of a sphere = 3.5 m

$\therefore$ Radius of a sphere $(r) = \frac{3.5}{2} = 1.75$ cm

$\therefore$ Surface area of a sphere $= 4\pi r^2 = 4 \times \frac{22}{7} \times 1.75 \times 1.75 = \frac{269.50}{7}$

$= 38.5 \text{cm}^2$

Question 3 Find the total surface area of a hemisphere of radius 10 cm. (use $\pi = 3.14$)

Sol. We have radius of a hemisphere, $r = 10$ cm

Total surface area of a hemisphere $= 3\pi r^2$

$= 3 \times 3.14 \times (10)^2$

$= 9.42 \times 100$

$= 942 \text{ cm}^2$

Question 4 The radius of a spherical balloon increases from 7 cm to 14 cm as air is being pumped into it. Find the ratio of surface areas of the balloon in the two cases.

Sol. Let initial radius of a spherical balloon, $(r_1) = 7$ cm

And after increases, $(r_2) = 14$cm

Surface area for initial balloon, $A_1 = 4\pi r_1^2 = 4 \times \frac{22}{7} \times 7 \times 7 = 88 \times 7$

$\Rightarrow$ $A_1 = 616 \text{ cm}^2$

Surface area for increasing balloon, $A_2 = 4\pi r_2^2 = 4 \times \frac{22}{7} \times 14 \times 14 = 88 \times 28$

$\Rightarrow$ $A_2 = 2464 \text{ cm}^2$

$\therefore$ Required ratio $= A_1 : A_2 = 616 : 2464 = 1 : 4$

Quick Solution

Let r_1 be the radius of spherical balloon and r_2 be the radius of a spherical balloon.

When air is pumped into it.

$\therefore$ $r_1 = 7$ cm and $r_2 = 14$ cm

Required ratio $= \frac{\text{Initial surface area}}{\text{Surface area after pumping air into balloon}}$

$= \frac{4\pi r_1^2}{4\pi r_2^2} = \left(\frac{r_1}{r_2}\right)^2 = \left(\frac{7}{14}\right)^2 = \left(\frac{1}{2}\right)^2 = \frac{1}{4}$

Question 5 A hemispherical bowl made of brass has inner diameter 10.5 cm. Find the cost of tin-plating it on the inside at the rate of ₹ 16 per 100 cm^2.

Sol. We have, inner diameter of a hemispherical bowl = 10.5 cm

$\therefore$ Inner radius of a hemispherical bowl $= \frac{10.5}{2} = 5.25$cm

Curved surface area of hemispherical bowl of inner side $= 2\pi r^2$

$$= 2 \times \frac{22}{7} \times (5.25)^2$$

$$= 2 \times \frac{22}{7} \times 5.25 \times 5.25 = 173.25\text{cm}^2$$

$\because$ Cost of tin-plating on inside for 100 cm^2 = ₹ 16

$\because$ Cost of tin-plating on the inside for 173.25 cm^2 = ₹ $\frac{16 \times 173.25}{100}$ = ₹ 27.72

Question 6 Find the radius of a sphere whose surface area is 154 cm^2.

Sol. Let the radius of the sphere be r.

Given, Surface area of a sphere = 154 cm^2

$$\therefore \quad 4\pi r^2 = 154 \Rightarrow 4 \times \frac{22}{7} \times r^2 = 154$$

$$\Rightarrow \quad r^2 = \frac{154 \times 7}{22 \times 4} = 12.25 \Rightarrow r = \sqrt{12.25}$$

$$\Rightarrow \quad r = 3.5 \text{ cm}$$

Hence, the radius of the sphere is 3.5 cm.

Question 7 The diameter of the Moon is approximately one-fourth of the diameter of the Earth. Find the ratio of their surface areas.

Sol. Let diameter of the Earth $= d_1$

Then, diameter of the Moon $= \frac{1}{4}d_1$

$\therefore$ Radius of the Earth, $(r_1) = \frac{d_1}{2}$

and radius of the Moon, $(r_2) = \frac{d_1}{2 \times 4} = \frac{d_1}{8}$

Now, Surface area of the Earth, $(S_1) = 4\pi r_1^2$

$$\Rightarrow \quad S_1 = 4\pi\left(\frac{d_1}{2}\right)^2 = \pi d_1^2$$

and surface area of the Moon, $(S_2) = 4\pi\left(\frac{d_1}{8}\right)^2 = 4\pi\frac{d_1^2}{64}$

$$\Rightarrow \quad S_2 = \frac{\pi d_1^2}{16}$$

Hence, ratio of their surface area $= \dfrac{\text{Surface area of Moon}}{\text{Surface area of Earth}}$

$$= S_2 : S_1 = \frac{\pi d_1^2}{16} : \frac{\pi d_1^2}{1} = 1 : 16$$

Question 8 A hemispherical bowl is made of steel, 0.25 cm thick. The inner radius of the bowl is 5 cm. Find the outer curved surface area of the bowl.

$\therefore$ Given inner radius of the bowl = 5 cm and thickness of the bowl = 0.25 cm,

Sol. $\therefore$ Outer radius of the bowl = (Inner radius + Thickness)

$$= (5 + 0.25)\ \text{cm} = 5.25\ \text{cm}$$

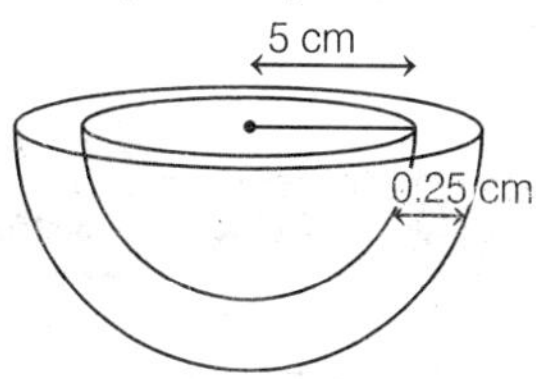

Outer curved surface area of the bowl $= 2\pi r^2$

$$= 2 \times \frac{22}{7} \times 5.25 \times 5.25$$

$$= 173.25\ \text{cm}^2$$

Question 9 A right circular cylinder just encloses a sphere of radius r (see figure). Find

(i) surface area of the sphere.

(ii) curved surface area of the cylinder.

(iii) ratio of the areas obtained in (i) and (ii).

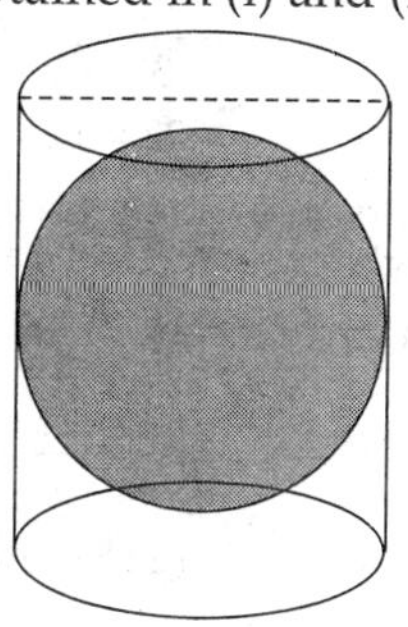

Sol. Given, radius of the sphere = r

$\therefore$ Radius of the cylinder = Radius of the sphere

$$= r$$

and height of the cylinder = Diameter of the sphere = $2r$

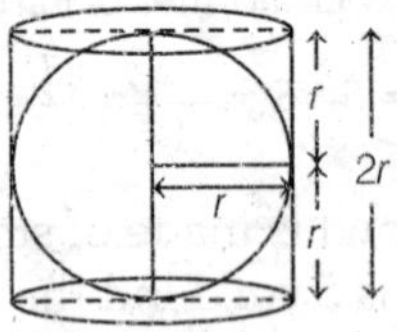

(i) Surface area of the sphere $(A_1) = 4\pi r^2$

(ii) Curved surface area of the cylinder $(A_2) = 2\pi rh$

$\Rightarrow \quad A_2 = 2\pi \times r \times 2r$

$\Rightarrow \quad A_2 = 4\pi r^2$

(iii) Required ratio $= A_1 : A_2 = 4\pi r^2 : 4\pi r^2 = 1 : 1$

Exercise 11.3

- Assume $\pi = \frac{22}{7}$, unless stated otherwise.

Question 1 Find the volume of the right circular cone with

(i) radius 6 cm, height 7 cm.

(ii) radius 3.5 cm, height 12 cm.

Sol. (i) We have, radius of the right circular cone $(r) = 6$ cm

and height of the right circular cone, $h = 7$cm.

Then, volume of the right circular cone $= \frac{1}{3}\pi r^2 h = \frac{1}{3} \times \frac{22}{7} \times 6^2 \times 7$

$= \frac{22}{3} \times 6 \times 6$

$= 22 \times 12 = 264 \text{ cm}^3$

(ii) Given, radius of the right circular cone, $(r) = 3.5$ cm

and height of the right circular cone, $h = 12$ cm.

Volume of the right circular cone $= \frac{1}{3}\pi r^2 h$

$= \left(\frac{1}{3} \times \frac{22}{7} \times 3.5 \times 3.5 \times 12\right) \text{cm}^3$

$= (22 \times 0.5 \times 3.5 \times 4) \text{ cm}^3 = 154 \text{ cm}^3$

Question 2 Find the capacity in litres of a conical vessel with

(i) radius 7 cm, slant height 25 cm.

(ii) height 12 cm, slant height 13 cm.

Sol. (i) We have, radius of a conical vessel, $r = 7$cm and slant height of a conical vessel, $l = 25$ cm

We know that $l^2 = r^2 + h^2$

$$\Rightarrow \quad h = \sqrt{l^2 - r^2} = \sqrt{25^2 - 7^2}$$

$$= \sqrt{625 - 49} = \sqrt{576} = 24 \text{ cm}$$

$$\text{Capacity of conical vessel} = \frac{1}{3}\pi r^2 h$$

$$= \frac{1}{3} \times \frac{22}{7} \times 7 \times 7 \times 24$$

$$= 22 \times 7 \times 8 = 1232 \text{ cm}^3$$

$$= \frac{1232}{1000} \text{L} = 1.232 \text{ L} \qquad \left(\because 1 \text{cm}^3 = \frac{1}{1000} \text{L}\right)$$

(ii) We have, height of the conical vessel, $h = 12$ cm and slant height of a conical vessel, $l = 13$ cm

We know that, $l^2 = h^2 + r^2$

$$\Rightarrow \quad r = \sqrt{l^2 - h^2} = \sqrt{13^2 - 12^2}$$

$$= \sqrt{169 - 144} = \sqrt{25} = 5 \text{ cm}$$

$$\text{Capacity of conical vessel} = \frac{1}{3}\pi r^2 h$$

$$= \frac{1}{3} \times \frac{22}{7} \times 5 \times 5 \times 12$$

$$= \frac{22 \times 100}{7} \text{cm}^3 = \frac{22 \times 100}{7 \times 1000} \text{L} = 0.314 \text{L}$$

$$\left(\because 1 \text{cm}^3 = \frac{1}{1000} \text{L}\right)$$

Mistake Alert Students make the mistake in mixing up units or failing to convert them properly.

Question 3 The height of a cone is 15 cm. If its volume is 1570 cm^3, find the radius of the base. (use $\pi = 3.14$)

Sol. Let r be the radius of the base of the cone given height of a cone, $h = 15$ cm and volume of a cone = 1570 cm^3

$$\Rightarrow \quad \frac{1}{3}\pi r^2 h = 1570$$

$$\Rightarrow \quad \frac{1}{3} \times 3.14 \times r^2 \times 15 = 1570$$

$$\Rightarrow \quad r^2 = \frac{1570}{3.14 \times 5} = \frac{15700}{157} = 100 \Rightarrow r = 10 \text{ cm}$$

Hence, radius of the base = 10 cm

Question 4 If the volume of a right circular cone of height 9 cm is 48π cm^3, find the diameter of its base.

Sol. Given, height of a right circular cone, $(h) = 9$ cm

and volume of a right circular cone, 48π cm^3

Let r be the radius of the base of the right circular cone.

$\therefore \quad \frac{1}{3}\pi r^2 h = 48\pi \Rightarrow \frac{1}{3} r^2 \times 9 = 48 \quad (\because h = 9 \text{ cm, given})$

$\Rightarrow \quad r^2 = 16 \Rightarrow r = 4$ cm

Hence, diameter of the base $= 2r = 2 \times 4 = 8$ cm $\quad (\because d = 2r)$

Question 5 A conical pit of top diameter 3.5 m is 12 m deep. What is its capacity in kilolitres?

Sol. We have, diameter of a conical pit = 3.5 m

$\therefore$ radius of a conical pit, $(r) = \frac{3.5}{2}$ m

and height of the conical pit, $h = 12$ m

$$\text{Capacity of a conical pit} = \frac{1}{3}\pi r^2 h$$

$$= \frac{1}{3} \times \frac{22}{7} \times \left(\frac{3.5}{2}\right)^2 \times 12$$

$$= \frac{1}{3} \times \frac{22}{7} \times \frac{3.5}{2} \times \frac{3.5}{2} \times 12$$

$$= 22 \times 0.5 \times 3.5$$

$$= 38.5 \text{ m}^3 \quad (1 \text{ m}^3 = 1 \text{kL})$$

$$= 38.5 \text{ kL}$$

Question 6 The volume of a right circular cone is 9856 cm^3. If the diameter of the base is 28 cm, find

(i) height of the cone.

(ii) slant height of the cone.

(iii) curved surface area of the cone.

Sol. (i) We have, diameter of a right circular cone $(d) = 28$ cm

$\therefore \quad r = 14$ cm $\quad \left(\because r = \frac{d}{2}\right)$

Let h be the height of the circular cone.

$\because$ Volume of a right circular cone = 9856 cm^3

$\therefore \quad \frac{1}{3}\pi r^2 h = 9856$

$\Rightarrow \quad \frac{1}{3} \times \frac{22}{7} \times 14^2 \times h = 9856$

$\Rightarrow \quad h = \frac{9856 \times 3 \times 7}{22 \times 14 \times 14}$

$\Rightarrow \quad h = \frac{448 \times 3}{28} = 48 \text{ cm}$

Hence, height of the cone is 48 cm.

(ii) We have, $h = 48$ cm

and $r = 14$ cm

Let l be the slant height of the circular cone.

$\because \quad l = \sqrt{h^2 + r^2}$

$= \sqrt{48^2 + 14^2}$

$= \sqrt{2304 + 196} = \sqrt{2500}$

$\Rightarrow \quad l = 50$ cm

Hence, slant height of the cone is 50 cm.

(iii) Curved surface area of the cone $= \pi r l = \frac{22}{7} \times 14 \times 50$

$= 44 \times 50$

$= 2200 \text{ cm}^2$

Question 7 A right triangle ABC with sides 5 cm, 12 cm and 13 cm is revolved about the side 12 cm. Find the volume of the solid so obtained.

Sol. On revolving the right $\Delta\, ABC$ about the side AB, we get a cone as shown in the adjoining figure.

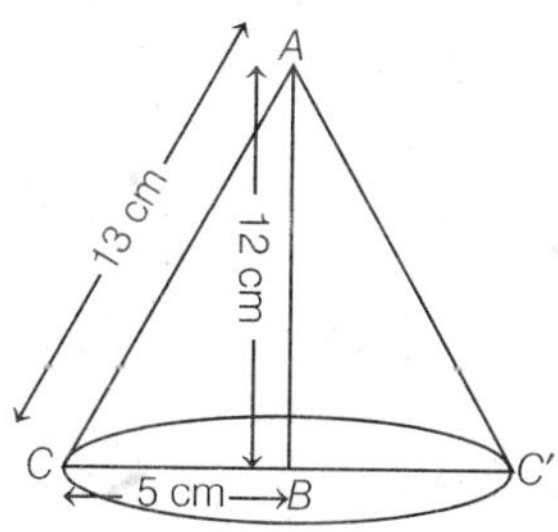

$\therefore$ Volume of the solid, so obtained $= \frac{1}{3} \pi r^2 h$

$= \frac{1}{3} \times \pi \times 5 \times 5 \times 12$

$= \pi \times 5 \times 5 \times 4 = 100\pi \text{ cm}^3$

Hence, the volume of the solid, so obtained is $100\pi \text{ cm}^3$.

Question 8 If the triangle ABC in the Question 7 above is revolved about the side 5 cm, then find the volume of the solid, so obtained. Find also the ratio of the volumes of the two solids obtained in Questions 7 and 8.

Sol. On revolving the right ΔABC about the side $BC(=5 \text{ cm})$, we get a cone as shown in the adjoining figure.

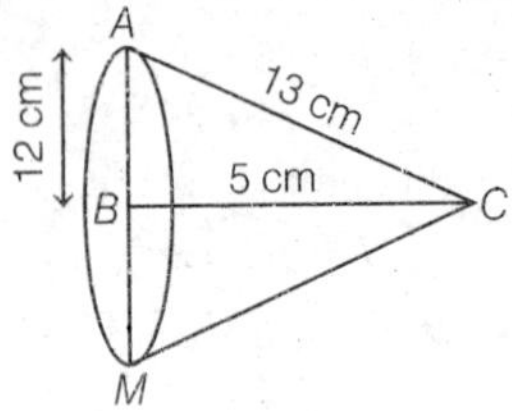

$$\text{Volume of solid, so obtained} = \frac{1}{3}\pi r^2 h$$

$$= \frac{1}{3} \times \pi \times 12 \times 12 \times 5 = 240\pi \text{ cm}^3$$

$$\text{So, the required ratio} = \frac{\text{Volume of solid in question 7}}{\text{Volume of solid in question 8}} = \frac{100\pi}{240\pi} = \frac{10}{24} = \frac{5}{12}$$

Question 9 A heap of wheat is in the form of a cone whose diameter is 10.5 m and height is 3 m. Find its volume. The heap is to be covered by canvas to protect it from rain. Find the area of the canvas required.

Sol. We have diameter of conical heap, $(d) = 10.5$ m,

and height of conical heap, $h = 3$ m

$\therefore$ Radius of conical heap, $(r) = \frac{10.5}{2} = 5.25$ m

Let l be the slant height of the conical heap

$$\because \quad l = \sqrt{r^2 + h^2} = \sqrt{(5.25)^2 + 3^2}$$

$$= \sqrt{27.5625 + 9} = \sqrt{36.5625} = 6.046$$

$$= 6.05 \text{ m} \quad \text{(approximately)}$$

$$\text{Volume of the heap of cone of wheat} = \frac{1}{3}\pi r^2 h$$

$$= \frac{1}{3} \times \frac{22}{7} \times 5.25 \times 5.25 \times 3 = 86.625 \text{ m}^3$$

Area of the canvas required = curved surface area of the heap

$$= \pi r l$$

$$= \frac{22}{7} \times 5.25 \times 6.05 \text{ m}^2$$

$$= 22 \times 0.75 \times 6.05 \text{ m}^2 = 99.825 \text{ m}^2$$

Exercise 11.4

- Assume $\pi = \frac{22}{7}$, unless stated otherwise.

Question 1 Find the volume of a sphere whose radius is

(i) 7 cm (ii) 0.63 m

Sol. (i) We have radius of a sphere, $r = 7\text{cm}$

Volume of a sphere, $= \frac{4}{3}\pi r^3$

$= \frac{4}{3} \times \frac{22}{7} \times (7)^3 = \frac{88 \times 7 \times 49}{3 \times 7}$

$= \frac{4312}{3} = 1437\frac{1}{3}\ \text{cm}^3$

(ii) We have radius of a sphere $r = 0.63$ m

Volume of a sphere $= \frac{4}{3}\pi r^3 = \frac{4}{3} \times \frac{22}{7}(0.63)^3$

$= \frac{4}{3} \times \frac{22}{7} \times 0.63 \times 0.63 \times 0.63$

$= 88 \times 0.9 \times 0.21 \times 0.63$

$= 1.0478 = 1.05\ \text{m}^3$

Question 2 Find the amount of water displaced by a solid spherical ball of diameter

(i) 28 cm (ii) 0.21 m

Sol. (i) We have, diameter of solid spherical ball = 28 cm

$\therefore$ Radius of solid spherical ball, $(r) = 14$ cm

Amount of water displaced by a solid spherical ball = Volume of sphere $= \frac{4}{3}\pi r^3$

$= \frac{4}{3} \times \frac{22}{7} \times (14)^3 = \frac{4}{3} \times \frac{22}{7} \times 14 \times 14 \times 14$

$= 11498.67\ \text{cm}^3$

(ii) We, have diameter of the spherical ball = 0.21 m

$\therefore$ Radius of the spherical ball, $r = \left(\frac{0.21}{2}\right)$ m $= 0.105$ m

Amount of water displaced by the spherical ball = Volume of sphere

$= \frac{4}{3}\pi r^3$

$= \frac{4}{3} \times \frac{22}{7} \times 0.105 \times 0.105 \times 0.105 = 0.004851\ \text{m}^3$

Question 3 The diameter of a metallic ball is 4.2 cm. What is the mass of the ball, if the density of the metal is 8.9 g per cm^3?

Sol. We have, diameter of a metallic ball = 4.2 cm

$\therefore$ Radius of the metallic ball, $r = \frac{4.2}{2} = 2.1\text{ cm}$

$$\text{Volume of the metallic ball} = \frac{4}{3}\pi r^3 = \frac{4}{3}\times\frac{22}{7}\times(2.1)^3$$
$$= \frac{4}{3}\times\frac{22}{7}\times 2.1\times 2.1\times 2.1$$
$$= 38.808\text{ cm}^3$$

The density of the metal per cm^3 = 8.9 g

The density of the metal 38.808 cm^3 = 38.808 × 8.9 g = 345.39 g

Hence, the mass of the ball = 345.39 g [$\because$ Mass = Density × Volume]

Question 4 The diameter of the Moon is approximately one-fourth of the diameter of the Earth. What fraction of the volume of the Earth is the volume of the Moon?

Sol. Let the diameter of the Earth = d

$\therefore$ Radius of the Earth = $\frac{d}{2}$

Given, diameter of Moon = $\frac{1}{4}$ × diameter of the Earth = $\frac{d}{4}$

$\therefore$ Radius of the Moon = $\frac{d}{8}$

$$\therefore \quad \text{Volume of the Earth }(V_1) = \frac{4}{3}\pi\left(\frac{d}{2}\right)^3 = \frac{4}{3}\pi\times\frac{d^3}{8}$$

$$\therefore \quad \text{Volume of the Moon }(V_2) = \frac{4}{3}\pi\left(\frac{d}{8}\right)^3 = \frac{4}{3}\pi\frac{d^3}{512}$$

$$\therefore \quad \text{Required fraction} = \frac{V_1}{V_2} = \frac{\frac{4}{3}\pi\left(\frac{d^3}{8}\right)}{\frac{4}{3}\pi\left(\frac{d^3}{512}\right)}$$

$$\frac{V_1}{V_2} = \frac{512}{8}$$

$$\Rightarrow \quad \frac{V_1}{V_2} = \frac{64}{1} \Rightarrow V_2 = \frac{1}{64}\times V_1$$

Therefore, volume of the Moon = $\frac{1}{64}$ × Volume of Earth.

Question 5 How many litres of milk can a hemispherical bowl of diameter 10.5 cm hold?

Sol. We have, diameter of a hemispherical bowl = 10.5 cm

$\therefore$ Radius of the hemispherical bowl, $r = \frac{10.5}{2} = 5.25$ cm

Volume of a hemisphere bowl $= \frac{2}{3}\pi r^3$

$$= \frac{2}{3} \times \frac{22}{7} \times 5.25 \times 5.25 \times 5.25 = 303.1875 \text{ cm}^3$$

Hemispherical bowl can hold milk $= \frac{303.1875}{1000}$ L $\quad \left(\because 1 \text{ cm}^3 = \frac{1}{1000} \text{ L}\right)$

$= 0.303$ L (Approx.)

Question 6 A hemispherical tank is made up of an iron sheet 1 cm thick. If the inner radius is 1 m, then find the volume of the iron used to make the tank.

◎ ***Thinking Process*** Firstly, find the inner and outer radius. Here, outer radius = Inner radius + Thickness. Then, volume of iron used to make the tank = Outer volume − Inner volume

Sol. Given, inner radius of the tank $(r_1) = 1$ m = 100 cm

$\therefore$ Outer radius of the tank $(r_2) = (100 + 1)$ cm

($\because$ Outer radius = Inner radius + Thickness)

= 101 cm

Outer volume of the tank $= \frac{2}{3}\pi(101)^3 \quad \left(\because \text{Volume} = \frac{4}{3}\pi r^3\right)$

Inner volume of the tank $= \frac{2}{3}\pi(100)^3$

Hence, volume of the iron used to make the tank

$$= (\text{Outer volume} - \text{Inner volume}) = \frac{2}{3}\pi[(101)^3 - (100)^3]$$

$$= \frac{2}{3} \times \frac{22}{7}(101 - 100)\,[(101)^2 + 101 \times 100 + (100)^2]$$

$$[\because a^3 - b^3 = (a - b)(a^2 + ab + b^2)]$$

$$= \frac{2}{3} \times \frac{22}{7}(10201 + 10100 + 10000)$$

$$= \frac{44}{21}(30301) = 63487.80 \text{ cm}^3$$

$$= \frac{63487.80}{100 \times 100 \times 100} \text{ m}^3 = 0.063 \text{ m}^3 \quad \text{(Approx.)}$$

Hence, volume of iron required to make the tank is 0.063 m^3.

Question 7 Find the volume of a sphere whose surface area is 154 cm^2.

Sol. Let r be the radius of a sphere.

Given, surface area of a sphere = 154 cm^2

$$\Rightarrow \quad 4\pi r^2 = 154$$

$$4 \times \frac{22}{7} r^2 = 154$$

$$\Rightarrow \quad r^2 = \frac{154 \times 7}{22 \times 4} = \frac{49}{4}$$

$$\Rightarrow \quad r = \frac{7}{2} \text{ cm}$$

Hence, volume of a sphere $= \frac{4}{3}\pi\left(\frac{7}{2}\right)^3 = \frac{4}{3} \times \frac{22}{7} \times \frac{7}{2} \times \frac{7}{2} \times \frac{7}{2}$

$$= \frac{11 \times 7 \times 7}{3}$$

$$= 179.666 \text{ cm}^3 = 179.67 \text{ cm}^3$$

Question 8 A dome of a building is in the form of a hemisphere. From inside, it was white washed at the cost of ₹ 498.96. If the cost of white washing is ₹ 2.00 per square metre, find the

(i) inside surface area of the dome,

(ii) volume of the air inside the dome.

Sol. (i) Given, cost of white washing the dome from inside = ₹ 498.96

Cost of white washing per square metre = ₹ 2.00

Surface area of the inner side of the dome

$$= \frac{\text{Cost of white washed}}{\text{Cost of white washing per square metre}}$$

$$= \frac{₹\ 498.96}{₹\ 2.00} = 249.48 \text{ sq m}$$

(ii) Let r be the inner radius of the hemispherical dome.

We have, surface area of the inner side of the dome = 249.48 sq m.

$$\therefore \quad 2\pi r^2 = 249.48$$

$$\Rightarrow \quad 2 \times \frac{22}{7} \times r^2 = 249.48$$

$$\Rightarrow \quad r^2 = \frac{249.48 \times 7}{44} \Rightarrow r^2 = 39.69$$

$$\Rightarrow \quad r = 6.3 \text{ m}$$

Volume of the air inside the dome $= \frac{2}{3}\pi r^3$

$$= \frac{2}{3} \times \frac{22}{7} \times (6.3)^3$$

$$= 523.908 \text{ m}^3 = 523.9 \text{ m}^3 \text{ (Approx.)}$$

Question 9 Twenty seven solid iron spheres, each of radius r and surface area S are melted to form a sphere with surface area S'. Find the

(i) radius r' of the new sphere.

(ii) ratio of S and S'.

Sol. (i) Volume of solid iron sphere $= \frac{4}{3}\pi r^3$

Volume of new sphere $= 27 \times \frac{4}{3}\pi r^3 = 36\pi r^3$

Since, 27 sphere are melted and formed into a single sphere

$\therefore \quad \frac{4}{3}\pi r'^3 = 36\pi r^3 \quad (\because r' = \text{radius of new sphere})$

$$r'^3 = \frac{36 \times 3r^3}{4} = 27\,r^3 = (3r)^3$$

$\Rightarrow \quad r' = 3r$

$\Rightarrow$ Hence, radius r' of the new sphere $= 3r$

(ii) Surface area (S) of solid iron sphere $= 4\pi r^2$

Surface area (S') of new sphere $= 4\pi(r')^2$

$$= 4\pi(3r)^2 = 36\pi r^2$$

$\therefore$ Required ratio $= S : S' = 4\pi r^2 : 36\pi r^2 = 1 : 9$

Question 10 A capsule of medicine is in the shape of a sphere of diameter 3.5 mm. How much medicine (in mm^3) is needed to fill this capsule?

Sol. We have, diameter of the capsule = 3.5 mm

$\Rightarrow$ Radius of the capsule, $r = \frac{3.5}{2}$ mm

Volume of capsule $= \frac{4}{3}\pi r^3$

$$= \frac{4}{3} \times \frac{22}{7} \times \frac{3.5}{2} \times \frac{3.5}{2} \times \frac{3.5}{2}$$

$$= \frac{11 \times 0.5 \times 3.5 \times 3.5}{3}$$

$$= 22.45833$$

$$= 22.46 \text{ mm}^3 \quad \text{(Approx.)}$$

Hence, capacity of medicine needed to fill the capsule is 22.46 mm^3.

DIKSHA APP Questions

☐ Multiple Choice Questions

Q.1 The total surface area of a hemisphere of radius 7 cm is

(a) 452 (b) 462
(c) 362 (d) 422

Sol. (b) Given, radius of a hemisphere = 7 cm

Total surface area of hemisphere $= 3\pi r^2$

$$= 3 \times \frac{22}{7} \times 7 \times 7$$

$$= 462 \text{ cm}^2$$

Q.2 If the radius of a sphere is doubled its volume will become how many times of its original volume?

(a) 2 times (b) 5 times (c) 8 times (d) 7 times

Sol. (c) Let the original radius be r.

So, volume of sphere $S_1 = \frac{4}{3}\pi r^3$

If the radius is doubled *i.e.*, $r' = 2r$

Then, volume of sphere $S_2 = \frac{4}{3}\pi (r')^3$

$$= \frac{4}{3}\pi (2r)^3 = \frac{4}{3} \times \pi \times 8r^3$$

$$= 8\left(\frac{4}{3}\pi r^3\right)$$

Therefore, it becomes 8 times to the original volume.

Q.3 Total surface area of a sphere is 154 cm^2. What is the radius of sphere?

(a) $\frac{5}{6}$ (b) $\frac{5}{9}$ (c) $\frac{9}{5}$ (d) $\frac{7}{2}$

Sol. (d) Let r be the radius of a sphere.

Given, total surface area of sphere = 154 cm^2

$\therefore$ $4\pi r^2 = 154$

$\Rightarrow$ $r^2 = \frac{154 \times 7}{4 \times 22} \Rightarrow r^2 = \frac{49}{4}$

$\Rightarrow$ $r = \frac{7}{2}$

☐ Subjective Type Questions

Q.1 A semicircular sheet of metal of diameter 28 cm is bent to form an open conical cup. Find the capacity of the cup.

Sol. Circumference of conical cup = Circumference of semicircle

Circumference of semicircle = $\pi r = 14\pi$ $(\because r = 14 \text{ cm})$

When a semicircular sheet is bent to form an open conical cup, the radius of sheet becomes the slant height of the cup and the circumference of sheet becomes the circumference of the base of the cone. Slant height of conical scup, l = Radius of semicircular sheet = 14 cm

Circumference of base of cone = 14π

$$\therefore \quad 2\pi r = 14\pi$$
$$2r = 14$$
$$r = 7 \text{ cm}$$

Let h be the height

$$l^2 = r^2 + h^2$$
$$(14)^2 = (7)^2 + h^2$$
$$h = \sqrt{196 - 49}$$
$$h = 7\sqrt{3} \text{ cm}$$

Now, Volume of cone $= \frac{1}{3} \times \frac{22}{7} \times 7 \times 7 \times 7\sqrt{3} = 622.4 \text{ cm}^3$

Hence, capacity of the conical cup is 622.4 cm^3.

Q.2 How many square meters of canvas is required for a conical tent whose height is 3.5 m and radius of whose base is 12 m?

Sol. Given, radius of a conical tent, (r) = 12 m

and height of a conical tent, (h) = 3.5 m

Let, l be the slant height of the conical tent.

We know that,

$$l^2 = r^2 + h^2 = 12^2 + 3.5^2$$
$$= 144 + 12.25 = 156.25$$
$$\Rightarrow \quad l = \sqrt{156.25}$$
$$\Rightarrow \quad l = 12.5 \text{ m}$$

Now, lateral surface area of conical tent = $\pi r l$

$$= \frac{22}{7} \times 12 \times 12.5 = \frac{3300}{7}$$
$$= 471.428 = 471.43 \text{ m}^2$$

Hence, the area of canvas required is 471.43 m^2.

Q.3 If h, C, V are respectively the height, the curved surface area and the volume of the cones, prove that
$3\pi Vh^3 - C^2h^2 + 9V^2 = 0$

Sol. We know that the curved surface area of cone (C) = πrl

$$\Rightarrow \quad C = \pi r\sqrt{h^2 + r^2} \qquad (\because l^2 = r^2 + h^2)$$

where h, l and r are the height, slant height and radius of the cone.

and volume of the cone $V = \frac{1}{3}\pi r^2 h$

Now,

$$\begin{aligned} \text{LHS} &= 3\pi Vh^3 - C^2h^2 + 9V^2 \\ &= 3\pi\left(\frac{1}{3}\pi r^2 h\right)h^3 - (\pi r\sqrt{h^2 + r^2})^2 h^2 + 9\left(\frac{1}{3}\pi r^2 h\right)^2 \\ &= \pi^2 r^2 h^4 - \pi^2 r^2 (h^2 + r^2)h^2 + 9 \times \frac{1}{9}\pi^2 r^4 h^2 \\ &= \pi^2 r^2 h^4 - \pi^2 r^2 h^4 - \pi^2 r^4 h^2 + \pi^2 r^4 h^2 = 0 = \text{RHS} \end{aligned}$$

Hence Proved.

Q.4 There are two cones. The *CSA* of one is twice that of the other. The slant height of the latter is twice that of the former. Find the ratio of the radii.

Sol. Let r_1, l_1 and r_2, l_2 be the radii and slant heights of the two cones respectively.

$\therefore$ CSA of the first cone = $\pi r_1 l_1$

and CSA of second cone = $\pi r_2 l_2$

It is given that $\pi r_1 l_1 = 2\pi r_2 l_2$

$$\Rightarrow \quad r_1 l_1 = 2r_2 l_2 \qquad \ldots \text{(i)}$$

and $\quad l_2 = 2l_1$

$$\Rightarrow \quad \frac{l_2}{l_1} = 2 \qquad \ldots \text{(ii)}$$

From Eq. (i), we have $\quad \frac{l_2}{l_1} = \frac{r_1}{2r_2} \qquad \ldots$(iii)

From Eqs. (ii) and (iii), we get

$$\frac{r_1}{2r_2} = 2 \Rightarrow \frac{r_1}{r_2} = 4$$

$$\Rightarrow \quad r_1 : r_2 = 4 : 1$$

Hence, the ratio of their radii is 4 : 1.

Q.5 The volume of the two spheres is in the ratio 64 : 27. Find the difference of their surface areas, if the sum of their radii is 7.

Sol. Let r_1 and r_2 be the radii of two spheres.

Given, ratio of volumes of two spheres = 64 : 27

$$\Rightarrow \quad \frac{\frac{4}{3}\pi r_1^3}{\frac{4}{3}\pi r_2^3} = \frac{64}{27} \qquad \left[\because \text{volume of sphere} = \frac{4}{3}\pi r^3\right]$$

$$\Rightarrow \quad \frac{r_1^3}{r_2^3} = \frac{4^3}{3^3}$$

$$\Rightarrow \quad \left(\frac{r_1}{r_2}\right)^3 = \left(\frac{4}{3}\right)^3$$

$$\Rightarrow \quad \frac{r_1}{r_2} = \frac{4}{3}$$

Also, given $\quad r_1 + r_2 = 7$

Let $\quad r_1 = 4k$ and $r_2 = 3k$

$\therefore \quad 4k + 3k = 7$

$\Rightarrow \quad 7k = 7$

$\Rightarrow \quad k = 1$

So, $r_1 = 4$ units and $r_2 = 3$ units

Difference of their surface areas

$$= 4\pi r_1^2 - 4\pi r_2^2$$
$$= 4\pi(r_1^2 - r_2^2)$$
$$= 4\pi(4^2 - 3^2)$$
$$= 4\pi(16 - 9)$$
$$= 4\pi \times 7$$
$$= 4 \times \frac{22}{7} \times 7 = 88 \text{ units.}$$

Q.6 The diameter of a sphere is decreased by 25%. By what percent its curved surface area decrease?

Sol. Let the diameter of sphere be d.

Radius (r_1) of the sphere $= \frac{d}{2}$

New radius (r_2) of the sphere $= \frac{d}{2}\left(1 - \frac{25}{100}\right) = \frac{3}{8}d$

CSA of sphere $(S_1) = 4\pi r_1^2 = 4\pi\left(\frac{d}{2}\right)^2 = \pi d^2$

CSA of sphere when radius is decreased $(S_2) = 4\pi r_2^2$

$$= 4\pi\left(\frac{3}{8}d\right)^2$$

$$= \frac{9}{16}\pi d^2$$

Decrease in the surface area of the sphere $= S_1 - S_2$

$$= \pi d^2 - \frac{9}{16}\pi d^2$$

$$= \frac{7}{16}\pi d^2$$

Percentage decrease in the surface area of sphere $= \frac{S_1 - S_2}{S_1} \times 100$

$$= \frac{\frac{7}{16}\pi d^2}{\pi d^2} \times 100$$

$$= \frac{7}{16} \times 100$$

$$= 43.75\%$$

Q.7 Determine the volume of a conical tin having radius of the base as 30 cm and its slant height as 50 cm?

Sol. Given, radius of the base of the conical tin, $(r) = 30$ cm

and slant height of the conical tin, $(l) = 50$ cm

Let h be the height of the conical tin.

We know that, $l^2 = r^2 + h^2$

$\Rightarrow$ $h = \sqrt{l^2 - r^2}$

$$= \sqrt{(50)^2 - (30)^2}$$

$$= \sqrt{2500 - 900} = \sqrt{1600} = 40 \text{ cm}$$

Volume of conical tin $= \frac{1}{3}\pi r^2 h$

$$= \frac{1}{3} \times \frac{22}{7} \times 30 \times 30 \times 40$$

$$= \frac{792000}{21} = 37714.29 \text{ cm}^3 \text{ (Approx.)}$$

Q.8 Into a conical tent of radius 8.4 m and vertical height 3.5 m, how many full bags of wheat can the be emptied, if space for the wheat in each bag is 1.96 m^3?

Sol. Given, radius of conical tent $(r) = 8.4$ m

Height of the tent, $(h) = 3.5$ m

Volume of conical tent $= \frac{1}{3}\pi r^2 h$

$$= \frac{1}{3} \times \frac{22}{7} \times 8.4 \times 8.4 \times 3.5 = \frac{5433.12}{21} = 258.72 \text{ m}^3$$

Given, volume of one bag $= 1.96 \text{ m}^3$

Number of bags can be emptied

$$= \frac{\text{Volume of tent}}{\text{Volume of bag}} = \frac{258.72}{1.96} = 132$$

Therefore, 132 bags of wheat can be emptied to fill the tent.

Q.9 In a flood hitted area, the volunteers of NSS erected a conical tent made of tarpaulin. The vertical height of the conical tent is 4 m and the base diameter is 6 m. If the width of tarpaulin is 1.5 m, then find the length of the used, assuming that 10% extra material is required for stitching margins and wastage in cutting (take $\pi = 3.14$).

Sol. Given, radius of conical tent $= \frac{6}{2} = 3$ m

and vertical height of coincal tent, $h = 4$ m

Now, $l = \sqrt{r^2 + h^2}$

$$= \sqrt{(3)^2 + (4)^2}$$

$$= \sqrt{9 + 16} = \sqrt{25} = 5 \text{ m}$$

Area of the canvas used for the tent

$$= \text{Curved surface area of the cone} = \pi r l$$

$$= 3.14 \times 3 \times 5 = 47.1 \text{ m}^2$$

$\therefore$ Length of tarpaulin required $= \frac{\text{Area of tarpaulin required}}{\text{Width of trapaulin}}$

$$= \frac{47.1}{1.5} = 31.4 \text{ m}$$

The extra material required for stitching margins and cutting is 10%

$$= 31.4 \times \frac{10}{100} = 3.14 \text{ m}$$

Hence, the total length of tarpaulin required $= 31.4 + 3.14 = 34.54$ m.

Q.10 What are the applications of surface area and volume in daily life?

Sol. Surface area and volume are fundamental concepts in mathematics and science with a wide range of applications across various fields.

Here are some key applications.

(i) Architecture and Construction

(ii) Manufacturing

(iii) Environmental science

(iv) Biology and Medicine

(v) Food industry

(vi) Cosmetics and Pharmaceuticals

(vii) Physics and Engineering

(viii) Mathematics and Education.

Statistics

CHAPTER 12

Important Points

01 Graphical Representation of Data To represent the data through the pictures or graph called graphical representation of data. The main graphical representations are as follows

(i) **Bar graphs** A bar graph is a pictorial representation of data in which usually bars of uniform width are drawn with equal spacing between them on one axis (say, the X-axis), depicting the variable. The values of the variable are shown on the other axis (say, the Y-axis) and heights of the bars depend on the values of the variable.

e.g.,

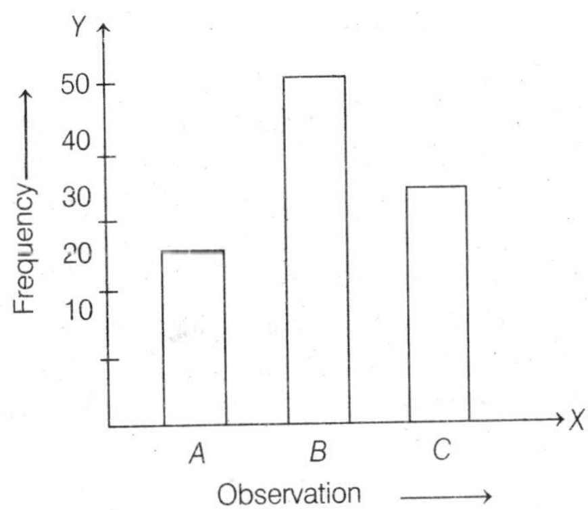

(ii) **Histogram** A histogram is a graphical representation of a grouped frequency distribution with continuous classes.

The steps of construction are as follows

(a) We represent along X-axis the class limits and frequencies along Y-axis on a suitable scale.

(b) We now draw rectangles (or rectangular bars) of width equal to the class size and lengths according to the frequencies of the corresponding class intervals.

Since, there are no gaps in between consecutive rectangles, the resultant graph appears like a solid figure. This is called a histogram.

e.g.,

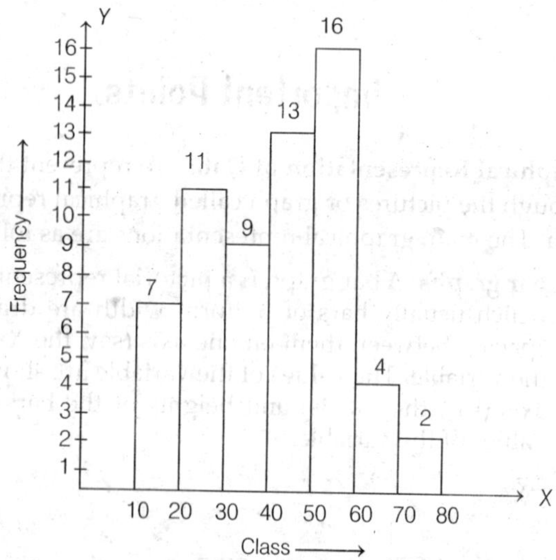

Note • If the first class interval is not starting from zero, then we show it on the graph by marking a kink or a break on the axis. Kink is a tool used to express that the first class interval does not start at zero.

• In a histogram, the areas of the rectangles eracted are proportional to the corresponding frequencies.

• If the widths of the rectangles are varying, then we need to make certain modifications in the lengths of the rectangles, so that the areas are again proportional to the frequencies. The steps to be followed for this are as given below

(a) Select a class interval with minimum class size.

(b) Then, the lengths of the rectangles are modified to be proportionate to the minimum class size.

(iii) **Frequency polygon** For an ungrouped distribution, the frequency polygon is obtained by plotting points with abscissa as the variate values and the ordinate as the corresponding frequencies and joining the plotted points by means of straight lines. For a grouped frequency distribution, the abscissa of points are mid-values of the class intervals. For equal class intervals the frequency polygon can be obtained by joining the middle points of the upper sides of the adjacent rectangles of the histogram by means of straight lines. Frequency polygons are used for understanding the snap of distributions.

$$\text{Class mark} = \frac{\text{Upper limit} + \text{Lower limit}}{2}$$

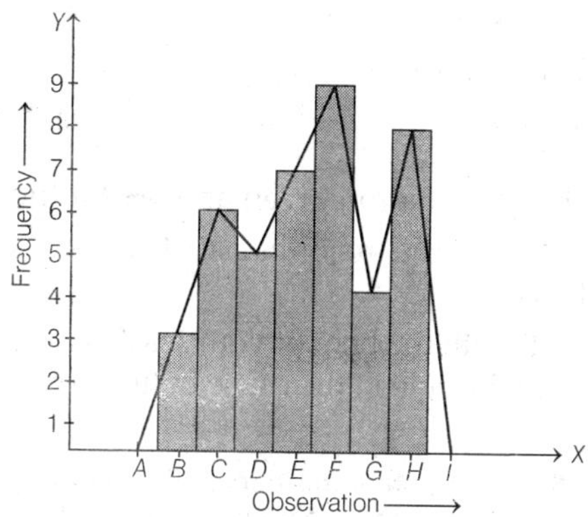

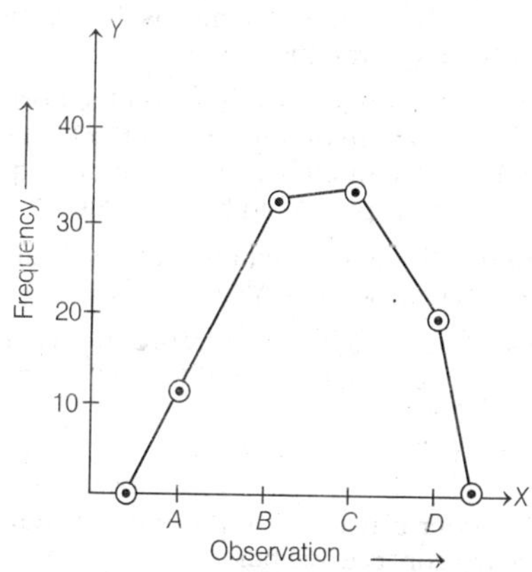

Note If both histogram and frequency polygon are to be drawn, then it is advisable first to draw histogram and then frequency polygon.

Exercise 12.1

Question 1 A survey conducted by an organisation for the cause of illness and death among the women between the ages 15-44 (in years) worldwide, found the following figures (in %)

S.No.	Causes	Female fatality rate (in %)
(a)	Reproductive health conditions	31.8
(b)	Neuropsychiatric conditions	25.4
(c)	Injuries	12.4
(d)	Cardiovascular conditions	4.3
(e)	Respiratory conditions	4.1
(f)	Other causes	22.0

(i) Represent the information given above graphically.

(ii) Which condition is the major cause of women's ill health and death worldwide?

(iii) Try to find out, with the help of your teacher, any two factors which play a major role in the cause in (ii) above being the major cause.

Sol. (i) We draw the bar graph of this data in the following steps. Note that, the unit in the second column is percentage. So, 31.8 against reproductive health conditions means 31.8% of illness and death among the women occurs due to RHC.

(a) We represent the causes (variable) on the horizontal axis choosing any scale, since width of the bar is not important but for clarity, we take equal widths for all bars and maintain equal gaps in between. Let one cause be represented by one unit.

(b) We represent the female fatality rate (value) on the vertical axis. Here, we can choose the scale as 1 unit = 4%.

(c) To represent our first cause *i.e.*, reproductive health conditions, we draw a rectangular bar with width 1 unit and height 7.95 units.

$$\left[\frac{31.8}{4} = 7.95\right]$$

(d) Similarly, other causes are represented leaving a gap of 1 unit in between two consecutive bars.

Now, the graph is drawn in figure.

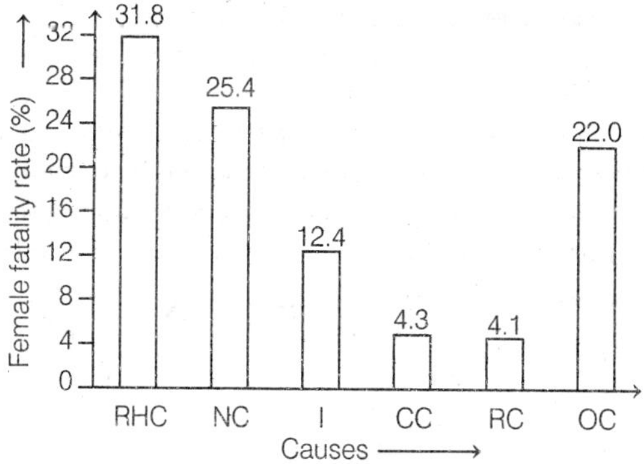

(ii) From graph, we observe that 'reproductive health conditions' is the major cause of women's ill health and death world wide because it has maximum percentage among the causes *i.e.*, 31.8%.

(iii) The factor are as follows.

(a) Lack of medical facilities

(b) Lack of correct knowledge of treatment.

Mistake Alert Students may not confuse in bar graph and histogram. The width of rectangles in bar graph remain same instead of varying width as histogram and the rectangles have equal spacing between them.

Question 2 The following data on the number of girls (to the nearest ten) per thousand boys in different sections of Indian society is given below.

Section	Number of girls per thousand boys
Scheduled Caste (SC)	940
Scheduled Tribe (ST)	970
Non SC/ST	920
Backward districts	950
Non-backward districts	920
Rural	930
Urban	910

(i) Represent the information above by a bar graph.

(ii) In the classroom discuss, what conclusions can be arrived at from the graph.

Thinking Process The variable is represented on horizontal axis and value of variable is represented on vertical axis.

Sol. (i) We draw the bar graph of this data, note that the unit in the second column is number of girls per thousand boys.

(a) We represent the section on the horizontal axis choosing any scale, since width of the bar is not important. But for clarity, we take equal widths for all bars and maintain equal gaps in between. Let one section be represented by one unit.

(b) We represent the number of girls per thousand boys on the vertical axis. Here, we can choose the scale as 1 unit = 100.

Now, the graph is drawn in figure.

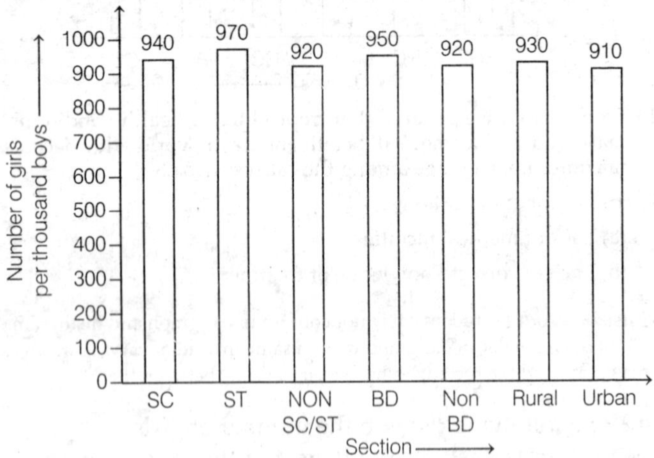

(ii) From graph, we observe that number of girls per thousand boys in scheduled tribe (ST) section is major section in different sections of Indian society, because it has maximum number of girls per thousand boys *i.e.*, 970 and minimum number of girls per thousand (*i.e.*, 910) is for urban.

Question 3 Given below are the seats won by different political parties in the polling outcome of a state assembly elections.

Political party	Seats won
A	75
B	55
C	37
D	29
E	10
F	37

(i) Draw a bar graph to represent the polling results.

(ii) Which political party won the maximum number of seats?

Sol. (i) We draw the bar graph of this data in the following steps note that the unit in the second column is seats won by political party.

(a) We represent the political party on the horizontal axis choosing any scale, since width of the bar is not important but for clarity, we take equal widths for all bars and maintain equal gaps in between. Let one political party be represented by one unit.

(b) We represent the seats won by political party on the vertical axis. Here, we can choose the scale as 1 unit = 10 seats

Now, the graph is drawn in figure

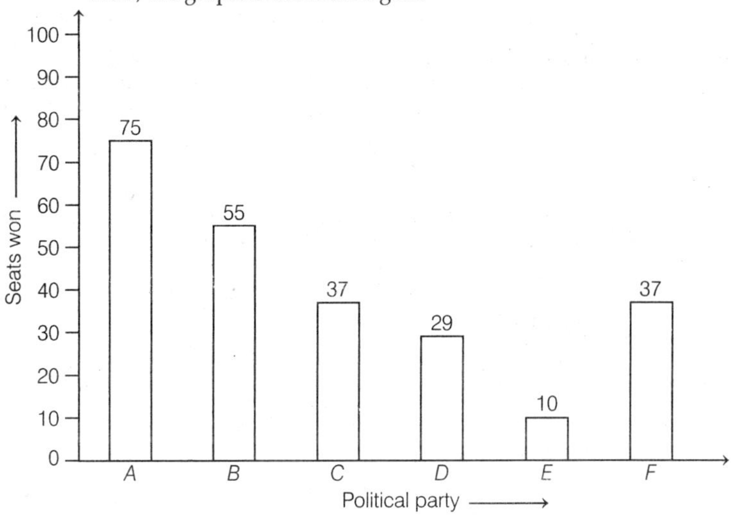

(ii) Party '*A*' won the maximum number of seats *i.e.*, 75.

Question 4 The length of 40 leaves of a plant measured correct to one millimetre and the obtained data is represented in the following table

Length (in mm)	**Number of leaves**
118 - 126	3
127 - 135	5
136 - 144	9
145 - 153	12
154 - 162	5
163 - 171	4
172 - 180	2

(i) Draw a histogram to represent the given data.

[**Hint** First make the class intervals continuous.]

(ii) Is there any other suitable graphical representation for the same data?

(iii) Is it correct to conclude that the maximum number of leaves are 153 mm long? Why?

◎ ***Thinking Process*** First convert this discontinuous data into continuous form, by adding 0.5 in upper limit and subtracting 0.5 in lower limit.

Sol. (i) We know that, the areas of the rectangles are proportional to the frequencies in a histogram. It can be observed that the length of leaves are represented in a discontinuous class interval having a difference of 1 mm between them. Therefore $\frac{1}{2} = 0.5$ has to be added to each upper class limit and also have to subtract 0.5 from the lower class limit as to make class interval continuous. Now, we get the following modified table by given data

Length (in mm)	Number of leaves	Width of the class
117.5 - 126.5	3	9
126.5 - 135.5	5	9
135.5 - 144.5	9	9
144.5 - 153.5	12	9
153.5 - 162.5	5	9
162.5 - 171.5	4	9
171.5 - 180.5	2	9

Now, the width of each class interval is 126.5-117.5 = 9.

Let us represent the data given above graphically as follows

(a) We represent the length on the horizontal axis on suitable scale.

Since, the first class interval is starting from 117.5 and not zero, we show it on the graph by marking a kink on the axis.

(b) We represent the number of leaves (frequency) on the vertical axis on a suitable scale. Since, the maximum frequency is 12, we need to choose the scale to accomodate this maximum frequency.

(c) Now, we draw rectangles of width equal to class size and lengths according to the frequencies of the correspnding class intervals.

Now, we draw the histogram for given data.

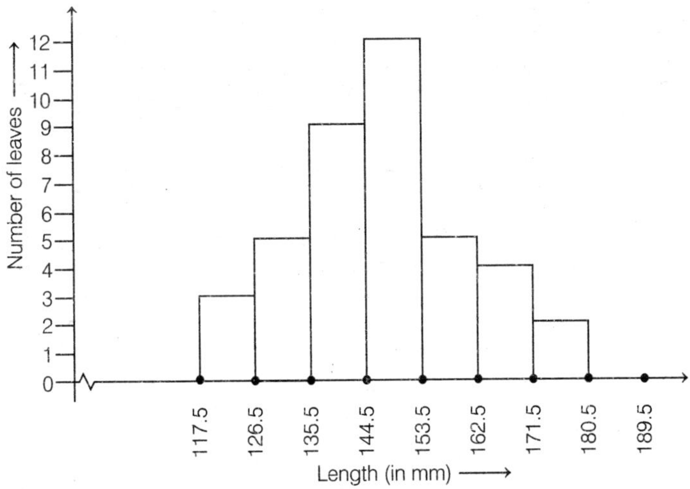

(ii) Yes, other suitable graphical representation of this data is frequency polygon.

(iii) No, because the length of the maximum number of leaves are lying in the interval of 145-153.

Question 5 The following table gives the life times of 400 neon lamps.

Life time (in hours)	Number of lamps
300 - 400	14
400 - 500	56
500 - 600	60
600 - 700	86
700 - 800	74
800 - 900	62
900 -1000	48

(i) Represent the given information with the help of a histogram.

(ii) How many lamps have a lifetime of more 700 h?

Thinking Process

First class interval is starting from 300 and not zero. So, we show it on the graph by marking a kink.

Sol. (i) Here, we will make a modified table by given data.

Lifetime (in hours)	Frequency	Width of the class
300 - 400	14	100
400 - 500	56	100
500 - 600	60	100
600 - 700	86	100
700 - 800	74	100
800 - 900	62	100
900 -1000	48	100

Now, we draw the histogram for above table. Here, 1 unit on Y-axis represents 10 lamps and X-axis represents the life time of neon lamps

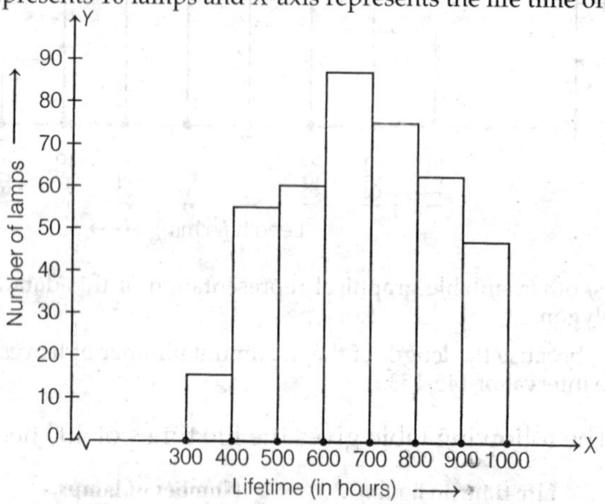

(ii) The number of neon lamps having their lifetime of more than 700 is the sum of number of neon lamps having their lifetime as 700 – 800, 800 – 900, 900 – 1000. Therefore, 184 lamps have a life time of more than 700 h *i.e.*, 74 + 62 + 48 = 184.

Question 6 The following table gives the distribution of students of two sections according to the marks obtained by them

Section A		Section B	
Marks	**Frequency**	**Marks**	**Frequency**
0 - 10	3	0 - 10	5
10 - 20	9	10 - 20	19
20 - 30	17	20 - 30	15
30 - 40	12	30 - 40	10
40 - 50	9	40 - 50	1

Represent the marks of the students of both the sections on the same graph by two frequency polygons. From the two polygons compare the performance of the two sections.

Sol. Here, we make modified tables with class mark by using formula

Class marks $= \dfrac{\text{Lower limit} + \text{Upper limit}}{2}$ by given data.

For section *A*,

Marks	Class marks	Frequency
0 - 10	5	3
10 - 20	15	9
20 - 30	25	17
30 - 40	35	12
40 - 50	45	9

For section *B*,

Marks	Class marks	Frequency
0 - 10	5	5
10 - 20	15	19
20 - 30	25	15
30 - 40	35	10
40 - 50	45	1

We can now draw a frequency polygon by plotting the class marks along the horizontal axis, the frequency along the vertical axis, and then plotting and joining the points.

Now, required frequency polygon curves are (1 unit = 2 for Y-axis)

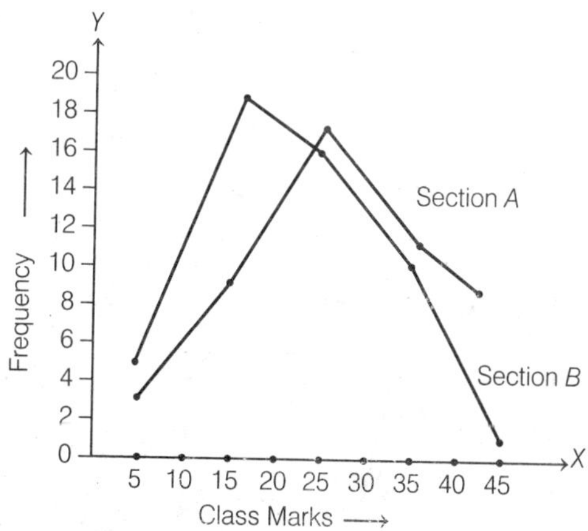

By observation we can conclude that the performance of students of section '*A*' is better than the students of section '*B*' in terms of good marks.

Mistake Alert Students may get confuse in applying the class-mark formulas as $\left(\dfrac{\text{Upper limit} - \text{Lower limit}}{2}\right)$ instead of $\left[\dfrac{\text{Upper limit} + \text{Lower limit}}{2}\right]$.

Question 7 The runs scored by two teams *A* and *B* on the first 60 balls in a cricket match are given below.

Number of balls	Team *A*	Team *B*
1 - 6	2	5
7 - 12	1	6
13 - 18	8	2
19 - 24	9	10
25 - 30	4	5
31 - 36	5	6
37 - 42	6	3
43 - 48	10	4
49 - 54	6	8
55 – 60	2	10

Represent the data of both the teams on the same graph by frequency polygons.

Sol. First make the class intervals continuous by adding 0.5 to the upper class limit and subtracting 0.5 to the lower class limit.

And find the class marks by the formula class marks $= \dfrac{\text{Upper limit} + \text{Lower limit}}{2}$

Modified table

Number of balls	Class marks	Team *A*	Team *B*
0.5 - 6.5	3.5	2	5
6.5 - 12.5	9.5	1	6
12.5 - 18.5	15.5	8	2
18.5 - 24.5	21.5	9	10
24.5 - 30.5	27.5	4	5
30.5 - 36.5	33.5	5	6
36.5 - 42.5	39.5	6	3
42.5 - 48.5	45.5	10	4
48.5 - 54.5	51.5	6	8
54.5 - 60.5	57.5	2	10

Now, draw a frequency polygon curve.

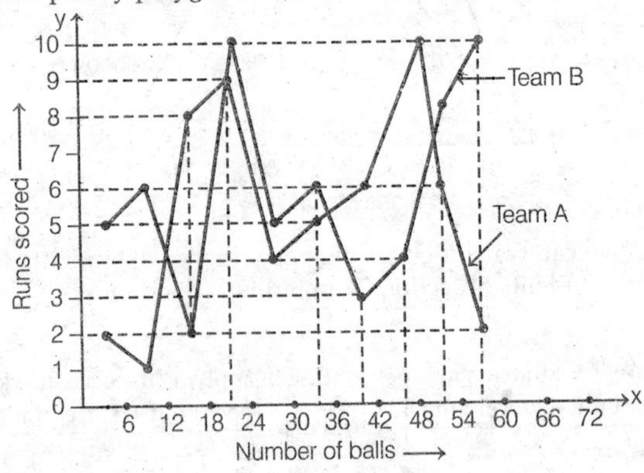

Mistake Alert Students are advised to draw proper line and mark a proper point on frequency polygon. So, that they can differentiate the two frequency polygon.

Question 8 A random survey of the number of children of various age groups playing in a park was found as follows

Age (in years)	Number of children
1 - 2	5
2 - 3	3
3 - 5	6
5 - 7	12
7 - 10	9
10 - 15	10
15 - 17	4

Draw a histogram to represent the data above.

Thinking Process The width of class = [Upper limit – Lower limit] and

$$\text{adjusted frequency} = \frac{\text{Minimum class size}}{\text{Class size of the class}} \times \text{Frequency of the class}$$

Sol. We know that, the areas of the rectangles are proportional to the frequencies in a histogram. Here, the widths of the rectangles are varying. So, we need to make certain modifications in the lengths of the rectangles, so that the areas are again proportional to the frequencies.

(i) Select a class interval with the minimum class size. The minimum class size is 1.

(ii) The lengths of the rectangles are then modified to be proportionate to the class size 1. Then, adjust the frequency of a class.

Adjusted frequency of a class

$$= \frac{\text{Minimum class size}}{\text{Class size of the class}} \times \text{Frequency of the class}$$

Now, we get the following table

Age (in years)	Number of children (frequency)	Width of the class	Adjusted frequency
1 - 2	5	1	$\frac{1}{1}\times 5=5$
2 - 3	3	1	$\frac{1}{1}\times 3=3$
3 - 5	6	2	$\frac{1}{2}\times 6=3$
5 - 7	12	2	$\frac{1}{2}\times 12=6$
7 - 10	9	3	$\frac{1}{3}\times 9=3$
10 - 15	10	5	$\frac{1}{5}\times 10=2$
15 - 17	4	2	$\frac{1}{2}\times 4=2$

So, the correct histogram with varying width is given below.

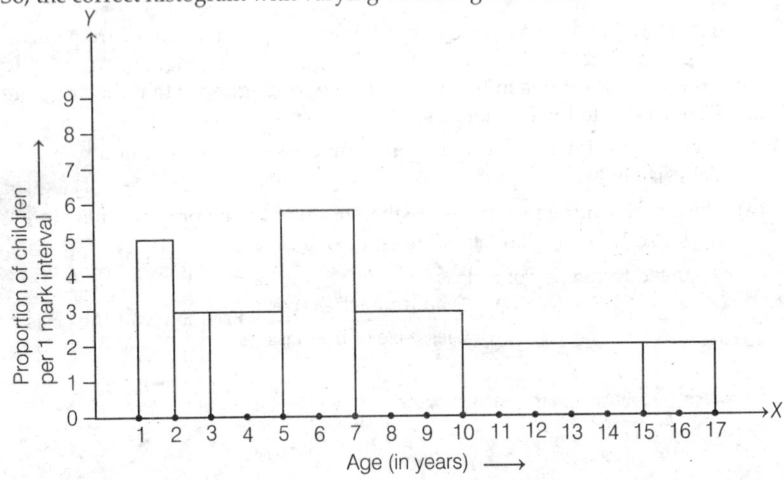

Question 9 100 surnames were randomly picked up from a local telephone directory and a frequency distribution of the number of letters in the English alphabet in the surnames was found as follows

Number of letters	Number of surnames
1 - 4	6
4 - 6	30
6 - 8	44
8 - 12	16
12 - 20	4

(i) Draw a histogram to depict the given information.

(ii) Write the class interval in which the maximum number of surnames lie.

Sol. (i) We know that, the areas of the rectangles are proportional to the frequencies in a histogram. Here, the widths of the rectangles are varying. So, we need to make certain modifications in the lengths of the rectangles. So that the areas are again proportional to the frequencies.

(a) Select a class interval with the minimum class size. The minimum class size is 2.

(b) The lengths of the rectangles are then modified to be proportionate to the class size 2.

Then, adjust the frequency of a class. Adjusted frequency of a class

$$= \frac{\text{Minimum class size}}{\text{Class size of the class}} \times \text{frequency of the class.}$$

Since, we have calculated these lengths for interval of 2 letters in each case, we may call these lengths as 'proportion of surnames per 2 mark interval'. So, the correct histogram with varying width is given below.

Here, we make a modified table by given data with minimum class size 2.

Number of letters	Number of surnames	Width of the class	Length of the rectangle or adjusted frequency
1 - 4	6	3	$\frac{2}{3} \times 6 = 4$
4 - 6	30	2	$\frac{2}{2} \times 30 = 30$
6 - 8	44	2	$\frac{2}{2} \times 44 = 44$
8 - 12	16	4	$\frac{2}{4} \times 16 = 8$
12 - 20	4	8	$\frac{2}{8} \times 4 = 1$

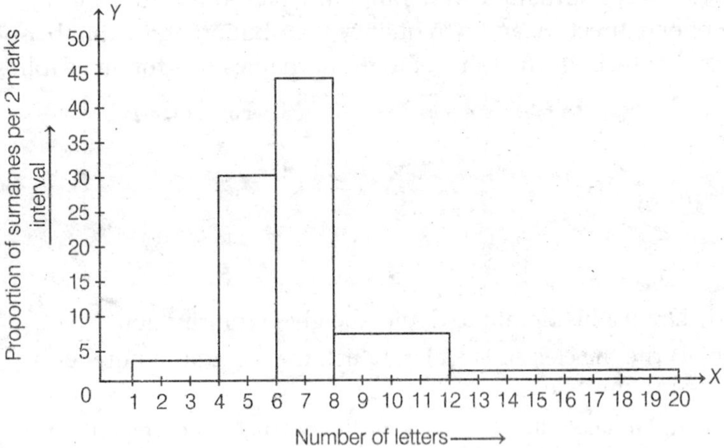

(ii) The class interval in which the maximum number of surnames lie is 6-8.

Mistake Alert Students should be remember that when class intervals are of unequal size, then they need to make modification in the lengths of rectangles.

It means, they use adjusted frequency instead of given frequency while drawing the histogram.

DIKSHA APP Questions

☐ Multiple Choice Questions

Q.1 In a continuous frequency distribution, class mark of a class is 85 and lower limit is 83, then its upper limit is-

(a) 80 (b) 89 (c) 86 (d) 87

Sol. (d) The formula of class mark is

$$\text{Class mark} = \frac{\text{Upper limit} + \text{Lower limit}}{2}$$

$$\Rightarrow \quad 85 = \frac{\text{Upper limit} + 83}{2} \quad [\because \text{Class mark} = 85, \text{Lower limit} = 83]$$

$$\Rightarrow \quad 170 = \text{Upper limit} + 83$$

$$\Rightarrow \text{Upper limit} = 87$$

Q.2 The class mark of a class is 10 and its class width is 6. The lower limit of the class is

(a) 4 (b) 7 (c) 6 (d) 5.7

◎ *Thinking Process* $\text{Class mark} = \frac{\text{Upper limit} + \text{Lower limit}}{2}$

and Class width = Upper limit – Lower limit

Sol. (b) $\text{Class mark} = \frac{\text{Upper limit} + \text{Lower limit}}{2}$

[∵ UL = Upper limit, LL = Lower limit]

Now, $10 = \frac{UL + LL}{2}$

$$\Rightarrow \quad UL + LL = 20 \quad \ldots \text{(i)}$$

Class width = Upper limit – lower limit

$$\Rightarrow \quad UL - LL = 6 \quad \ldots \text{(ii)}$$

On adding Eqs. (i) and (ii), we get

$$\begin{aligned} UL + LL &= 20 \\ UL - LL &= 6 \\ \hline 2UL &= 26 \end{aligned}$$

$$\Rightarrow \quad UL = 13$$

On putting UL = 13 in Eq. (i), we get

$$UL + LL = 20 \quad \Rightarrow 13 + LL = 20$$

$$\Rightarrow \quad LL = 20 - 13 \Rightarrow \quad LL = 7$$

Therefore, the required class is 7 – 13.